SON OF SUPERMAN

HOWARD CHAYKIN
DAVID TISCHMAN

writers

J.H. WILLIAMS III

penciller

MICK GRAY

inker

LEE LOUGHRIDGE

colorist

KURT HATHAWAY

letterer

Superman created by
JERRY SIEGEL &
JOE SHUSTER

™

SON OF SUPERMAN.
Published by DC Comics,
1700 Broadway,
New York, NY 10019.
Copyright © 1999 DC Comics.
All Rights Reserved.
All characters featured in this issue,
the distinctive likenesses thereof,
and all related indicia are trademarks
of DC Comics. The stories, characters
and incidents mentioned in this
magazine are entirely fictional.
Printed on recyclable paper.
DC Comics. A division of Warner Bros.-
A Time Warner Entertainment Company.

Printed in Canada. First printing.

Hard Cover ISBN: 1-56389-595-1
Soft Cover ISBN: 1-56389-596-X

Publication design by Kim Grzybek.

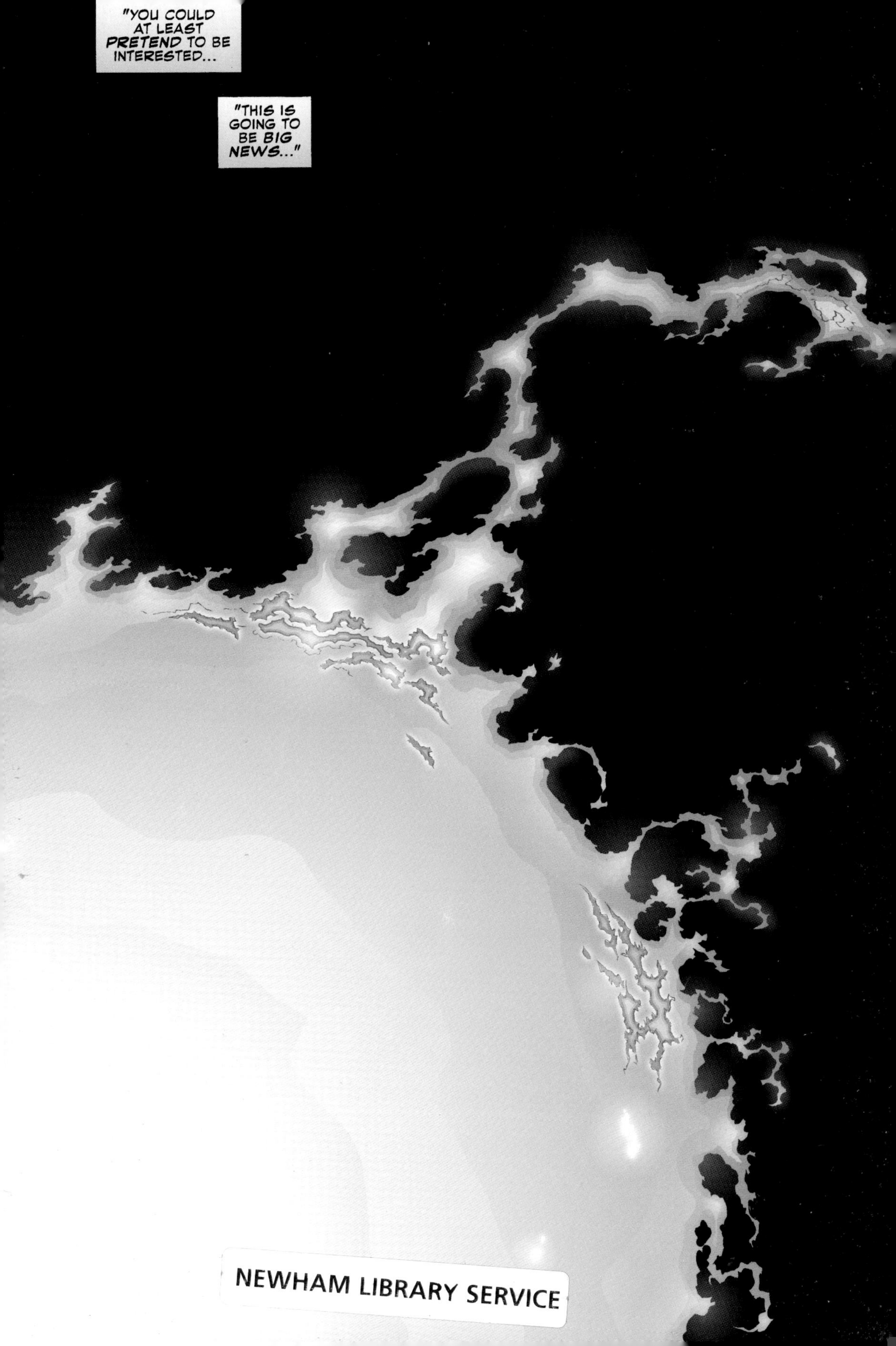
"YOU COULD AT LEAST PRETEND TO BE INTERESTED...
"THIS IS GOING TO BE BIG NEWS..."

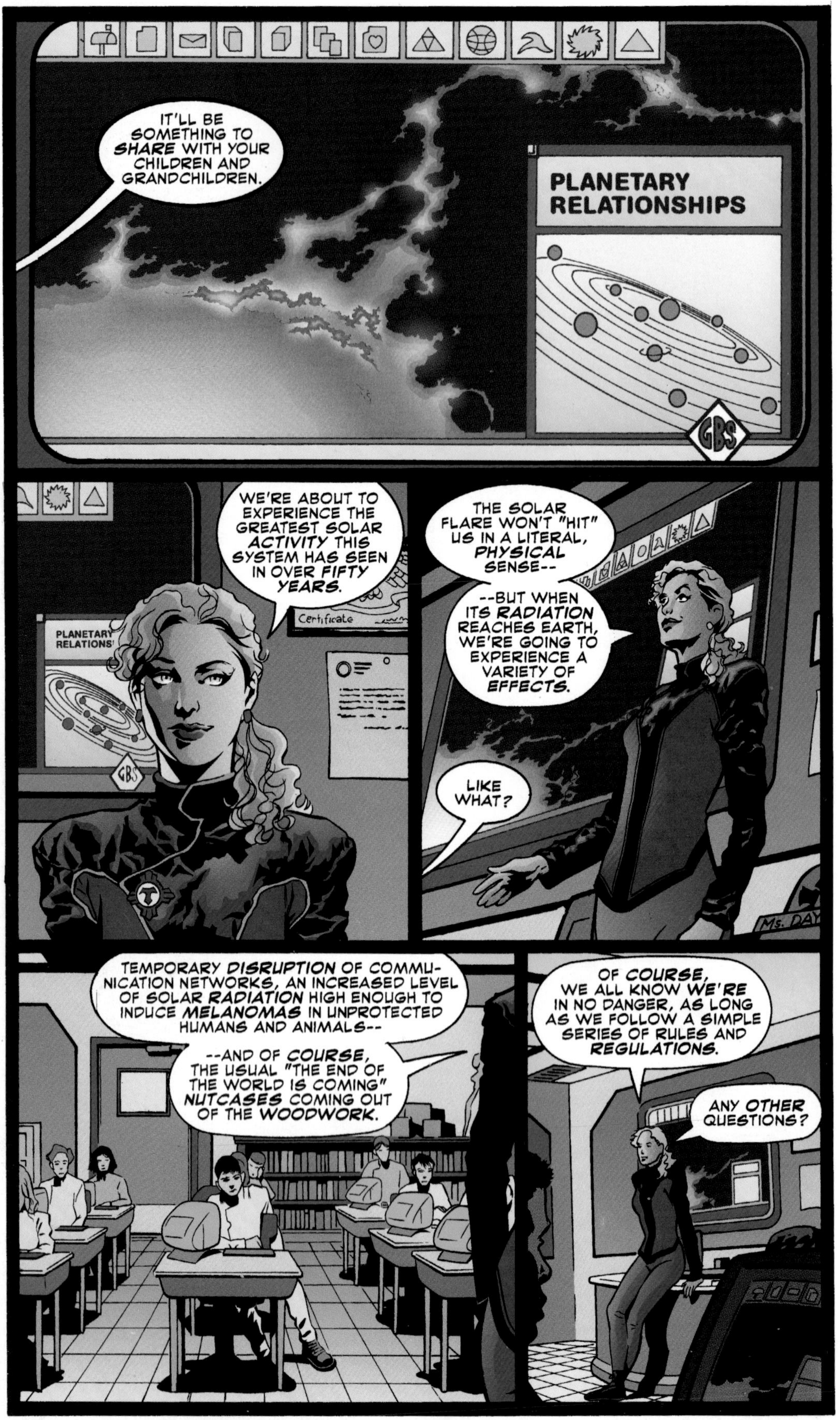
IT'LL BE SOMETHING TO SHARE WITH YOUR CHILDREN AND GRANDCHILDREN.
PLANETARY RELATIONSHIPS
GBS
WE'RE ABOUT TO EXPERIENCE THE GREATEST SOLAR ACTIVITY THIS SYSTEM HAS SEEN IN OVER FIFTY YEARS.
Certificate
PLANETARY RELATIONS
GBS
THE SOLAR FLARE WON'T "HIT" US IN A LITERAL, PHYSICAL SENSE--
--BUT WHEN ITS RADIATION REACHES EARTH, WE'RE GOING TO EXPERIENCE A VARIETY OF EFFECTS.
LIKE WHAT?
Ms. DAY
TEMPORARY DISRUPTION OF COMMUNICATION NETWORKS, AN INCREASED LEVEL OF SOLAR RADIATION HIGH ENOUGH TO INDUCE MELANOMAS IN UNPROTECTED HUMANS AND ANIMALS--
--AND OF COURSE, THE USUAL "THE END OF THE WORLD IS COMING" NUTCASES COMING OUT OF THE WOODWORK.
OF COURSE, WE ALL KNOW WE'RE IN NO DANGER, AS LONG AS WE FOLLOW A SIMPLE SERIES OF RULES AND REGULATIONS.
ANY OTHER QUESTIONS?

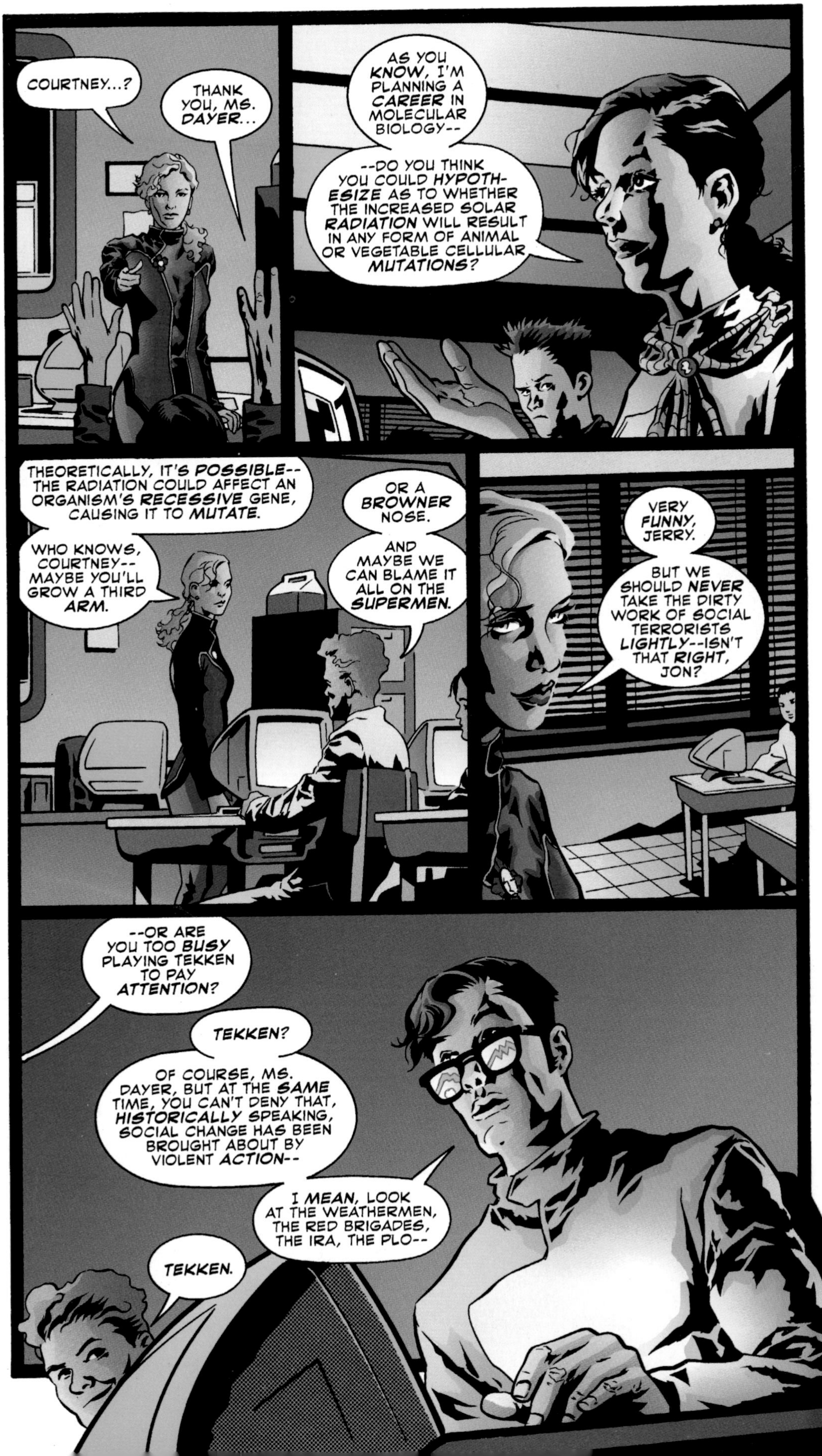
COURTNEY...?
THANK YOU, MS. DAYER...
AS YOU KNOW, I'M PLANNING A CAREER IN MOLECULAR BIOLOGY--
--DO YOU THINK YOU COULD HYPOTH-ESIZE AS TO WHETHER THE INCREASED SOLAR RADIATION WILL RESULT IN ANY FORM OF ANIMAL OR VEGETABLE CELLULAR MUTATIONS?
THEORETICALLY, IT'S POSSIBLE--THE RADIATION COULD AFFECT AN ORGANISM'S RECESSIVE GENE, CAUSING IT TO MUTATE.
WHO KNOWS, COURTNEY--MAYBE YOU'LL GROW A THIRD ARM.
OR A BROWNER NOSE.
AND MAYBE WE CAN BLAME IT ALL ON THE SUPERMEN.
VERY FUNNY, JERRY.
BUT WE SHOULD NEVER TAKE THE DIRTY WORK OF SOCIAL TERRORISTS LIGHTLY--ISN'T THAT RIGHT, JON?
--OR ARE YOU TOO BUSY PLAYING TEKKEN TO PAY ATTENTION?
TEKKEN?
OF COURSE, MS. DAYER, BUT AT THE SAME TIME, YOU CAN'T DENY THAT, HISTORICALLY SPEAKING, SOCIAL CHANGE HAS BEEN BROUGHT ABOUT BY VIOLENT ACTION--
I MEAN, LOOK AT THE WEATHERMEN, THE RED BRIGADES, THE IRA, THE PLO--
TEKKEN.

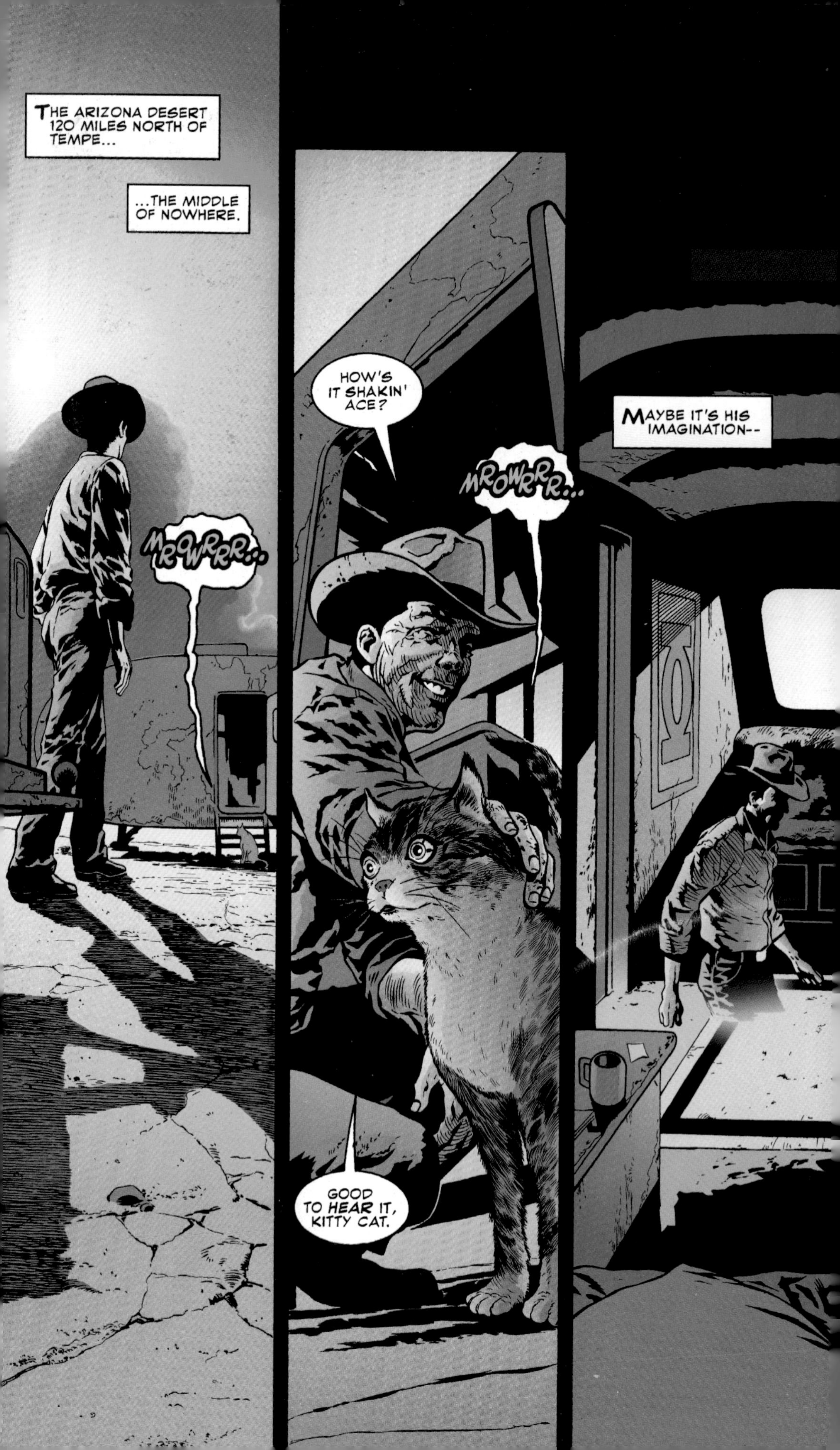
THE ARIZONA DESERT
120 MILES NORTH OF
TEMPE...
...THE MIDDLE
OF NOWHERE.
MRROWRRR...
HOW'S
IT SHAKIN'
ACE?
MROWRRR...
GOOD
TO HEAR IT,
KITTY CAT.
MAYBE IT'S HIS
IMAGINATION--

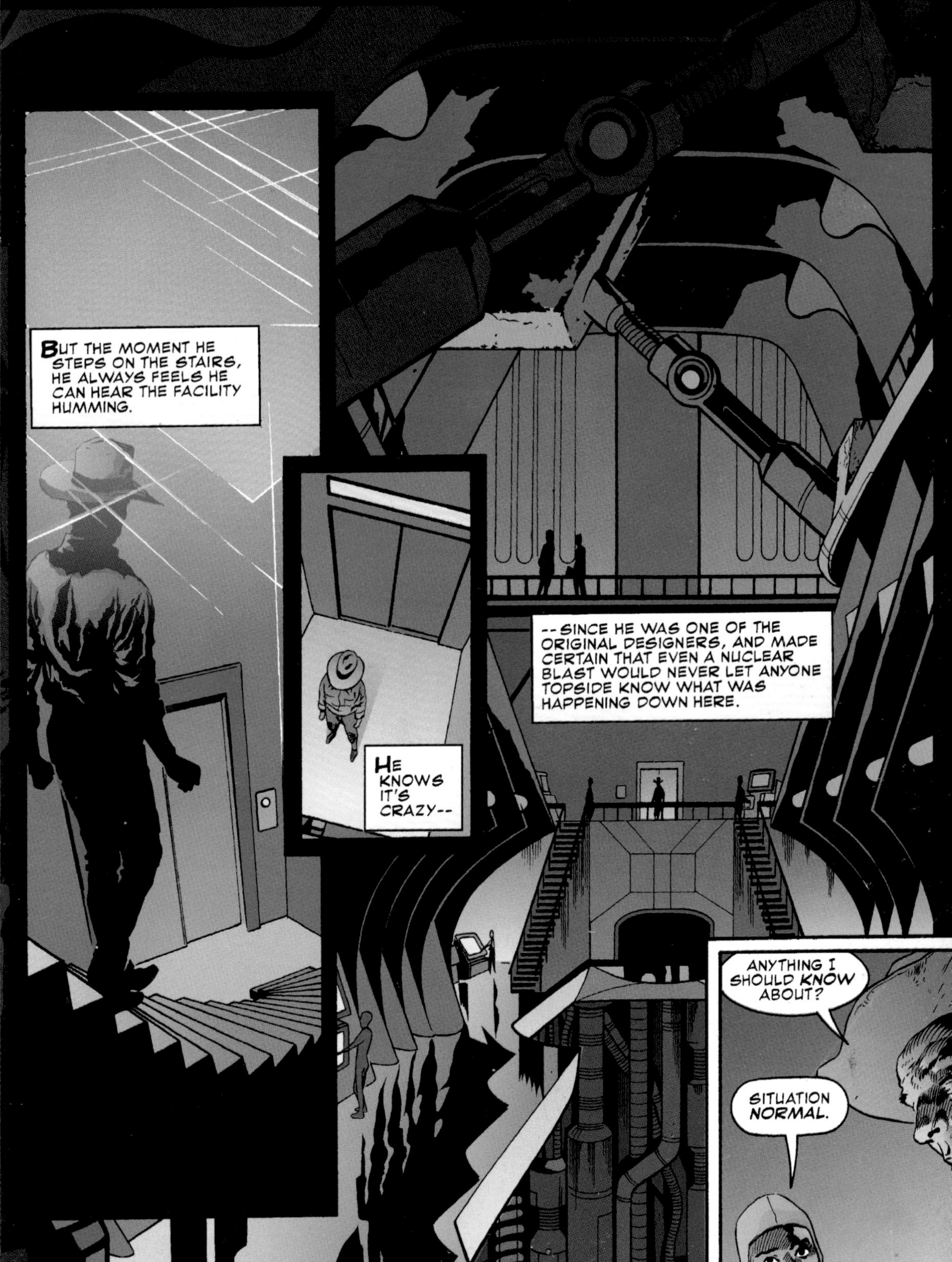
BUT THE MOMENT HE STEPS ON THE STAIRS, HE ALWAYS FEELS HE CAN HEAR THE FACILITY HUMMING.
HE KNOWS IT'S CRAZY--
--SINCE HE WAS ONE OF THE ORIGINAL DESIGNERS, AND MADE CERTAIN THAT EVEN A NUCLEAR BLAST WOULD NEVER LET ANYONE TOPSIDE KNOW WHAT WAS HAPPENING DOWN HERE.
ANYTHING I SHOULD KNOW ABOUT?
SITUATION NORMAL.

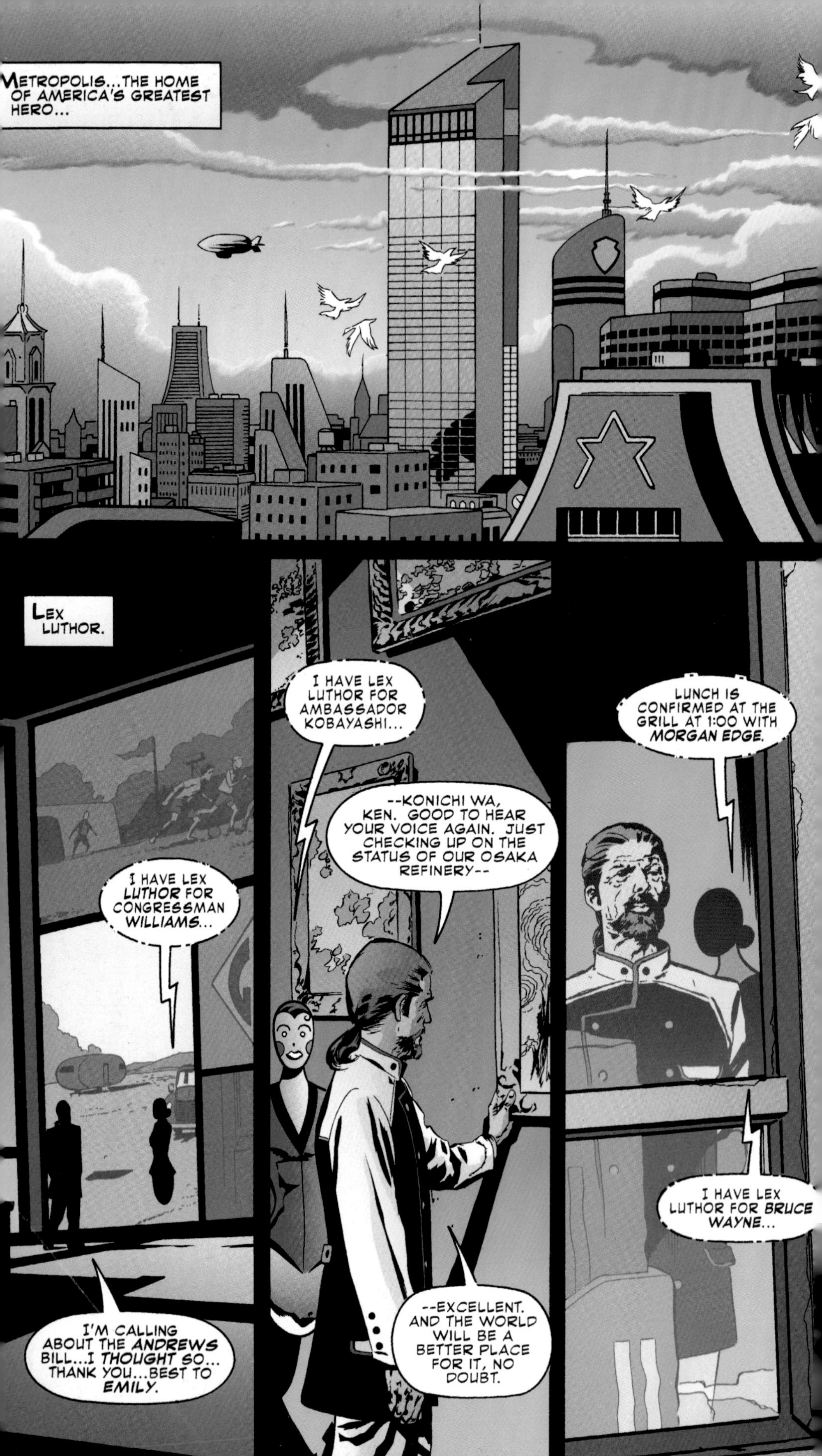
METROPOLIS...THE HOME OF AMERICA'S GREATEST HERO...
LEX LUTHOR.
I HAVE LEX LUTHOR FOR CONGRESSMAN WILLIAMS...
I'M CALLING ABOUT THE ANDREWS BILL...I THOUGHT SO... THANK YOU...BEST TO EMILY.
I HAVE LEX LUTHOR FOR AMBASSADOR KOBAYASHI...
--KONICHI WA, KEN. GOOD TO HEAR YOUR VOICE AGAIN. JUST CHECKING UP ON THE STATUS OF OUR OSAKA REFINERY--
--EXCELLENT. AND THE WORLD WILL BE A BETTER PLACE FOR IT, NO DOUBT.
LUNCH IS CONFIRMED AT THE GRILL AT 1:00 WITH MORGAN EDGE.
I HAVE LEX LUTHOR FOR BRUCE WAYNE...

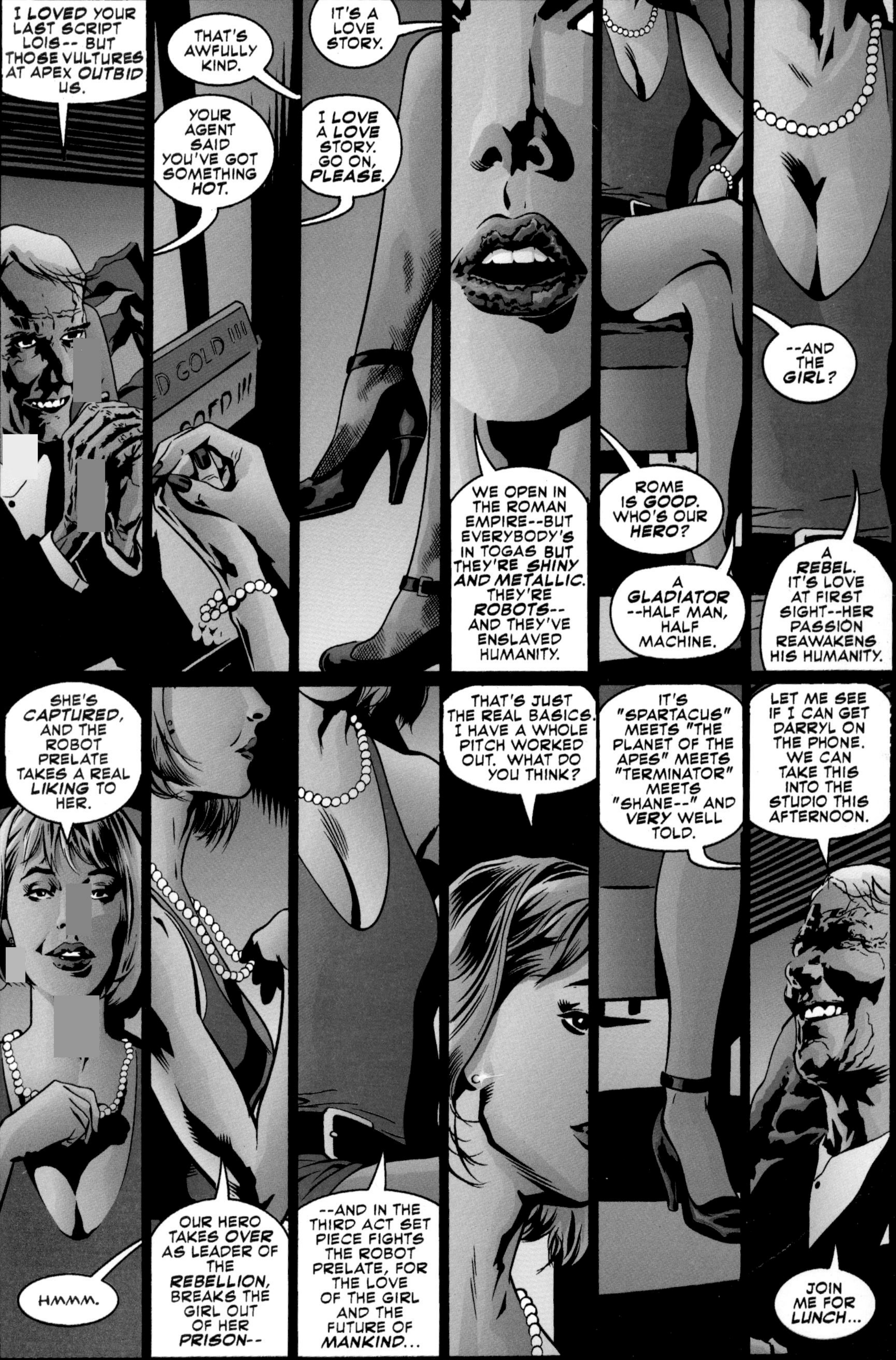
I LOVED YOUR LAST SCRIPT LOIS-- BUT THOSE VULTURES AT APEX OUTBID US.
THAT'S AWFULLY KIND.
YOUR AGENT SAID YOU'VE GOT SOMETHING HOT.
IT'S A LOVE STORY.
I LOVE A LOVE STORY. GO ON, PLEASE.
WE OPEN IN THE ROMAN EMPIRE--BUT EVERYBODY'S IN TOGAS BUT THEY'RE SHINY AND METALLIC. THEY'RE ROBOTS-- AND THEY'VE ENSLAVED HUMANITY.
ROME IS GOOD. WHO'S OUR HERO?
A GLADIATOR --HALF MAN, HALF MACHINE.
--AND THE GIRL?
A REBEL. IT'S LOVE AT FIRST SIGHT--HER PASSION REAWAKENS HIS HUMANITY.
SHE'S CAPTURED, AND THE ROBOT PRELATE TAKES A REAL LIKING TO HER.
HMMM.
OUR HERO TAKES OVER AS LEADER OF THE REBELLION, BREAKS THE GIRL OUT OF HER PRISON--
--AND IN THE THIRD ACT SET PIECE FIGHTS THE ROBOT PRELATE, FOR THE LOVE OF THE GIRL AND THE FUTURE OF MANKIND...
THAT'S JUST THE REAL BASICS. I HAVE A WHOLE PITCH WORKED OUT. WHAT DO YOU THINK?
IT'S "SPARTACUS" MEETS "THE PLANET OF THE APES" MEETS "TERMINATOR" MEETS "SHANE--" AND VERY WELL TOLD.
LET ME SEE IF I CAN GET DARRYL ON THE PHONE. WE CAN TAKE THIS INTO THE STUDIO THIS AFTERNOON.
JOIN ME FOR LUNCH...

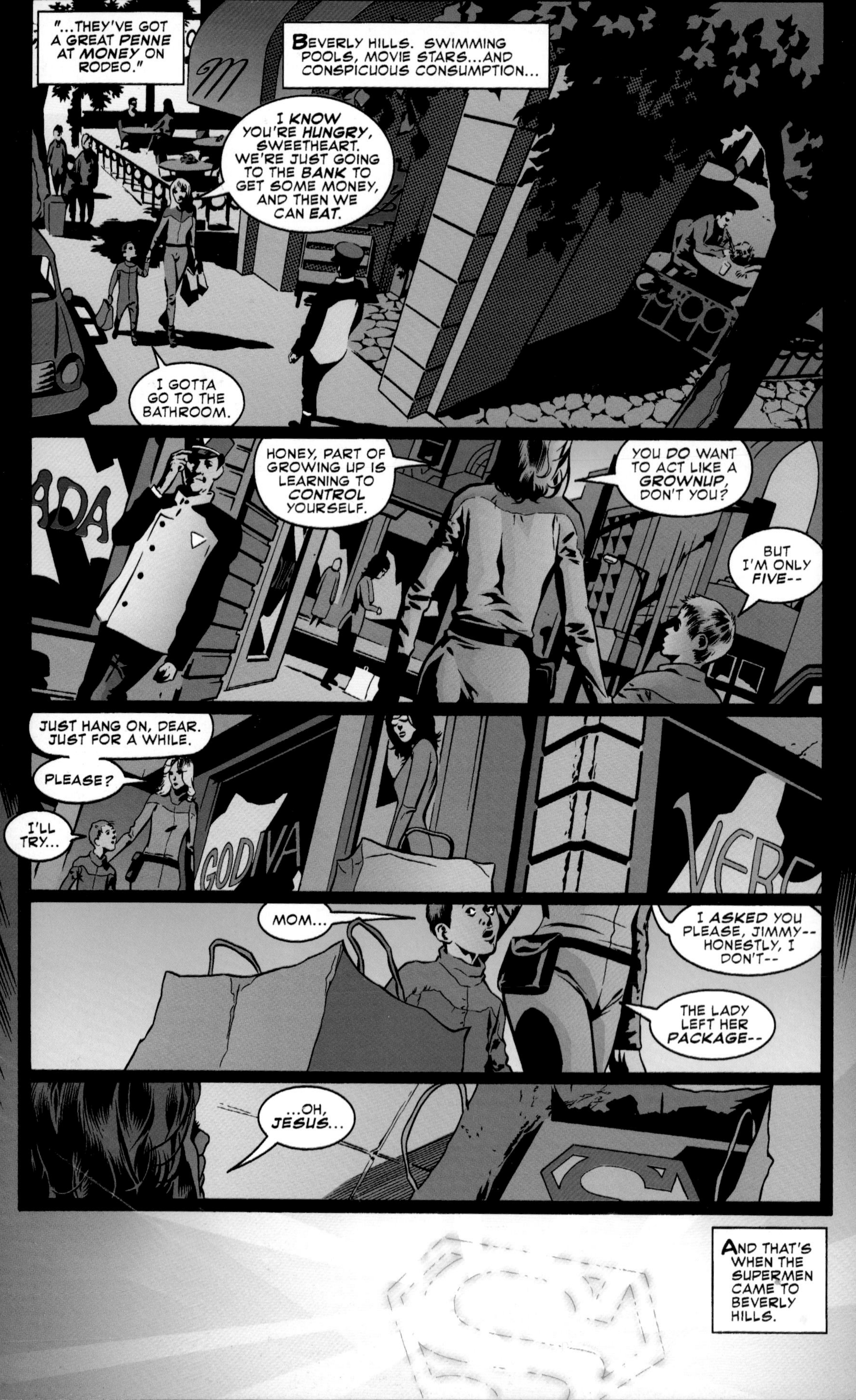
"...THEY'VE GOT A GREAT PENNE AT MONEY ON RODEO."
BEVERLY HILLS. SWIMMING POOLS, MOVIE STARS...AND CONSPICUOUS CONSUMPTION...
I KNOW YOU'RE HUNGRY, SWEETHEART. WE'RE JUST GOING TO THE BANK TO GET SOME MONEY, AND THEN WE CAN EAT.
I GOTTA GO TO THE BATHROOM.
HONEY, PART OF GROWING UP IS LEARNING TO CONTROL YOURSELF.
YOU DO WANT TO ACT LIKE A GROWNUP, DON'T YOU?
BUT I'M ONLY FIVE--
ADA
JUST HANG ON, DEAR. JUST FOR A WHILE.
PLEASE?
I'LL TRY...
GODIVA
VERS
MOM...
I ASKED YOU PLEASE, JIMMY-- HONESTLY, I DON'T--
THE LADY LEFT HER PACKAGE--
...OH, JESUS...
AND THAT'S WHEN THE SUPERMEN CAME TO BEVERLY HILLS.

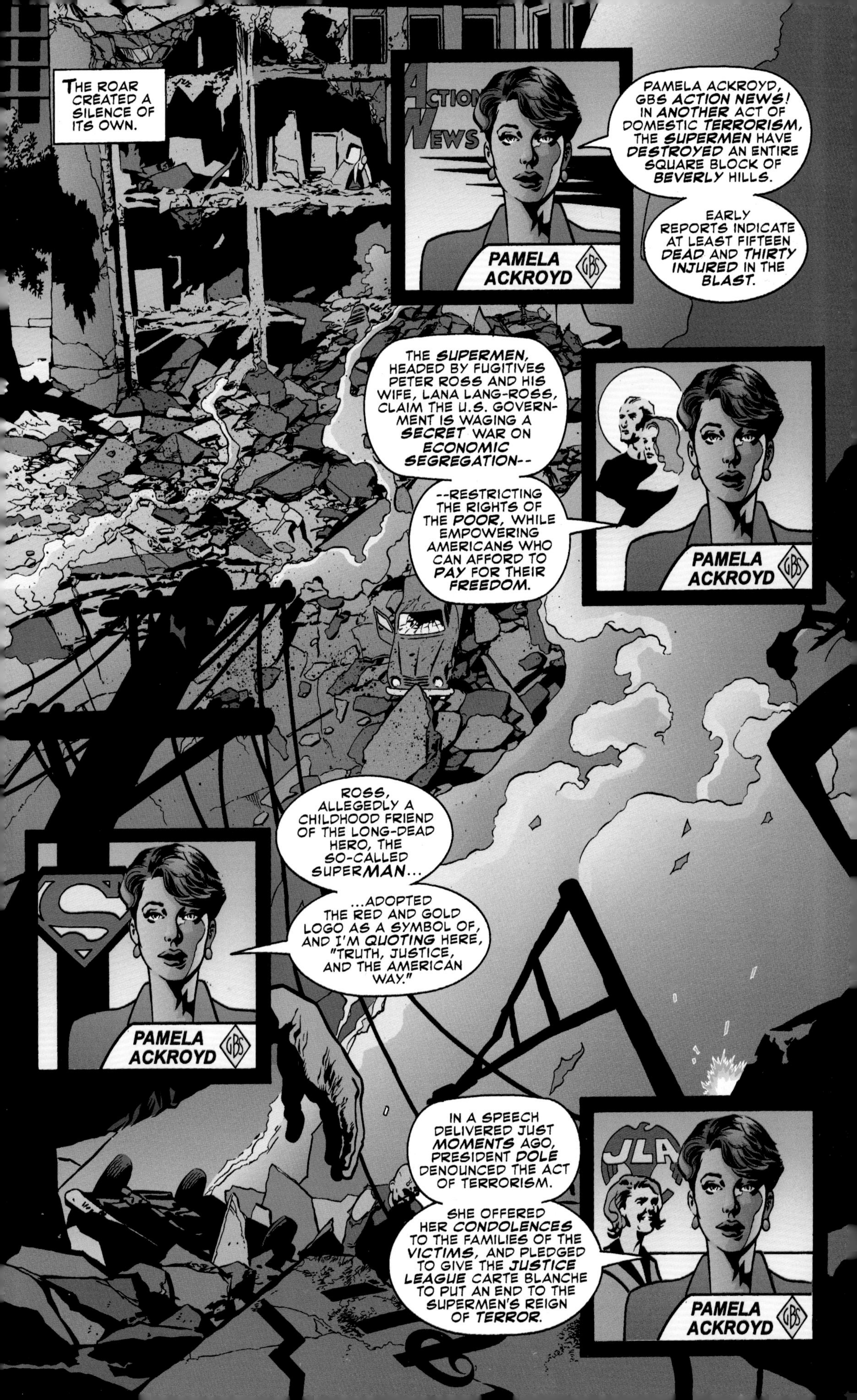
THE ROAR CREATED A SILENCE OF ITS OWN.
ACTION NEWS
PAMELA ACKROYD, GBS ACTION NEWS! IN ANOTHER ACT OF DOMESTIC TERRORISM, THE SUPERMEN HAVE DESTROYED AN ENTIRE SQUARE BLOCK OF BEVERLY HILLS.
EARLY REPORTS INDICATE AT LEAST FIFTEEN DEAD AND THIRTY INJURED IN THE BLAST.
PAMELA ACKROYD
GBS
THE SUPERMEN, HEADED BY FUGITIVES PETER ROSS AND HIS WIFE, LANA LANG-ROSS, CLAIM THE U.S. GOVERNMENT IS WAGING A SECRET WAR ON ECONOMIC SEGREGATION--
--RESTRICTING THE RIGHTS OF THE POOR, WHILE EMPOWERING AMERICANS WHO CAN AFFORD TO PAY FOR THEIR FREEDOM.
PAMELA ACKROYD
GBS
ROSS, ALLEGEDLY A CHILDHOOD FRIEND OF THE LONG-DEAD HERO, THE SO-CALLED SUPERMAN...
...ADOPTED THE RED AND GOLD LOGO AS A SYMBOL OF, AND I'M QUOTING HERE, "TRUTH, JUSTICE, AND THE AMERICAN WAY."
PAMELA ACKROYD
GBS
IN A SPEECH DELIVERED JUST MOMENTS AGO, PRESIDENT DOLE DENOUNCED THE ACT OF TERRORISM.
SHE OFFERED HER CONDOLENCES TO THE FAMILIES OF THE VICTIMS, AND PLEDGED TO GIVE THE JUSTICE LEAGUE CARTE BLANCHE TO PUT AN END TO THE SUPERMEN'S REIGN OF TERROR.
JLA
PAMELA ACKROYD
GBS

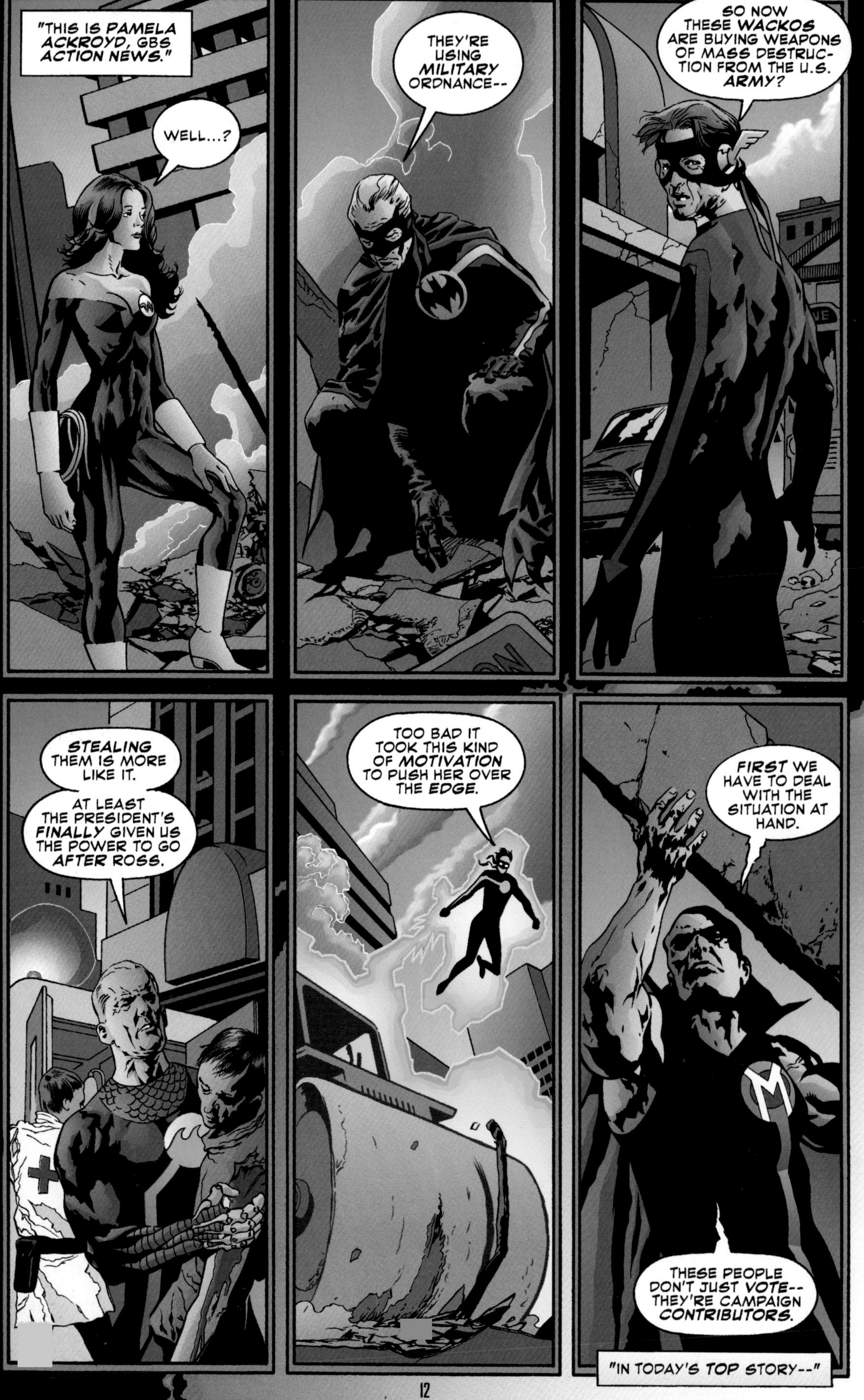
"THIS IS PAMELA ACKROYD, GBS ACTION NEWS."
WELL...?
THEY'RE USING MILITARY ORDNANCE--
SO NOW THESE WACKOS ARE BUYING WEAPONS OF MASS DESTRUCTION FROM THE U.S. ARMY?
STEALING THEM IS MORE LIKE IT.
AT LEAST THE PRESIDENT'S FINALLY GIVEN US THE POWER TO GO AFTER ROSS.
TOO BAD IT TOOK THIS KIND OF MOTIVATION TO PUSH HER OVER THE EDGE.
FIRST WE HAVE TO DEAL WITH THE SITUATION AT HAND.
THESE PEOPLE DON'T JUST VOTE-- THEY'RE CAMPAIGN CONTRIBUTORS.
"IN TODAY'S TOP STORY--"

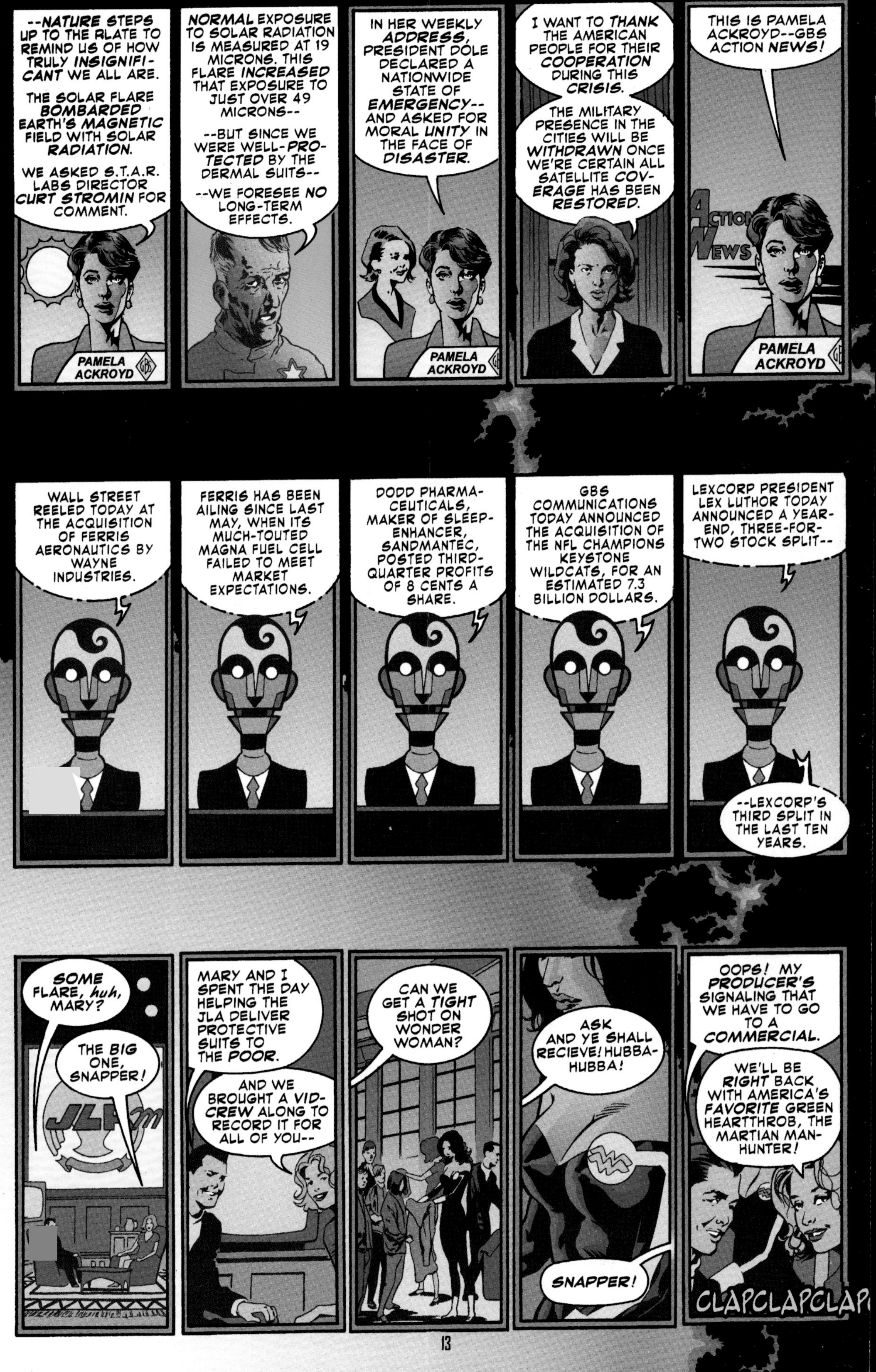
--NATURE STEPS UP TO THE PLATE TO REMIND US OF HOW TRULY INSIGNIFICANT WE ALL ARE.
THE SOLAR FLARE BOMBARDED EARTH'S MAGNETIC FIELD WITH SOLAR RADIATION.
WE ASKED S.T.A.R. LABS DIRECTOR CURT STROMIN FOR COMMENT.
PAMELA ACKROYD
GBS
NORMAL EXPOSURE TO SOLAR RADIATION IS MEASURED AT 19 MICRONS. THIS FLARE INCREASED THAT EXPOSURE TO JUST OVER 49 MICRONS--
--BUT SINCE WE WERE WELL-PROTECTED BY THE DERMAL SUITS--
--WE FORESEE NO LONG-TERM EFFECTS.
IN HER WEEKLY ADDRESS, PRESIDENT DOLE DECLARED A NATIONWIDE STATE OF EMERGENCY--AND ASKED FOR MORAL UNITY IN THE FACE OF DISASTER.
PAMELA ACKROYD
I WANT TO THANK THE AMERICAN PEOPLE FOR THEIR COOPERATION DURING THIS CRISIS.
THE MILITARY PRESENCE IN THE CITIES WILL BE WITHDRAWN ONCE WE'RE CERTAIN ALL SATELLITE COVERAGE HAS BEEN RESTORED.
THIS IS PAMELA ACKROYD--GBS ACTION NEWS!
ACTION NEWS
PAMELA ACKROYD
WALL STREET REELED TODAY AT THE ACQUISITION OF FERRIS AERONAUTICS BY WAYNE INDUSTRIES.
FERRIS HAS BEEN AILING SINCE LAST MAY, WHEN ITS MUCH-TOUTED MAGNA FUEL CELL FAILED TO MEET MARKET EXPECTATIONS.
DODD PHARMACEUTICALS, MAKER OF SLEEP-ENHANCER, SANDMANTEC, POSTED THIRD-QUARTER PROFITS OF 8 CENTS A SHARE.
GBS COMMUNICATIONS TODAY ANNOUNCED THE ACQUISITION OF THE NFL CHAMPIONS KEYSTONE WILDCATS, FOR AN ESTIMATED 7.3 BILLION DOLLARS.
LEXCORP PRESIDENT LEX LUTHOR TODAY ANNOUNCED A YEAR-END, THREE-FOR-TWO STOCK SPLIT--
--LEXCORP'S THIRD SPLIT IN THE LAST TEN YEARS.
SOME FLARE, huh, MARY?
THE BIG ONE, SNAPPER!
MARY AND I SPENT THE DAY HELPING THE JLA DELIVER PROTECTIVE SUITS TO THE POOR.
AND WE BROUGHT A VID-CREW ALONG TO RECORD IT FOR ALL OF YOU--
CAN WE GET A TIGHT SHOT ON WONDER WOMAN?
ASK AND YE SHALL RECIEVE! HUBBA-HUBBA!
SNAPPER!
OOPS! MY PRODUCER'S SIGNALING THAT WE HAVE TO GO TO A COMMERCIAL.
WE'LL BE RIGHT BACK WITH AMERICA'S FAVORITE GREEN HEARTTHROB, THE MARTIAN MANHUNTER!
CLAPCLAPCLAP

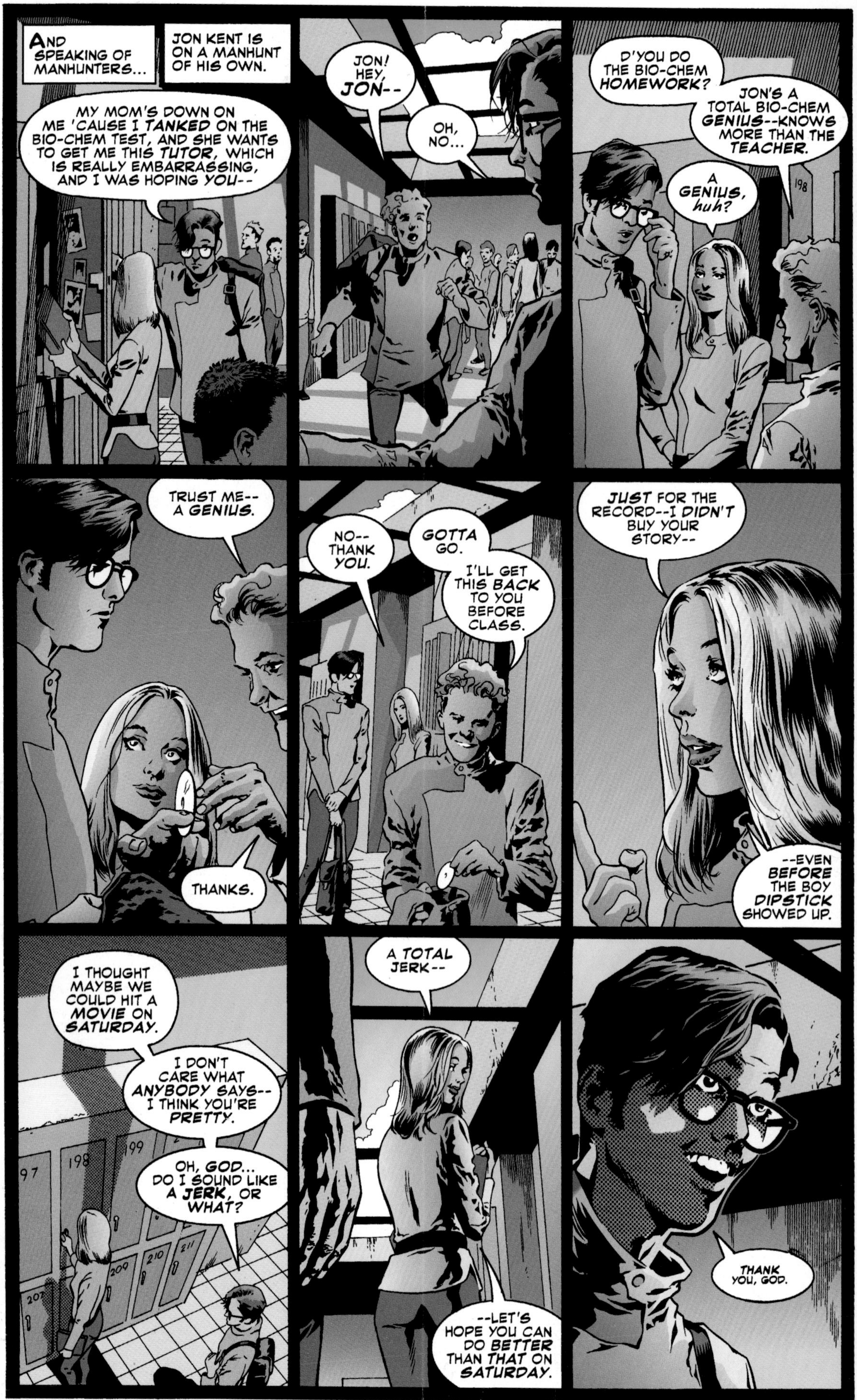
AND SPEAKING OF MANHUNTERS...
JON KENT IS ON A MANHUNT OF HIS OWN.
MY MOM'S DOWN ON ME 'CAUSE I TANKED ON THE BIO-CHEM TEST, AND SHE WANTS TO GET ME THIS TUTOR, WHICH IS REALLY EMBARRASSING, AND I WAS HOPING YOU--
JON! HEY, JON--
OH, NO...
D'YOU DO THE BIO-CHEM HOMEWORK?
JON'S A TOTAL BIO-CHEM GENIUS--KNOWS MORE THAN THE TEACHER.
A GENIUS, huh?
TRUST ME-- A GENIUS.
THANKS.
NO-- THANK YOU.
GOTTA GO.
I'LL GET THIS BACK TO YOU BEFORE CLASS.
JUST FOR THE RECORD--I DIDN'T BUY YOUR STORY--
--EVEN BEFORE THE BOY DIPSTICK SHOWED UP.
I THOUGHT MAYBE WE COULD HIT A MOVIE ON SATURDAY.
I DON'T CARE WHAT ANYBODY SAYS-- I THINK YOU'RE PRETTY.
OH, GOD... DO I SOUND LIKE A JERK, OR WHAT?
A TOTAL JERK--
--LET'S HOPE YOU CAN DO BETTER THAN THAT ON SATURDAY.
THANK YOU, GOD.

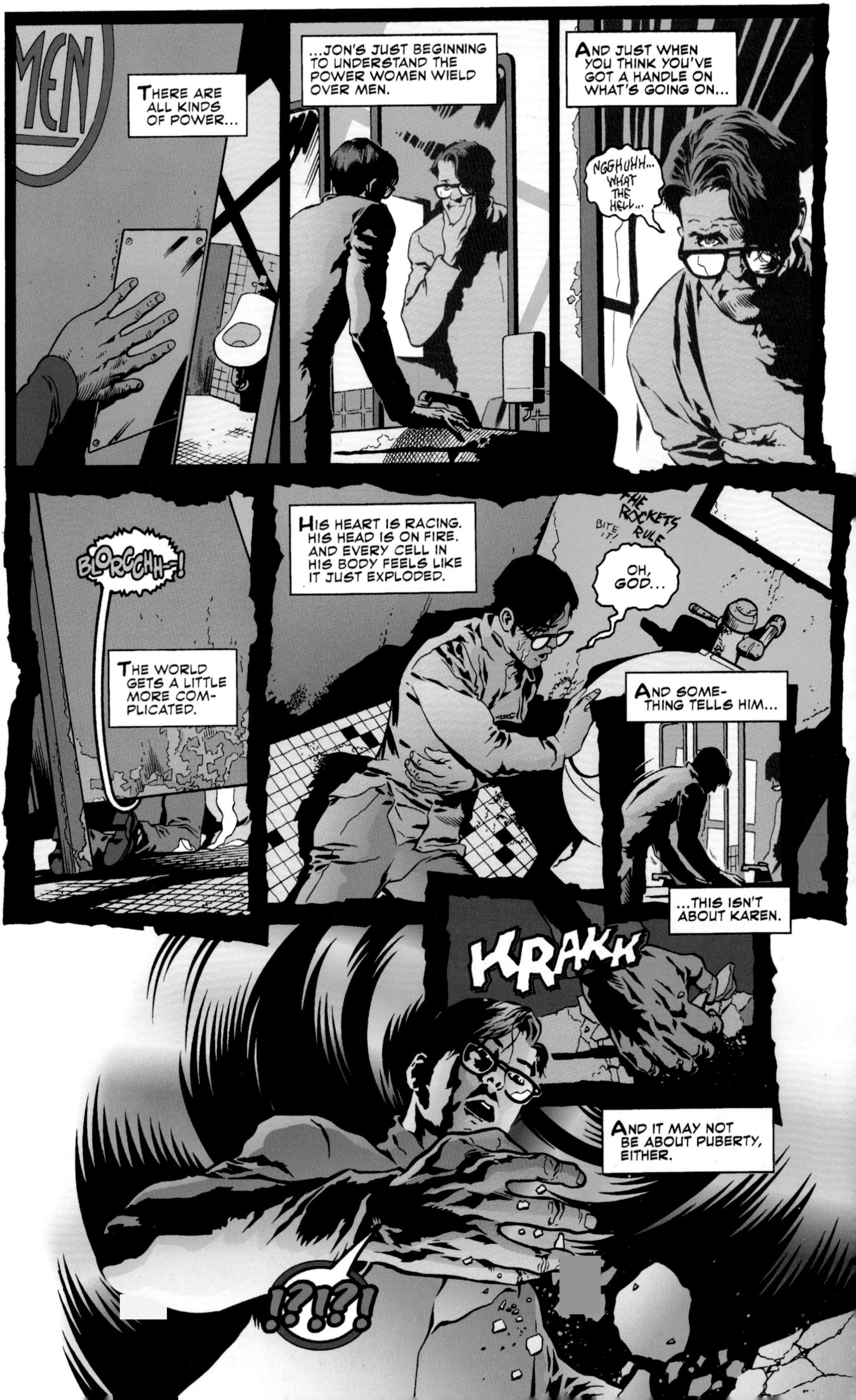
MEN
THERE ARE ALL KINDS OF POWER...
...JON'S JUST BEGINNING TO UNDERSTAND THE POWER WOMEN WIELD OVER MEN.
AND JUST WHEN YOU THINK YOU'VE GOT A HANDLE ON WHAT'S GOING ON...
NGGHUHH... WHAT THE HELL...
BLORGCHH--!
THE WORLD GETS A LITTLE MORE COMPLICATED.
HIS HEART IS RACING. HIS HEAD IS ON FIRE. AND EVERY CELL IN HIS BODY FEELS LIKE IT JUST EXPLODED.
THE ROCKETS RULE
BITE IT!
OH, GOD...
AND SOMETHING TELLS HIM...
...THIS ISN'T ABOUT KAREN.
KRAKK
AND IT MAY NOT BE ABOUT PUBERTY, EITHER.
!?!?!

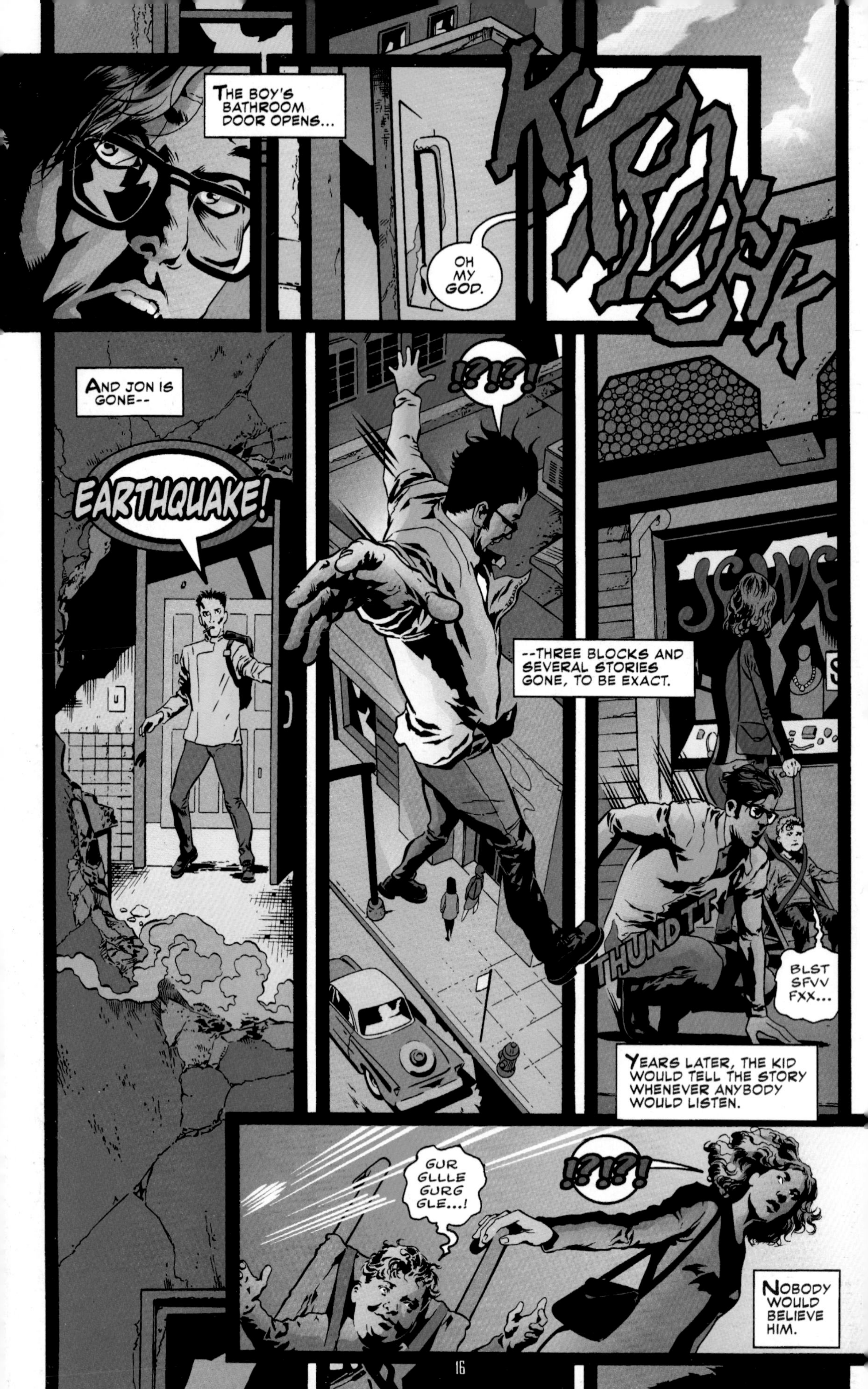
THE BOY'S BATHROOM DOOR OPENS...
OH MY GOD.
KTHOOK
AND JON IS GONE--
EARTHQUAKE!
!?!?!
--THREE BLOCKS AND SEVERAL STORIES GONE, TO BE EXACT.
THUNDTT
BLST SFVV FXX...
YEARS LATER, THE KID WOULD TELL THE STORY WHENEVER ANYBODY WOULD LISTEN.
GUR GLLLE GURG GLE...!
!?!?!
NOBODY WOULD BELIEVE HIM.

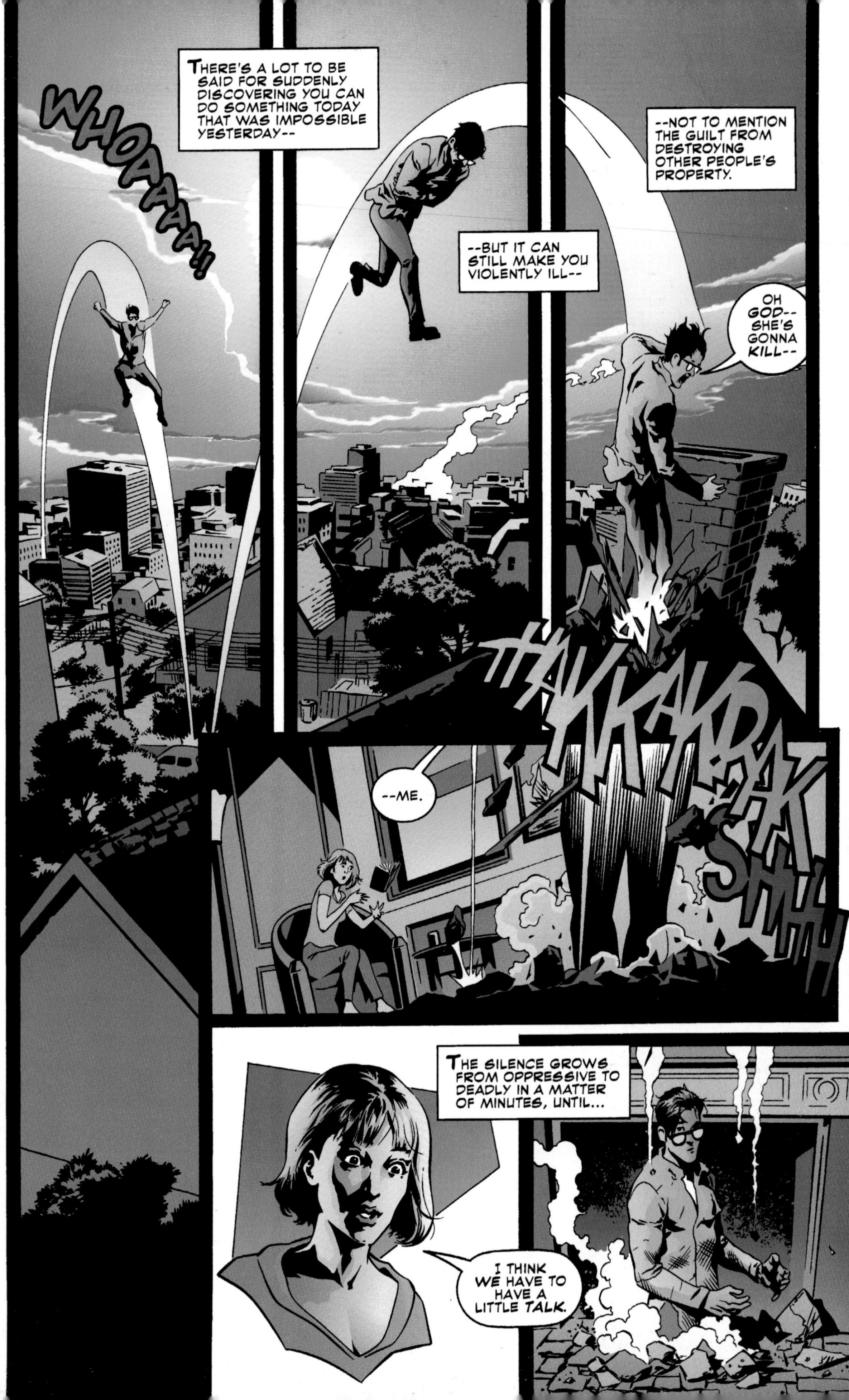
WHOAAAAA!!
THERE'S A LOT TO BE SAID FOR SUDDENLY DISCOVERING YOU CAN DO SOMETHING TODAY THAT WAS IMPOSSIBLE YESTERDAY--
--BUT IT CAN STILL MAKE YOU VIOLENTLY ILL--
--NOT TO MENTION THE GUILT FROM DESTROYING OTHER PEOPLE'S PROPERTY.
OH GOD-- SHE'S GONNA KILL--
THAKKAKRAKK
--ME.
SHHH
THE SILENCE GROWS FROM OPPRESSIVE TO DEADLY IN A MATTER OF MINUTES, UNTIL...
I THINK WE HAVE TO HAVE A LITTLE TALK.

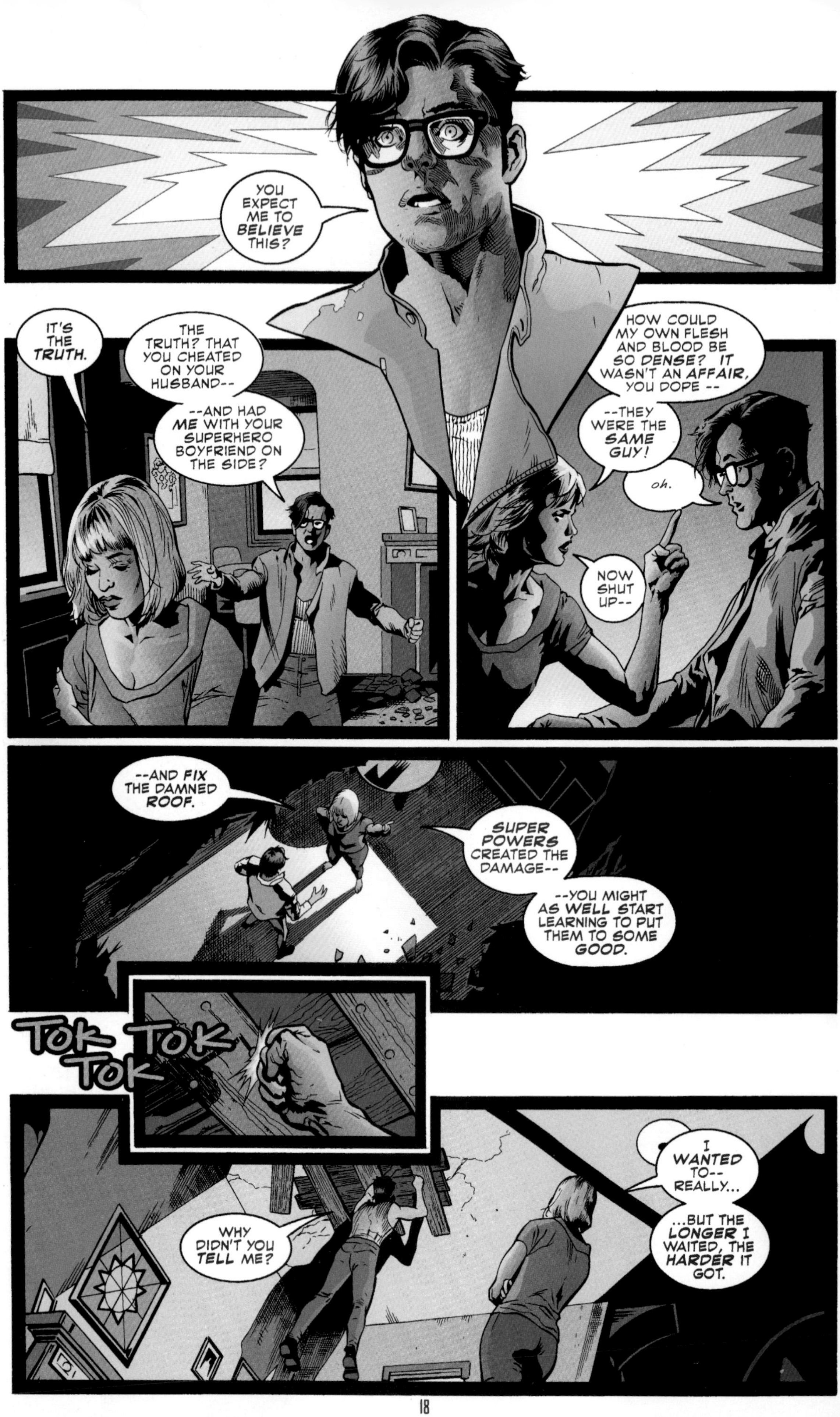
YOU EXPECT ME TO BELIEVE THIS?
IT'S THE TRUTH.
THE TRUTH? THAT YOU CHEATED ON YOUR HUSBAND--
--AND HAD ME WITH YOUR SUPERHERO BOYFRIEND ON THE SIDE?
HOW COULD MY OWN FLESH AND BLOOD BE SO DENSE? IT WASN'T AN AFFAIR, YOU DOPE --
--THEY WERE THE SAME GUY!
oh.
NOW SHUT UP--
--AND FIX THE DAMNED ROOF.
SUPER POWERS CREATED THE DAMAGE--
--YOU MIGHT AS WELL START LEARNING TO PUT THEM TO SOME GOOD.
TOK TOK TOK
WHY DIDN'T YOU TELL ME?
I WANTED TO-- REALLY...
...BUT THE LONGER I WAITED, THE HARDER IT GOT.

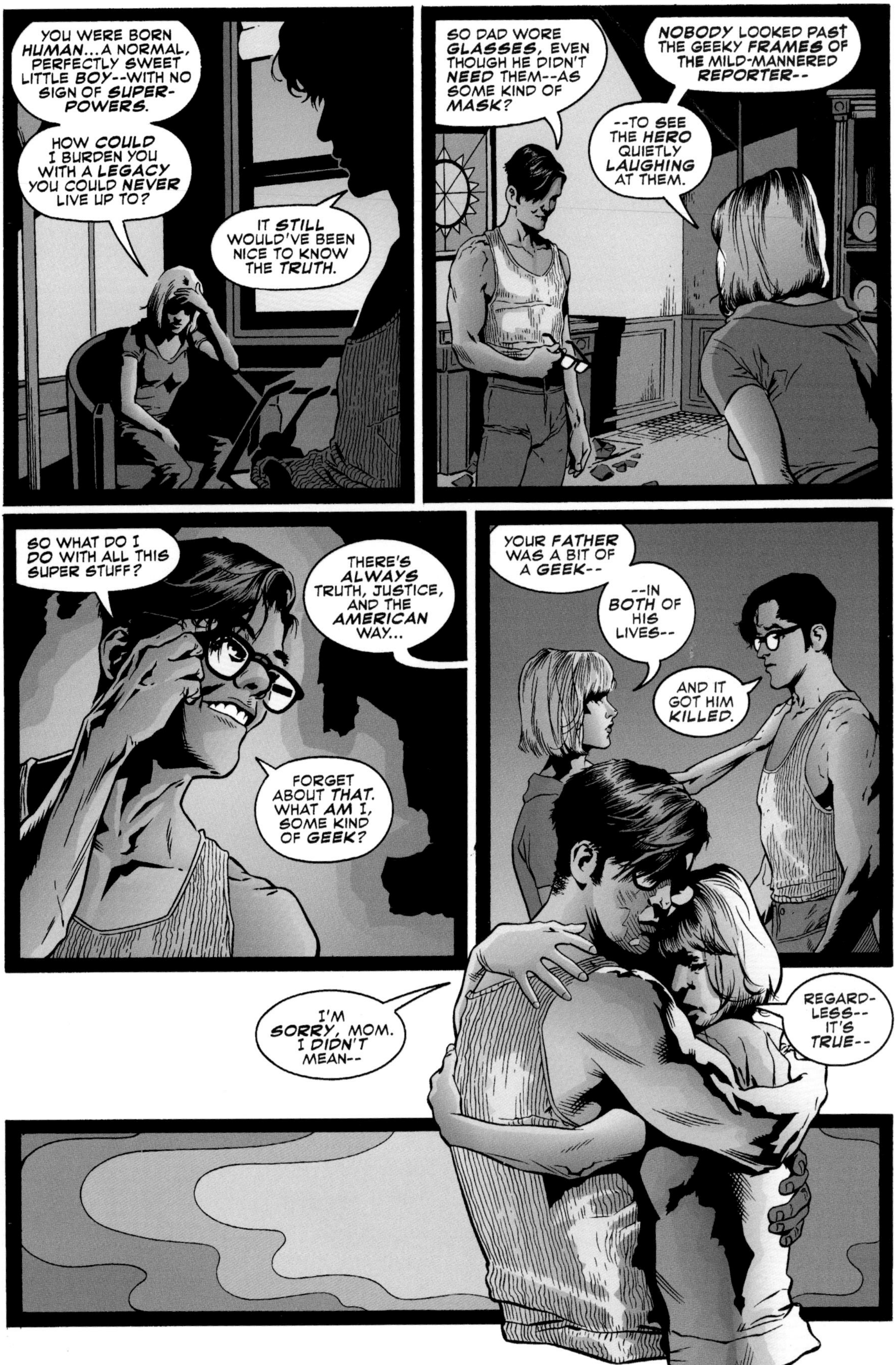
YOU WERE BORN HUMAN... A NORMAL, PERFECTLY SWEET LITTLE BOY--WITH NO SIGN OF SUPER-POWERS.
HOW COULD I BURDEN YOU WITH A LEGACY YOU COULD NEVER LIVE UP TO?
IT STILL WOULD'VE BEEN NICE TO KNOW THE TRUTH.
SO DAD WORE GLASSES, EVEN THOUGH HE DIDN'T NEED THEM--AS SOME KIND OF MASK?
NOBODY LOOKED PAST THE GEEKY FRAMES OF THE MILD-MANNERED REPORTER--
--TO SEE THE HERO QUIETLY LAUGHING AT THEM.
SO WHAT DO I DO WITH ALL THIS SUPER STUFF?
THERE'S ALWAYS TRUTH, JUSTICE, AND THE AMERICAN WAY...
FORGET ABOUT THAT. WHAT AM I, SOME KIND OF GEEK?
YOUR FATHER WAS A BIT OF A GEEK--
--IN BOTH OF HIS LIVES--
AND IT GOT HIM KILLED.
I'M SORRY, MOM. I DIDN'T MEAN--
REGARD-LESS-- IT'S TRUE--

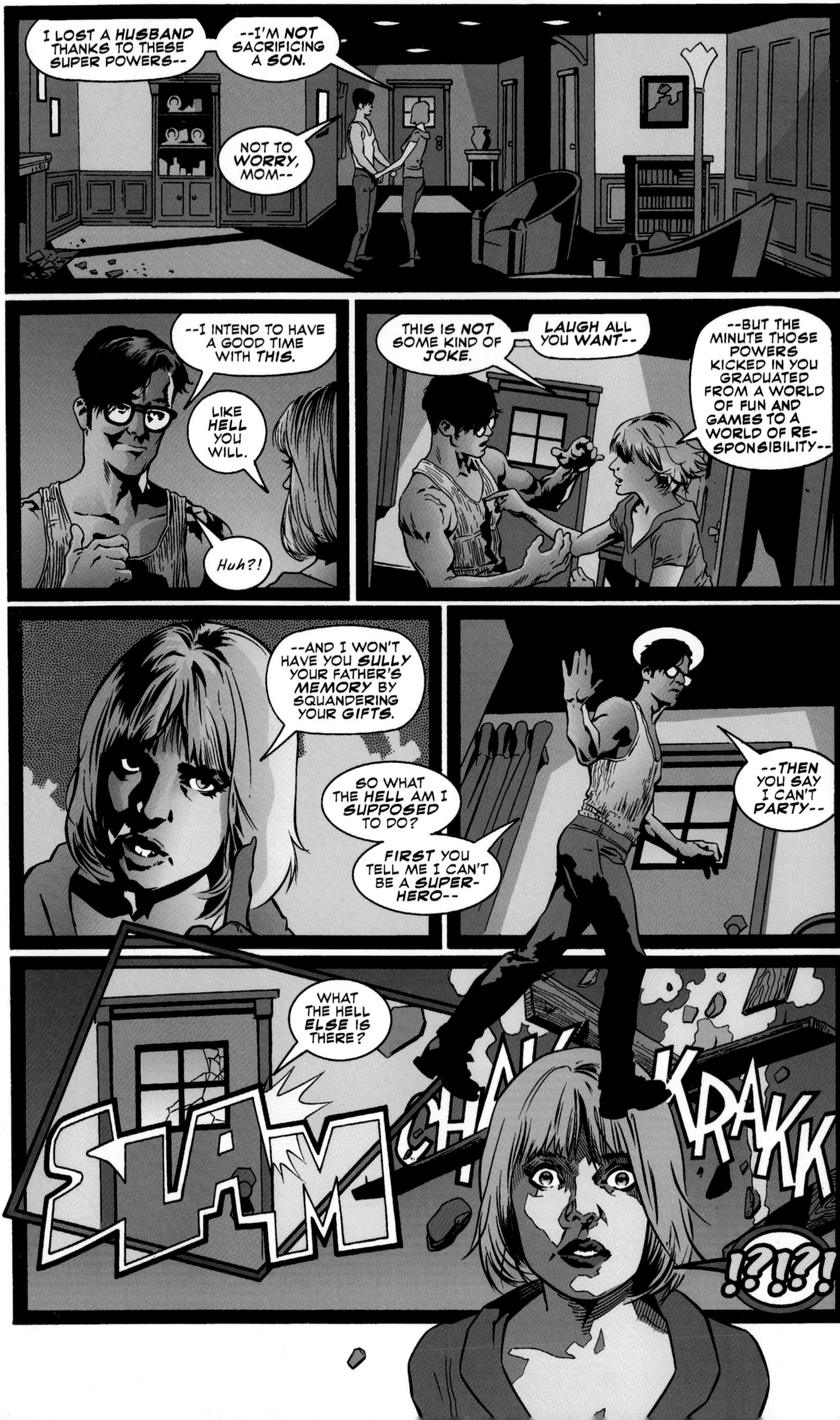
I LOST A HUSBAND THANKS TO THESE SUPER POWERS--
--I'M NOT SACRIFICING A SON.
NOT TO WORRY, MOM--
--I INTEND TO HAVE A GOOD TIME WITH THIS.
LIKE HELL YOU WILL.
Huh?!
THIS IS NOT SOME KIND OF JOKE.
LAUGH ALL YOU WANT--
--BUT THE MINUTE THOSE POWERS KICKED IN YOU GRADUATED FROM A WORLD OF FUN AND GAMES TO A WORLD OF RE-SPONSIBILITY--
--AND I WON'T HAVE YOU SULLY YOUR FATHER'S MEMORY BY SQUANDERING YOUR GIFTS.
SO WHAT THE HELL AM I SUPPOSED TO DO?
FIRST YOU TELL ME I CAN'T BE A SUPER-HERO--
--THEN YOU SAY I CAN'T PARTY--
WHAT THE HELL ELSE IS THERE?
SLAM
KRAKK
!?!?!

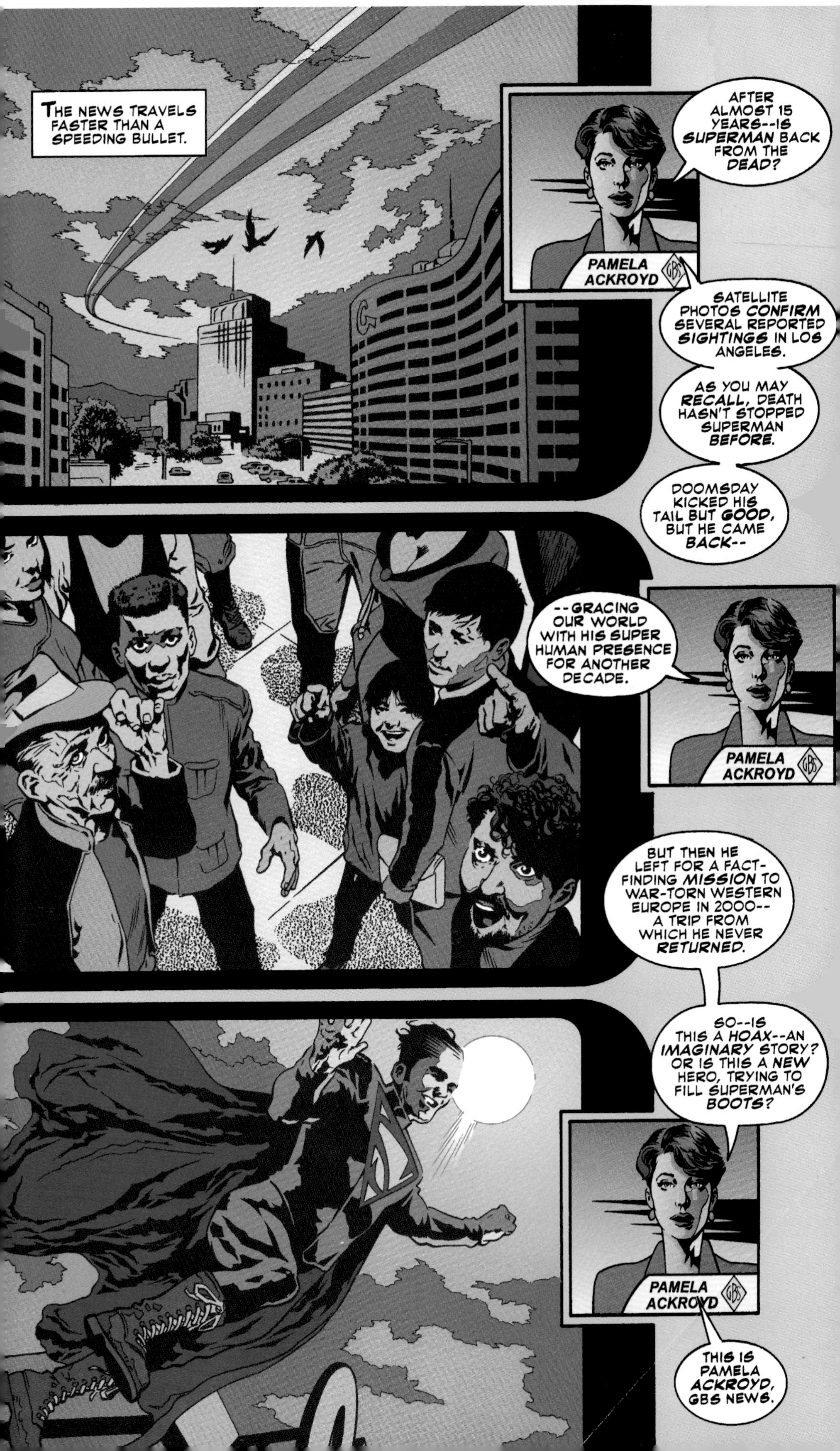
THE NEWS TRAVELS FASTER THAN A SPEEDING BULLET.
AFTER ALMOST 15 YEARS--IS SUPERMAN BACK FROM THE DEAD?
PAMELA ACKROYD GBS
SATELLITE PHOTOS CONFIRM SEVERAL REPORTED SIGHTINGS IN LOS ANGELES.
AS YOU MAY RECALL, DEATH HASN'T STOPPED SUPERMAN BEFORE.
DOOMSDAY KICKED HIS TAIL BUT GOOD, BUT HE CAME BACK--
--GRACING OUR WORLD WITH HIS SUPER HUMAN PRESENCE FOR ANOTHER DECADE.
PAMELA ACKROYD GBS
BUT THEN HE LEFT FOR A FACT-FINDING MISSION TO WAR-TORN WESTERN EUROPE IN 2000--A TRIP FROM WHICH HE NEVER RETURNED.
SO--IS THIS A HOAX--AN IMAGINARY STORY? OR IS THIS A NEW HERO, TRYING TO FILL SUPERMAN'S BOOTS?
PAMELA ACKROYD GBS
THIS IS PAMELA ACKROYD, GBS NEWS.

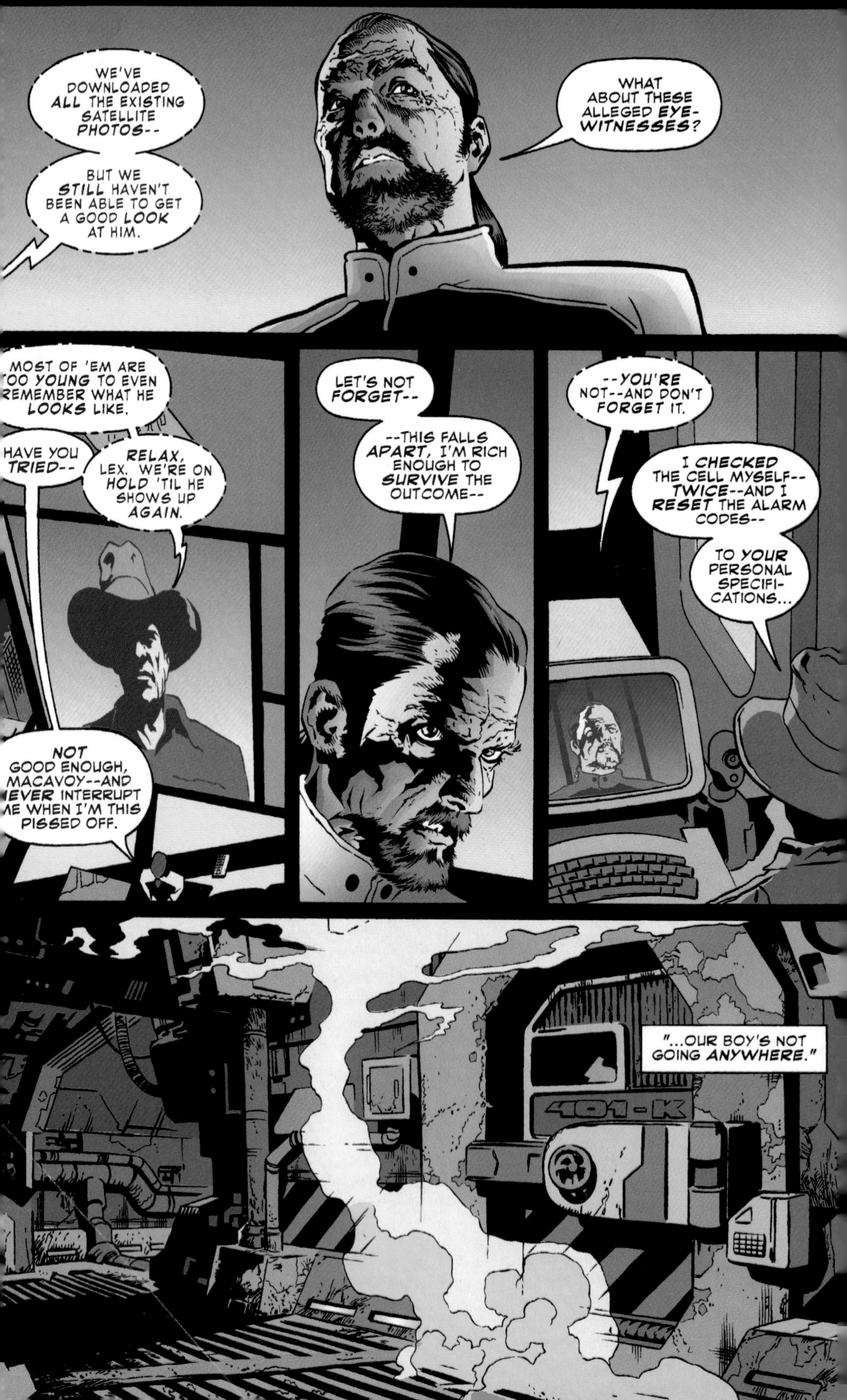
WE'VE DOWNLOADED ALL THE EXISTING SATELLITE PHOTOS--
BUT WE STILL HAVEN'T BEEN ABLE TO GET A GOOD LOOK AT HIM.
WHAT ABOUT THESE ALLEGED EYE-WITNESSES?
MOST OF 'EM ARE TOO YOUNG TO EVEN REMEMBER WHAT HE LOOKS LIKE.
HAVE YOU TRIED--
RELAX, LEX. WE'RE ON HOLD 'TIL HE SHOWS UP AGAIN.
NOT GOOD ENOUGH, MACAVOY--AND NEVER INTERRUPT ME WHEN I'M THIS PISSED OFF.
LET'S NOT FORGET--
--THIS FALLS APART, I'M RICH ENOUGH TO SURVIVE THE OUTCOME--
--YOU'RE NOT--AND DON'T FORGET IT.
I CHECKED THE CELL MYSELF--TWICE--AND I RESET THE ALARM CODES--
TO YOUR PERSONAL SPECIFI-CATIONS...
"...OUR BOY'S NOT GOING ANYWHERE."
401-K

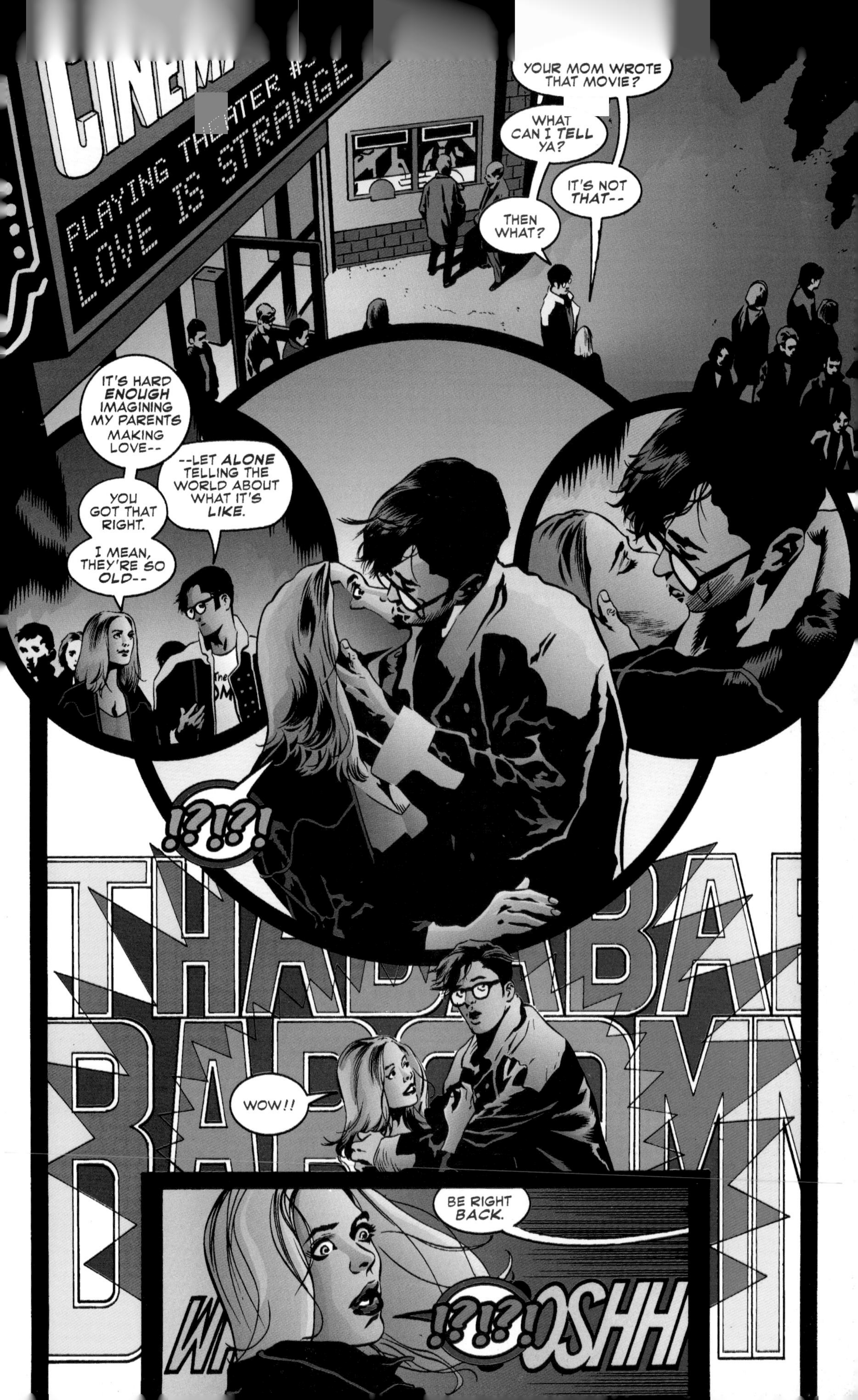
PLAYING THEATER #
LOVE IS STRANGE
YOUR MOM WROTE THAT MOVIE?
WHAT CAN I TELL YA?
IT'S NOT THAT--
THEN WHAT?
IT'S HARD ENOUGH IMAGINING MY PARENTS MAKING LOVE--
--LET ALONE TELLING THE WORLD ABOUT WHAT IT'S LIKE.
YOU GOT THAT RIGHT.
I MEAN, THEY'RE SO OLD--
!?!?!
WOW!!
BE RIGHT BACK.
!?!?!

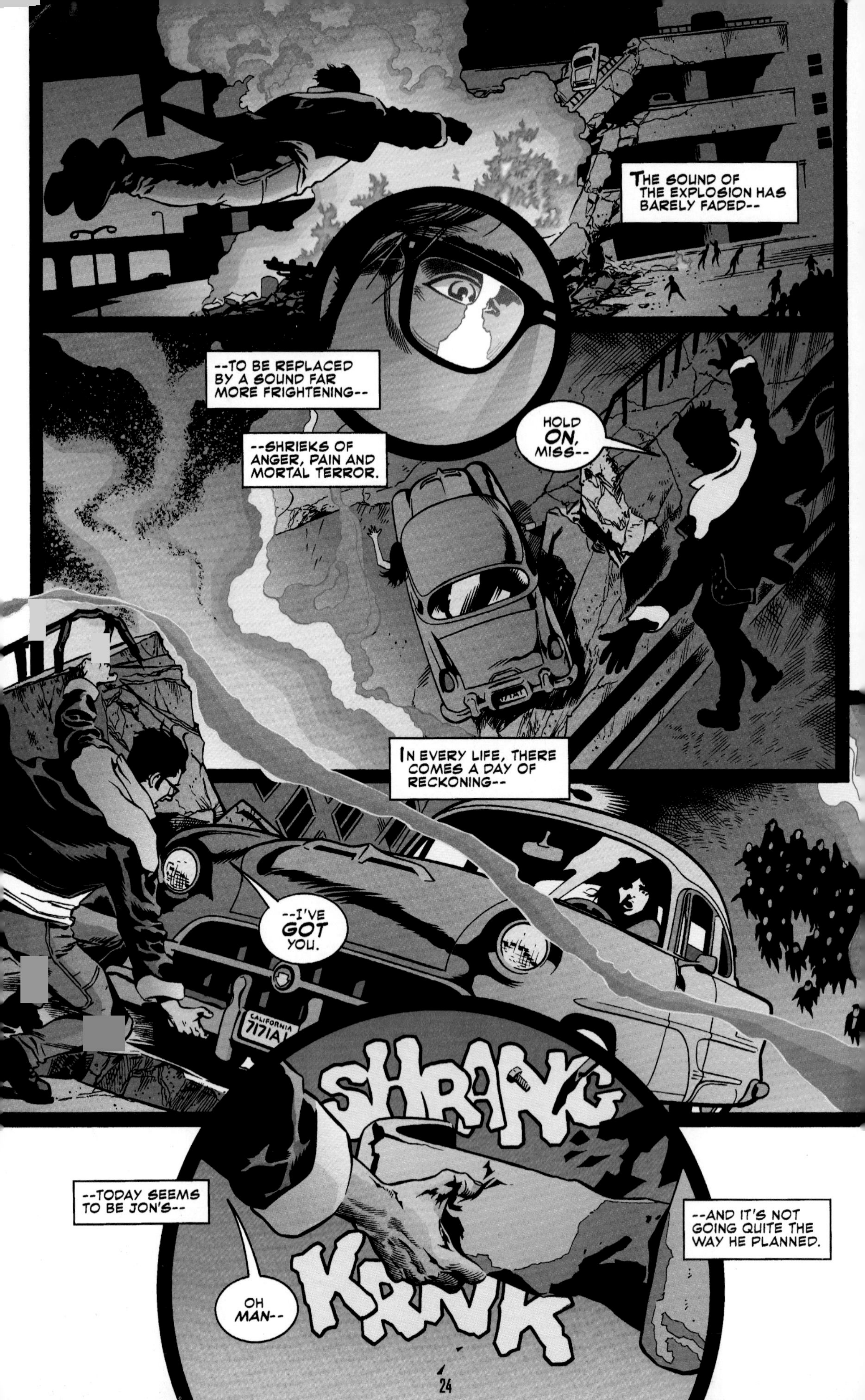
THE SOUND OF THE EXPLOSION HAS BARELY FADED--
--TO BE REPLACED BY A SOUND FAR MORE FRIGHTENING--
--SHRIEKS OF ANGER, PAIN AND MORTAL TERROR.
HOLD ON, MISS--
IN EVERY LIFE, THERE COMES A DAY OF RECKONING--
--I'VE GOT YOU.
CALIFORNIA
7171AL
SHRANG
--TODAY SEEMS TO BE JON'S--
--AND IT'S NOT GOING QUITE THE WAY HE PLANNED.
OH MAN--
KRNK

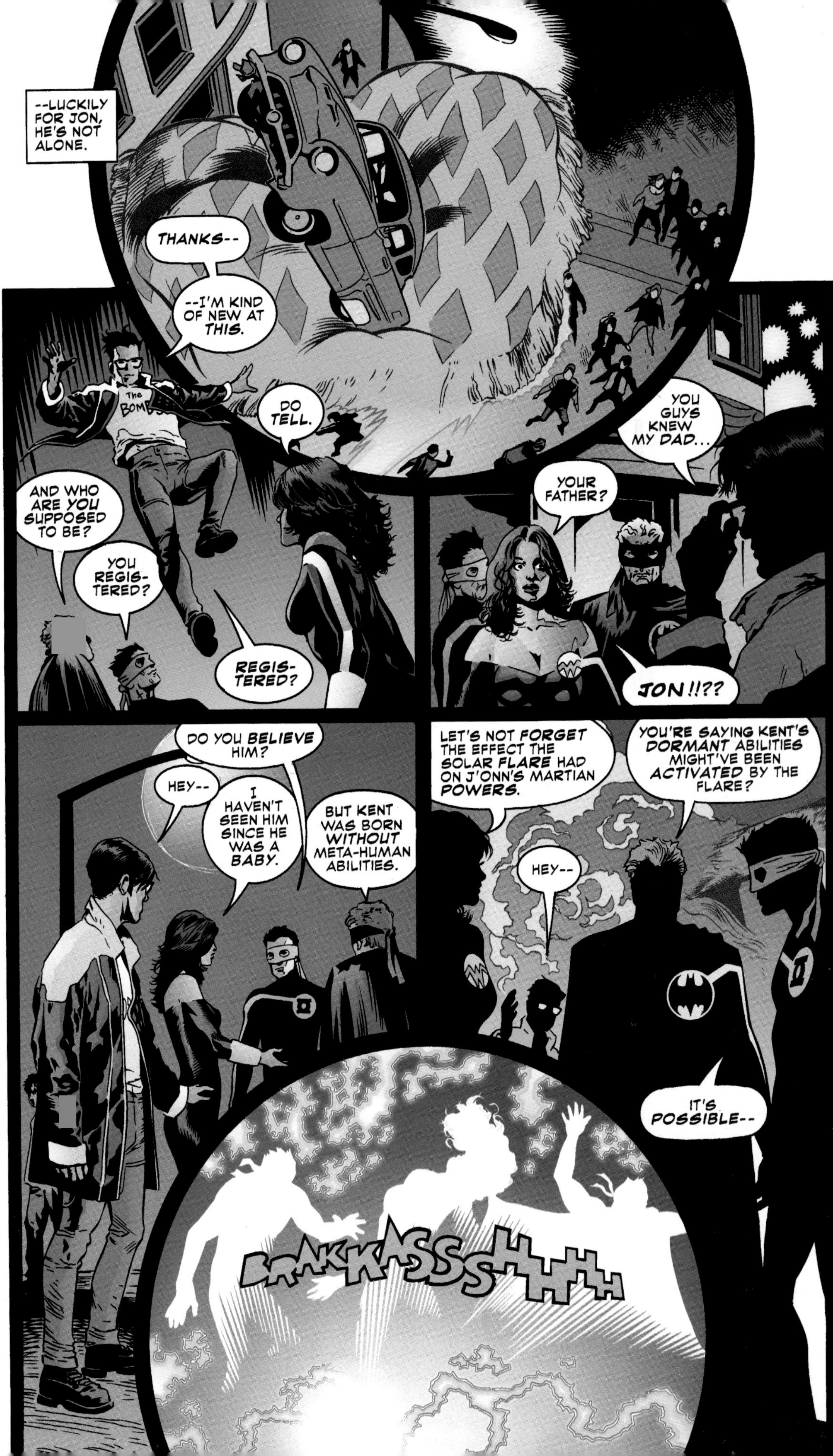
--LUCKILY FOR JON, HE'S NOT ALONE.
THANKS--
--I'M KIND OF NEW AT THIS.
DO TELL.
AND WHO ARE YOU SUPPOSED TO BE?
YOU REGIS-TERED?
REGIS-TERED?
YOU GUYS KNEW MY DAD...
YOUR FATHER?
JON!!??
DO YOU BELIEVE HIM?
HEY--
I HAVEN'T SEEN HIM SINCE HE WAS A BABY.
BUT KENT WAS BORN WITHOUT META-HUMAN ABILITIES.
LET'S NOT FORGET THE EFFECT THE SOLAR FLARE HAD ON J'ONN'S MARTIAN POWERS.
YOU'RE SAYING KENT'S DORMANT ABILITIES MIGHT'VE BEEN ACTIVATED BY THE FLARE?
HEY--
IT'S POSSIBLE--
BRAKKASSSHHHHH

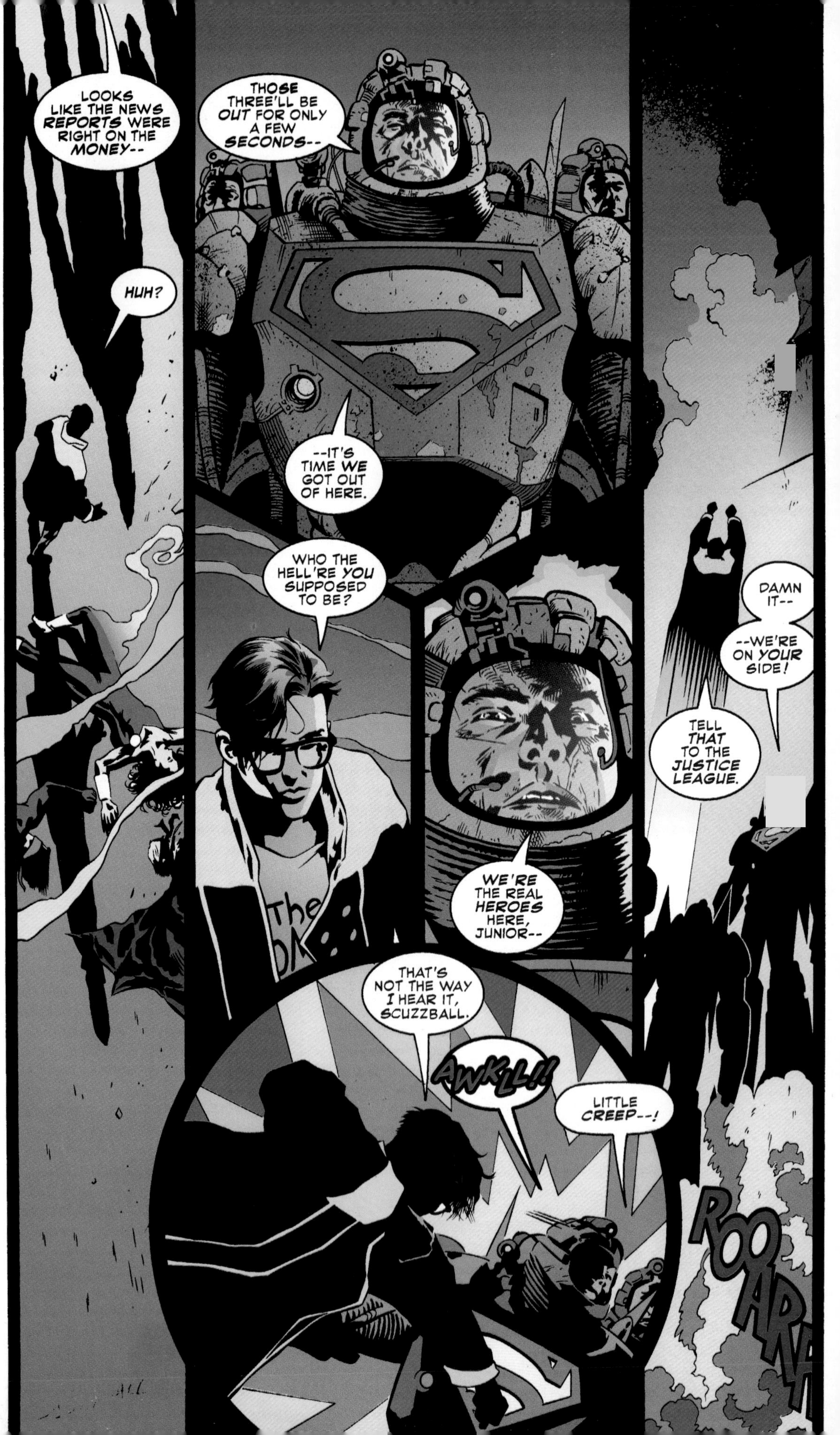
LOOKS LIKE THE NEWS REPORTS WERE RIGHT ON THE MONEY--
THOSE THREE'LL BE OUT FOR ONLY A FEW SECONDS--
HUH?
--IT'S TIME WE GOT OUT OF HERE.
WHO THE HELL'RE YOU SUPPOSED TO BE?
WE'RE THE REAL HEROES HERE, JUNIOR--
THAT'S NOT THE WAY I HEAR IT, SCUZZBALL.
AWKLL!!
LITTLE CREEP--!
DAMN IT--
--WE'RE ON YOUR SIDE!
TELL THAT TO THE JUSTICE LEAGUE.
ROOARR

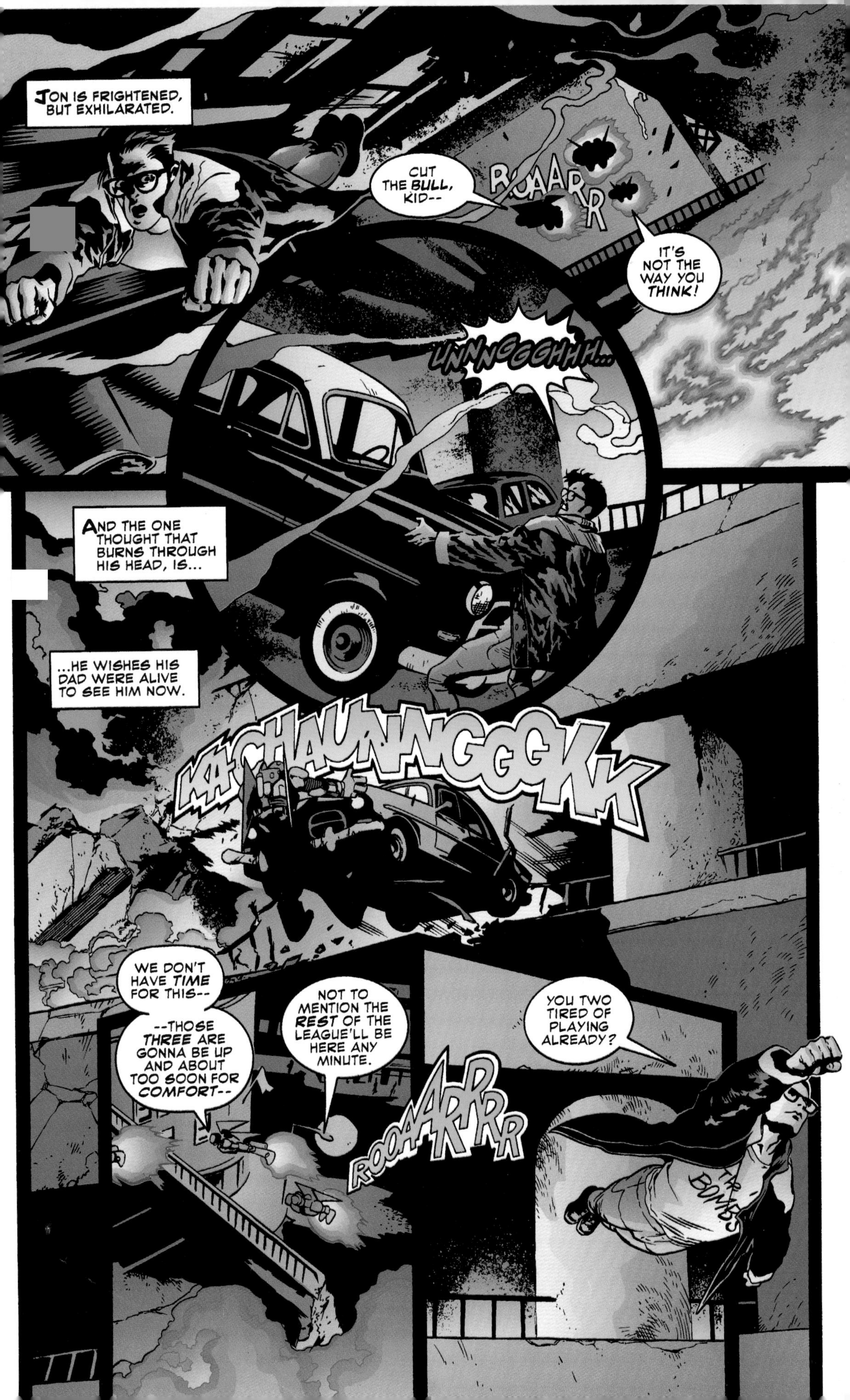
JON IS FRIGHTENED, BUT EXHILARATED.
CUT THE BULL, KID--
ROAARRR
IT'S NOT THE WAY YOU THINK!
UNNNGGGHHH...
AND THE ONE THOUGHT THAT BURNS THROUGH HIS HEAD, IS...
...HE WISHES HIS DAD WERE ALIVE TO SEE HIM NOW.
KACHAUNNGGGKK
WE DON'T HAVE TIME FOR THIS--
--THOSE THREE ARE GONNA BE UP AND ABOUT TOO SOON FOR COMFORT--
NOT TO MENTION THE REST OF THE LEAGUE'LL BE HERE ANY MINUTE.
YOU TWO TIRED OF PLAYING ALREADY?
ROOAARRRR

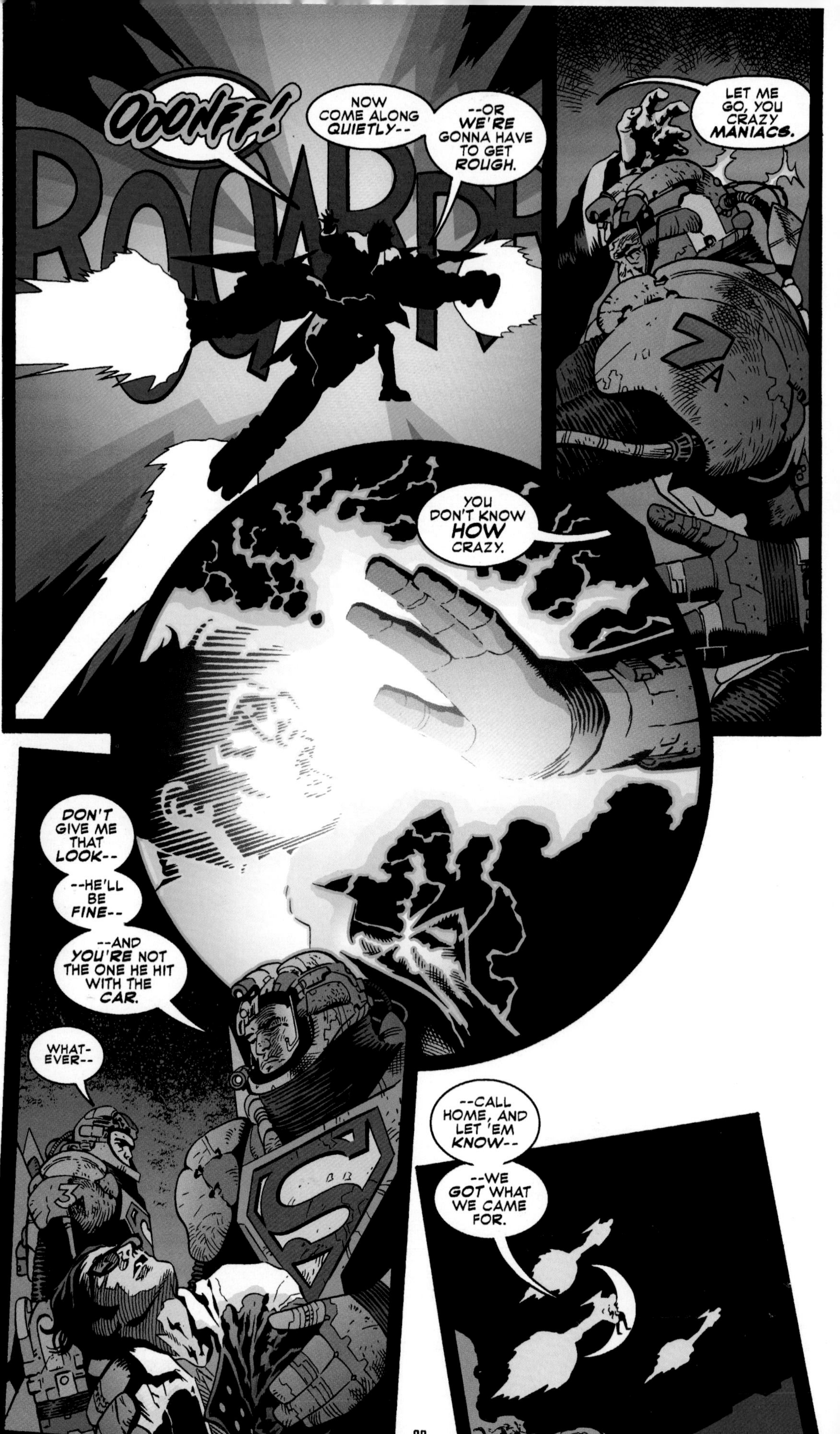
OOONFF!
ROOARR
NOW COME ALONG QUIETLY--
--OR WE'RE GONNA HAVE TO GET ROUGH.
LET ME GO, YOU CRAZY MANIACS.
YOU DON'T KNOW HOW CRAZY.
DON'T GIVE ME THAT LOOK--
--HE'LL BE FINE--
--AND YOU'RE NOT THE ONE HE HIT WITH THE CAR.
WHAT-EVER--
--CALL HOME, AND LET 'EM KNOW--
--WE GOT WHAT WE CAME FOR.

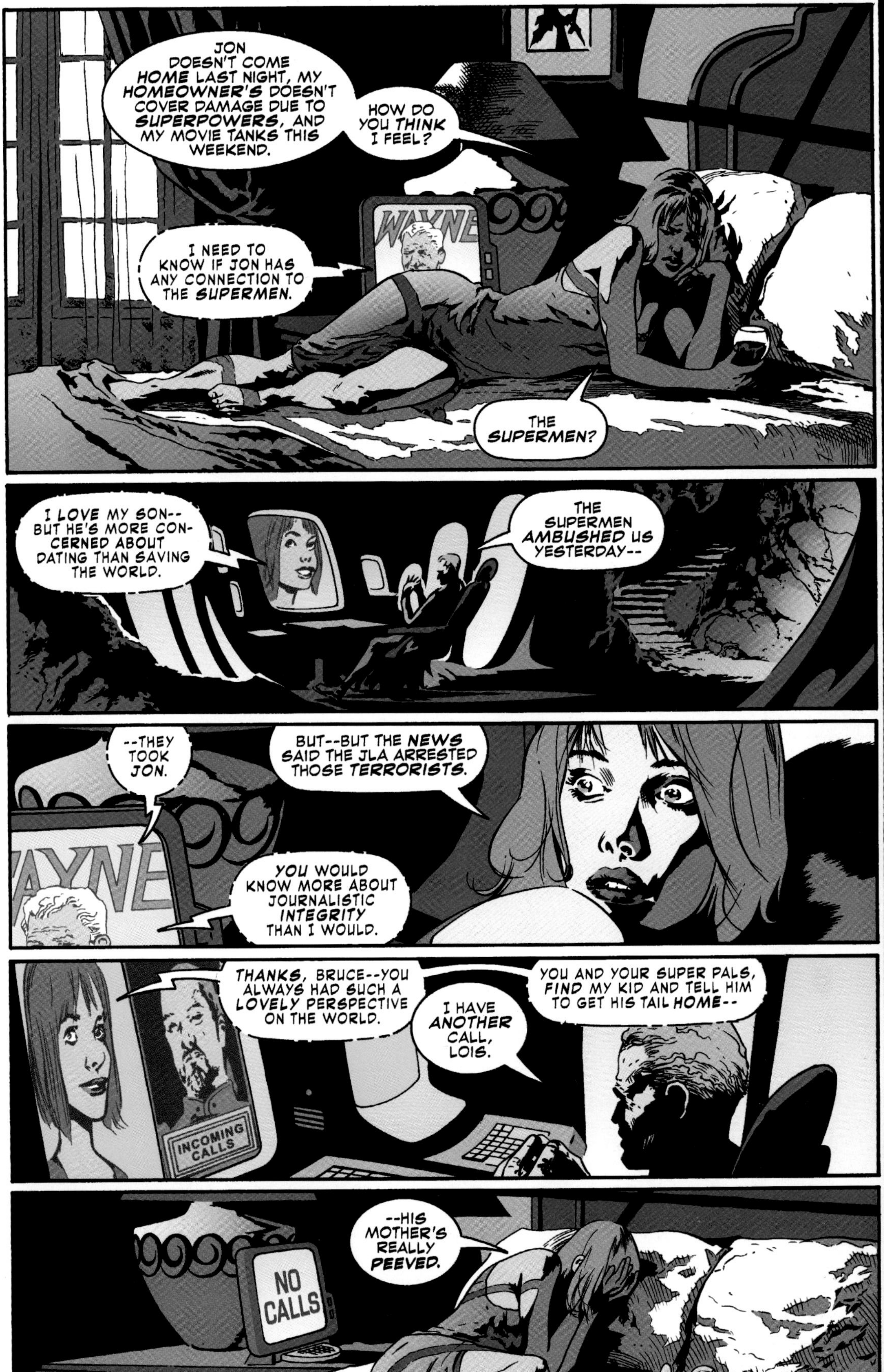
JON DOESN'T COME HOME LAST NIGHT, MY HOMEOWNER'S DOESN'T COVER DAMAGE DUE TO SUPERPOWERS, AND MY MOVIE TANKS THIS WEEKEND.
HOW DO YOU THINK I FEEL?
WAYNE
I NEED TO KNOW IF JON HAS ANY CONNECTION TO THE SUPERMEN.
THE SUPERMEN?
I LOVE MY SON-- BUT HE'S MORE CON-CERNED ABOUT DATING THAN SAVING THE WORLD.
THE SUPERMEN AMBUSHED US YESTERDAY--
--THEY TOOK JON.
BUT--BUT THE NEWS SAID THE JLA ARRESTED THOSE TERRORISTS.
YOU WOULD KNOW MORE ABOUT JOURNALISTIC INTEGRITY THAN I WOULD.
THANKS, BRUCE--YOU ALWAYS HAD SUCH A LOVELY PERSPECTIVE ON THE WORLD.
I HAVE ANOTHER CALL, LOIS.
YOU AND YOUR SUPER PALS, FIND MY KID AND TELL HIM TO GET HIS TAIL HOME--
INCOMING CALLS
--HIS MOTHER'S REALLY PEEVED.
NO CALLS

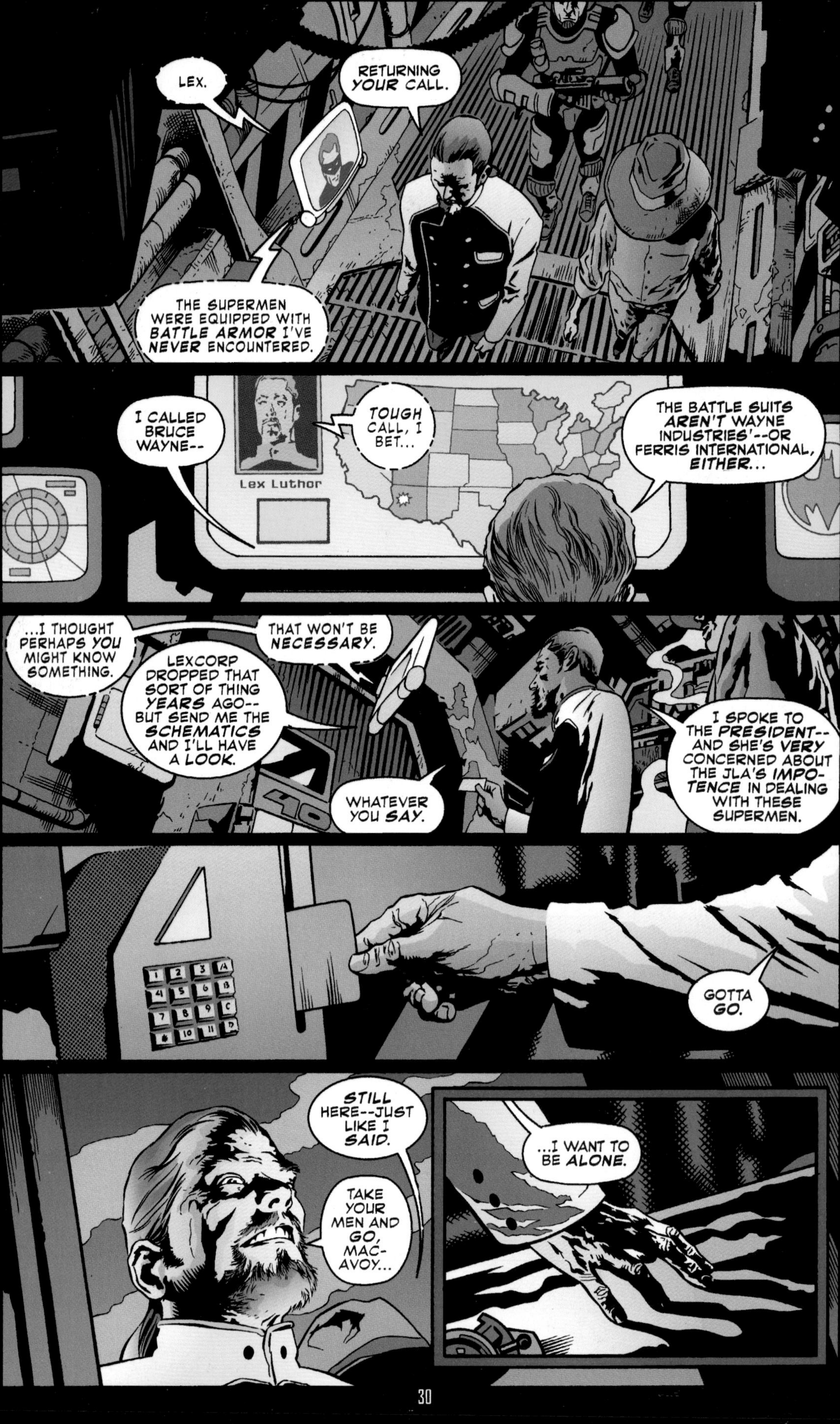
LEX.
RETURNING YOUR CALL.
THE SUPERMEN WERE EQUIPPED WITH BATTLE ARMOR I'VE NEVER ENCOUNTERED.
Lex Luthor
I CALLED BRUCE WAYNE--
TOUGH CALL, I BET...
THE BATTLE SUITS AREN'T WAYNE INDUSTRIES'--OR FERRIS INTERNATIONAL, EITHER...
...I THOUGHT PERHAPS YOU MIGHT KNOW SOMETHING.
LEXCORP DROPPED THAT SORT OF THING YEARS AGO--BUT SEND ME THE SCHEMATICS AND I'LL HAVE A LOOK.
THAT WON'T BE NECESSARY.
WHATEVER YOU SAY.
I SPOKE TO THE PRESIDENT--AND SHE'S VERY CONCERNED ABOUT THE JLA'S IMPOTENCE IN DEALING WITH THESE SUPERMEN.
GOTTA GO.
STILL HERE--JUST LIKE I SAID.
TAKE YOUR MEN AND GO, MAC-AVOY...
...I WANT TO BE ALONE.

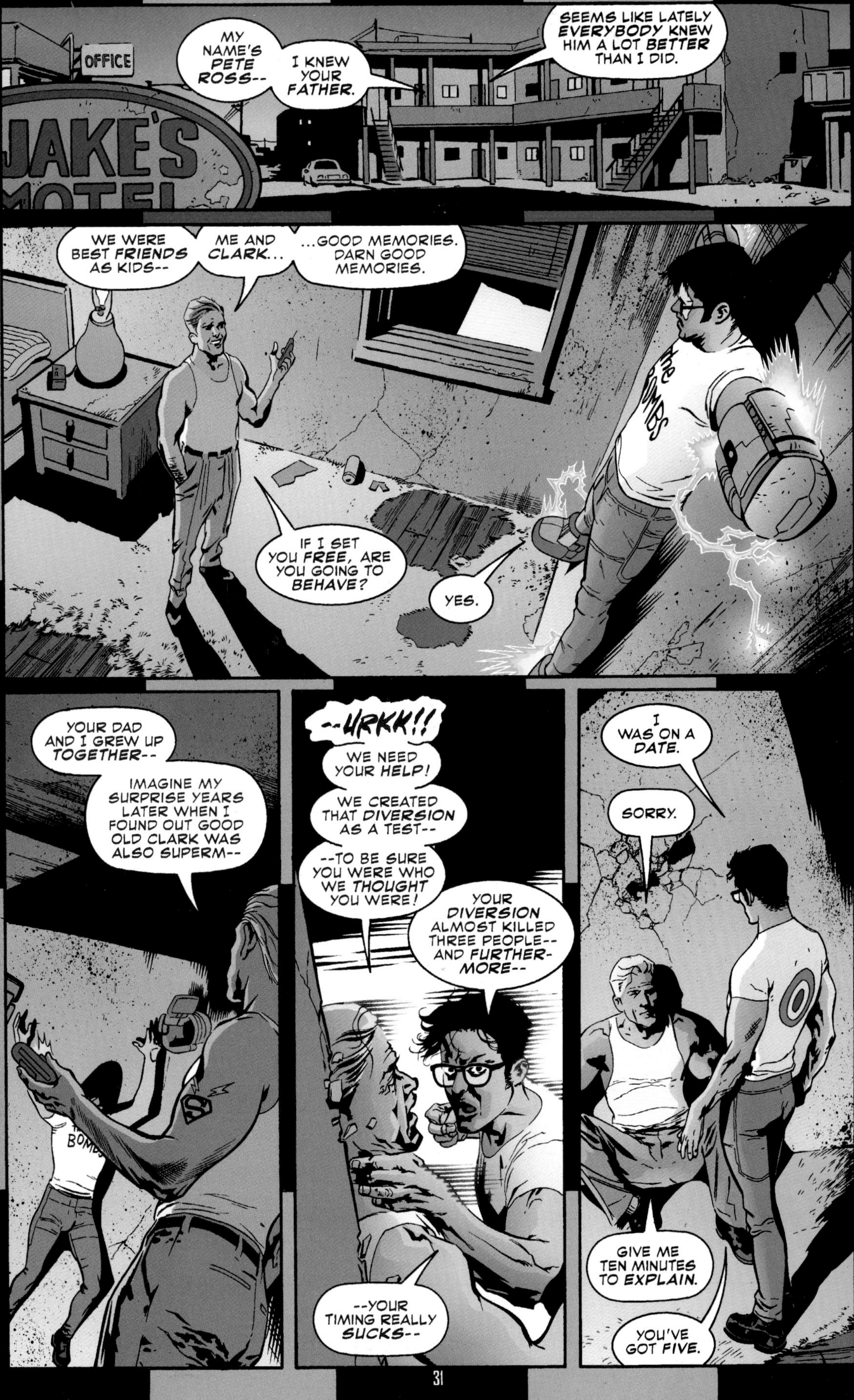

OFFICE
JAKE'S MOTEL
MY NAME'S PETE ROSS--
I KNEW YOUR FATHER.
SEEMS LIKE LATELY EVERYBODY KNEW HIM A LOT BETTER THAN I DID.
WE WERE BEST FRIENDS AS KIDS--
ME AND CLARK...
...GOOD MEMORIES. DARN GOOD MEMORIES.
IF I SET YOU FREE, ARE YOU GOING TO BEHAVE?
YES.
YOUR DAD AND I GREW UP TOGETHER--
IMAGINE MY SURPRISE YEARS LATER WHEN I FOUND OUT GOOD OLD CLARK WAS ALSO SUPERM--
--URKK!!
WE NEED YOUR HELP!
WE CREATED THAT DIVERSION AS A TEST--
--TO BE SURE YOU WERE WHO WE THOUGHT YOU WERE!
YOUR DIVERSION ALMOST KILLED THREE PEOPLE--AND FURTHER-MORE--
--YOUR TIMING REALLY SUCKS--
I WAS ON A DATE.
SORRY.
GIVE ME TEN MINUTES TO EXPLAIN.
YOU'VE GOT FIVE.

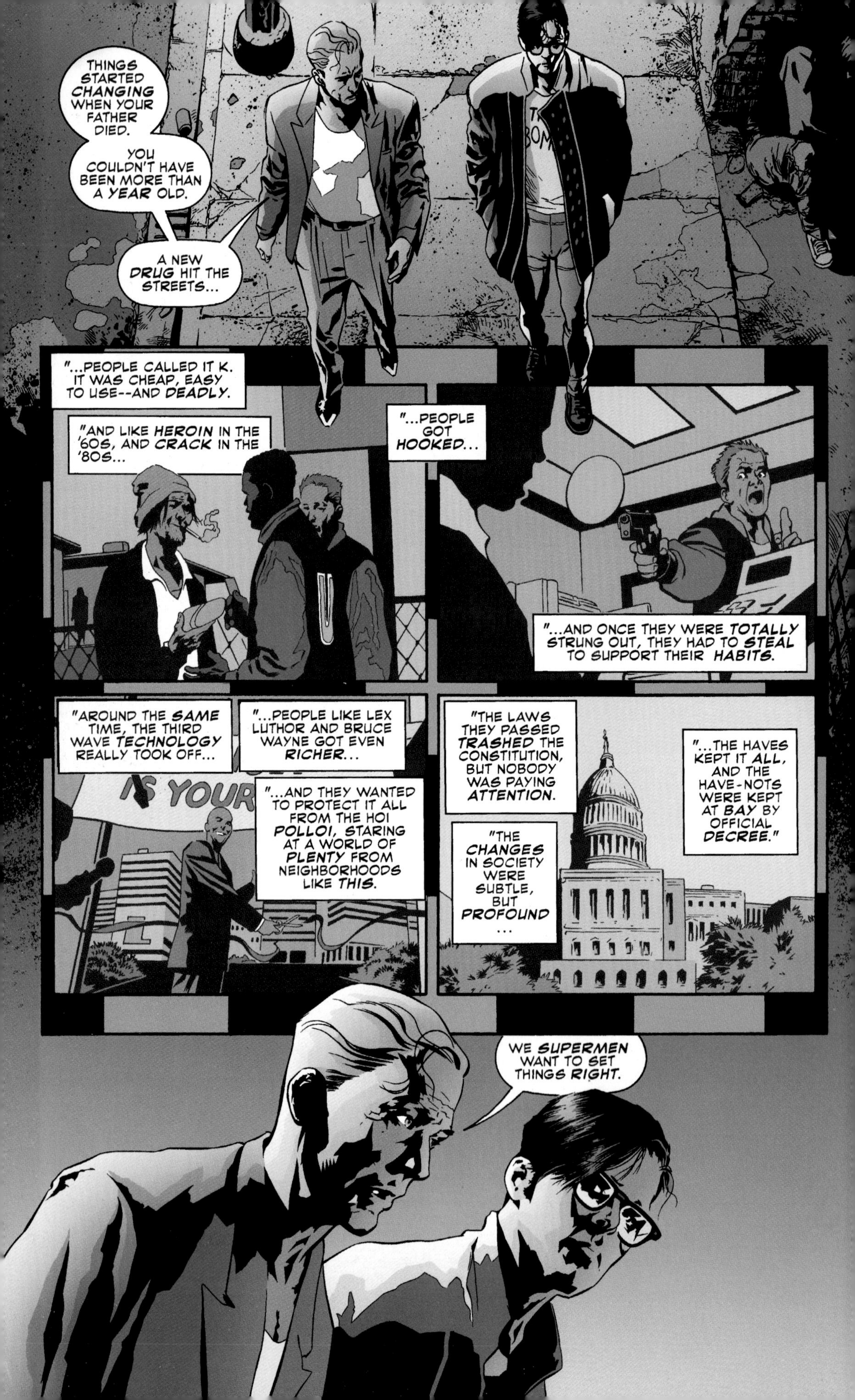
THINGS STARTED CHANGING WHEN YOUR FATHER DIED.
YOU COULDN'T HAVE BEEN MORE THAN A YEAR OLD.
A NEW DRUG HIT THE STREETS...
"...PEOPLE CALLED IT K. IT WAS CHEAP, EASY TO USE--AND DEADLY.
"AND LIKE HEROIN IN THE '60S, AND CRACK IN THE '80S...
"...PEOPLE GOT HOOKED...
"...AND ONCE THEY WERE TOTALLY STRUNG OUT, THEY HAD TO STEAL TO SUPPORT THEIR HABITS.
"AROUND THE SAME TIME, THE THIRD WAVE TECHNOLOGY REALLY TOOK OFF...
"...PEOPLE LIKE LEX LUTHOR AND BRUCE WAYNE GOT EVEN RICHER...
IS YOUR
"...AND THEY WANTED TO PROTECT IT ALL FROM THE HOI POLLOI, STARING AT A WORLD OF PLENTY FROM NEIGHBORHOODS LIKE THIS.
"THE LAWS THEY PASSED TRASHED THE CONSTITUTION, BUT NOBODY WAS PAYING ATTENTION.
"THE CHANGES IN SOCIETY WERE SUBTLE, BUT PROFOUND...
"...THE HAVES KEPT IT ALL, AND THE HAVE-NOTS WERE KEPT AT BAY BY OFFICIAL DECREE."
WE SUPERMEN WANT TO SET THINGS RIGHT.

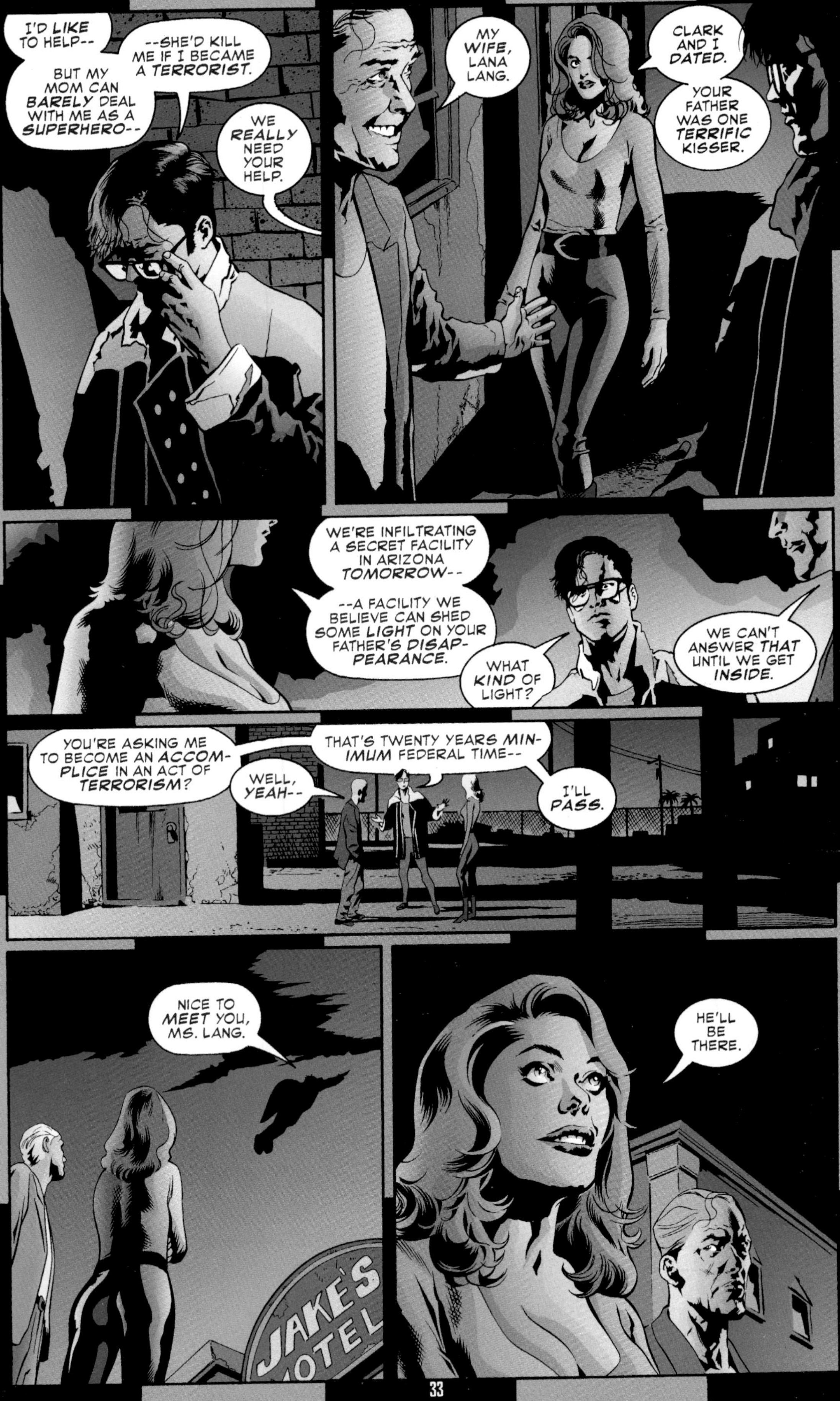
I'D LIKE TO HELP--
BUT MY MOM CAN BARELY DEAL WITH ME AS A SUPERHERO--
--SHE'D KILL ME IF I BECAME A TERRORIST.
WE REALLY NEED YOUR HELP.
MY WIFE, LANA LANG.
CLARK AND I DATED.
YOUR FATHER WAS ONE TERRIFIC KISSER.
WE'RE INFILTRATING A SECRET FACILITY IN ARIZONA TOMORROW--
--A FACILITY WE BELIEVE CAN SHED SOME LIGHT ON YOUR FATHER'S DISAPPEARANCE.
WHAT KIND OF LIGHT?
WE CAN'T ANSWER THAT UNTIL WE GET INSIDE.
YOU'RE ASKING ME TO BECOME AN ACCOMPLICE IN AN ACT OF TERRORISM?
WELL, YEAH--
THAT'S TWENTY YEARS MINIMUM FEDERAL TIME--
I'LL PASS.
NICE TO MEET YOU, MS. LANG.
JAKE'S MOTEL
HE'LL BE THERE.

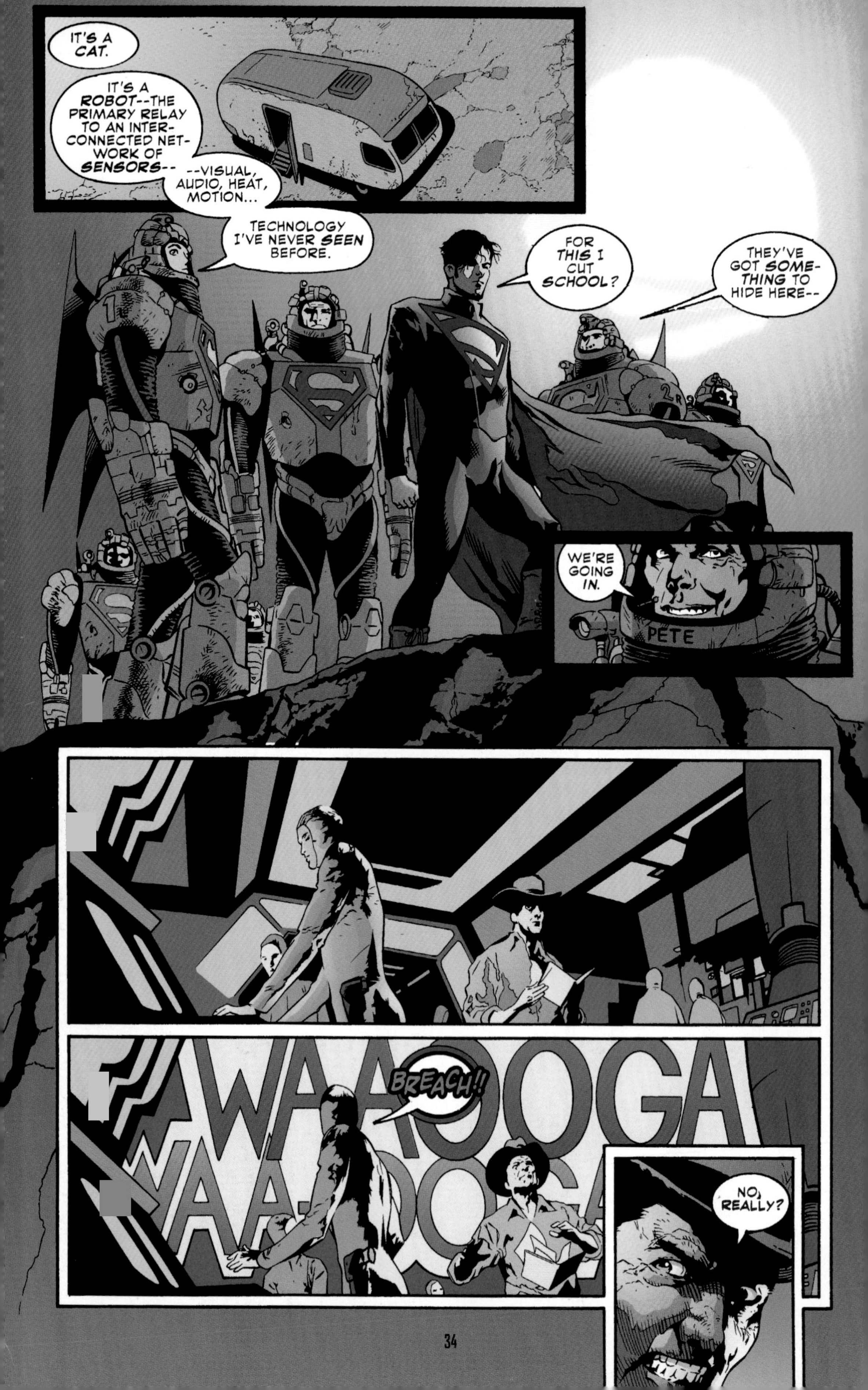
IT'S A CAT.
IT'S A ROBOT--THE PRIMARY RELAY TO AN INTER-CONNECTED NET-WORK OF SENSORS--
--VISUAL, AUDIO, HEAT, MOTION...
TECHNOLOGY I'VE NEVER SEEN BEFORE.
FOR THIS I CUT SCHOOL?
THEY'VE GOT SOME-THING TO HIDE HERE--
WE'RE GOING IN.
PETE
WAAOOGA
BREACH!!
WAAOOGA
NO, REALLY?

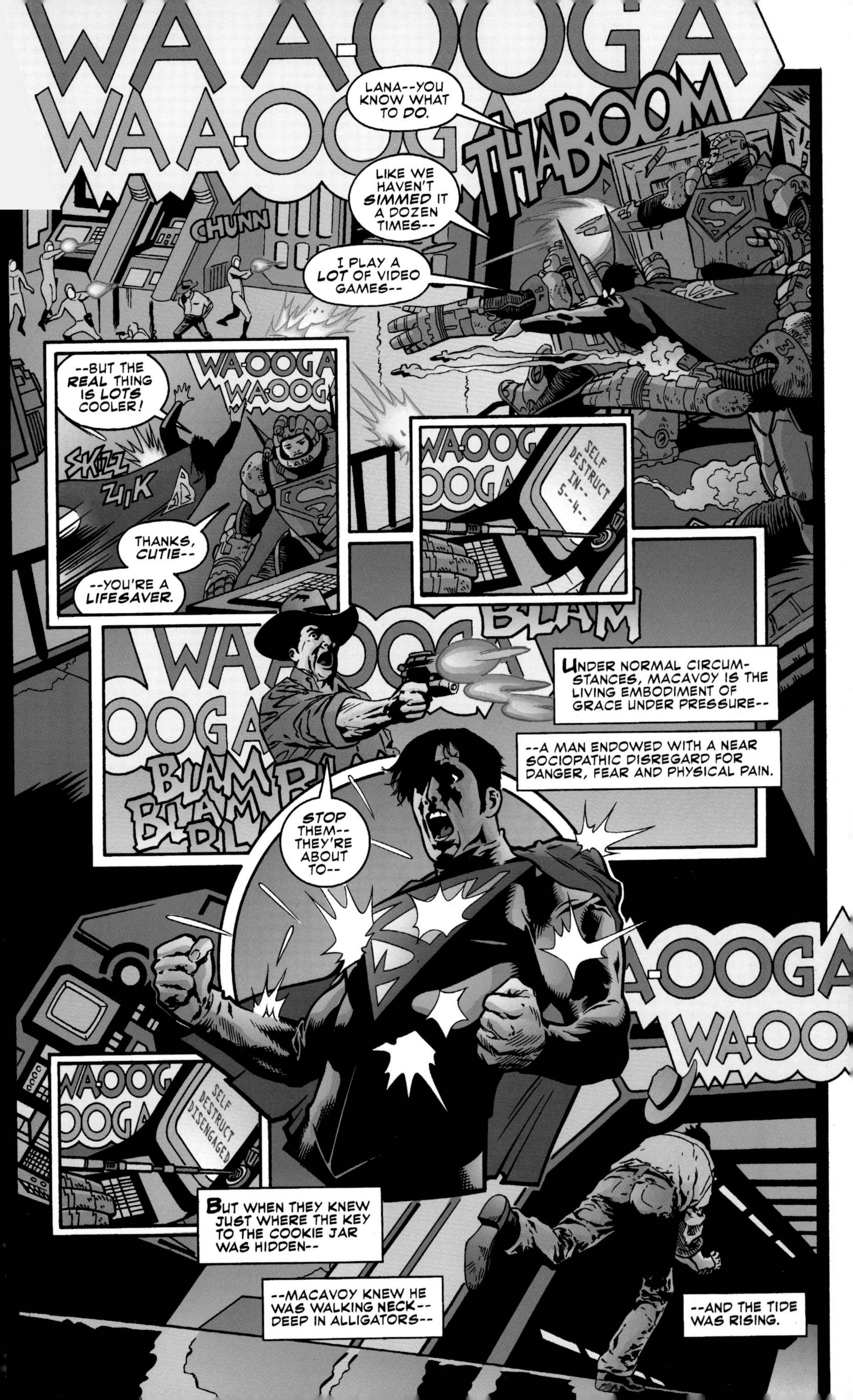
WA A-OOGA
WA A-OOGA
LANA--YOU KNOW WHAT TO DO.
THABOOM
LIKE WE HAVEN'T SIMMED IT A DOZEN TIMES--
CHUNN
I PLAY A LOT OF VIDEO GAMES--
--BUT THE REAL THING IS LOTS COOLER!
WA-OOGA
WA-OOG
SKZZ
ZIK
THANKS, CUTIE--
--YOU'RE A LIFESAVER.
WA-OOG
OOGA
SELF DESTRUCT IN-- 5--4--
BLAM
WA-OOG
OOGA
UNDER NORMAL CIRCUMSTANCES, MACAVOY IS THE LIVING EMBODIMENT OF GRACE UNDER PRESSURE--
--A MAN ENDOWED WITH A NEAR SOCIOPATHIC DISREGARD FOR DANGER, FEAR AND PHYSICAL PAIN.
BLAM
BLAM
STOP THEM--THEY'RE ABOUT TO--
A-OOGA
WA-OO
WA-OOG
OOGA
SELF DESTRUCT DISENGAGED
BUT WHEN THEY KNEW JUST WHERE THE KEY TO THE COOKIE JAR WAS HIDDEN--
--MACAVOY KNEW HE WAS WALKING NECK--DEEP IN ALLIGATORS--
--AND THE TIDE WAS RISING.

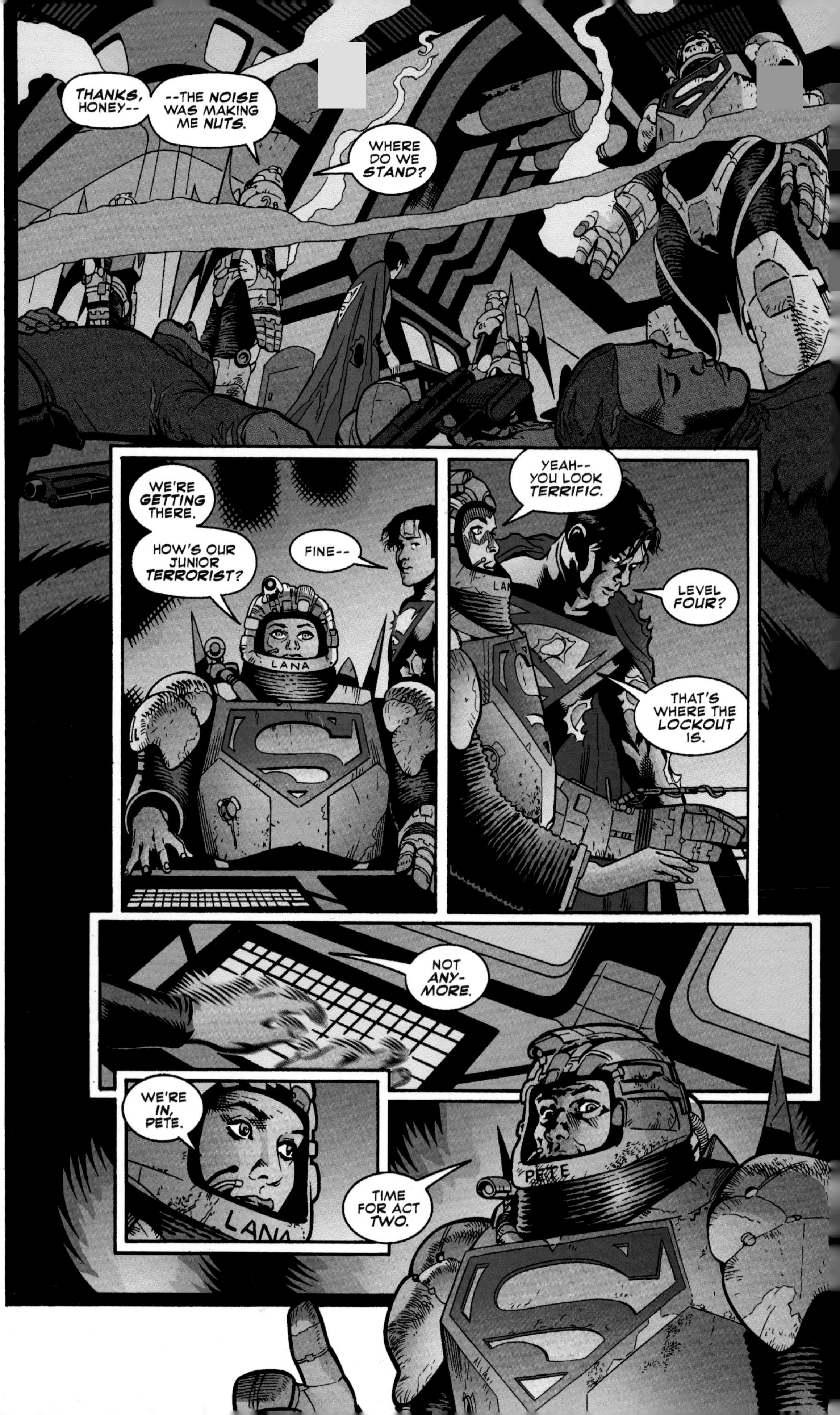
THANKS, HONEY--
--THE NOISE WAS MAKING ME NUTS.
WHERE DO WE STAND?
WE'RE GETTING THERE.
HOW'S OUR JUNIOR TERRORIST?
FINE--
YEAH-- YOU LOOK TERRIFIC.
LEVEL FOUR?
THAT'S WHERE THE LOCKOUT IS.
NOT ANY-MORE.
WE'RE IN, PETE.
TIME FOR ACT TWO.

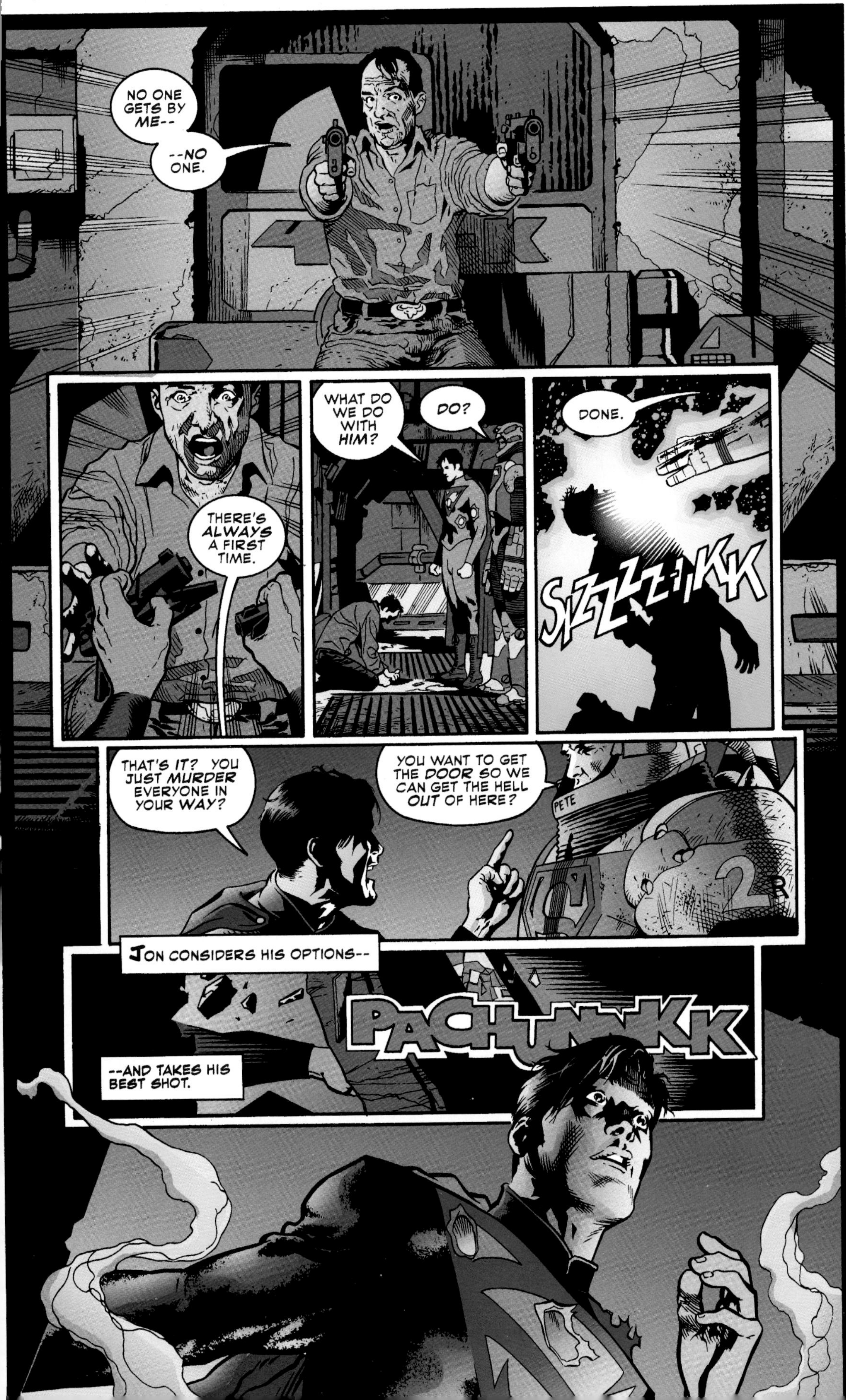
NO ONE GETS BY ME--
--NO ONE.
THERE'S ALWAYS A FIRST TIME.
WHAT DO WE DO WITH HIM?
DO?
DONE.
SIZZZZZ-IKK
THAT'S IT? YOU JUST MURDER EVERYONE IN YOUR WAY?
YOU WANT TO GET THE DOOR SO WE CAN GET THE HELL OUT OF HERE?
PETE
JON CONSIDERS HIS OPTIONS--
PACHUNNKK
--AND TAKES HIS BEST SHOT.

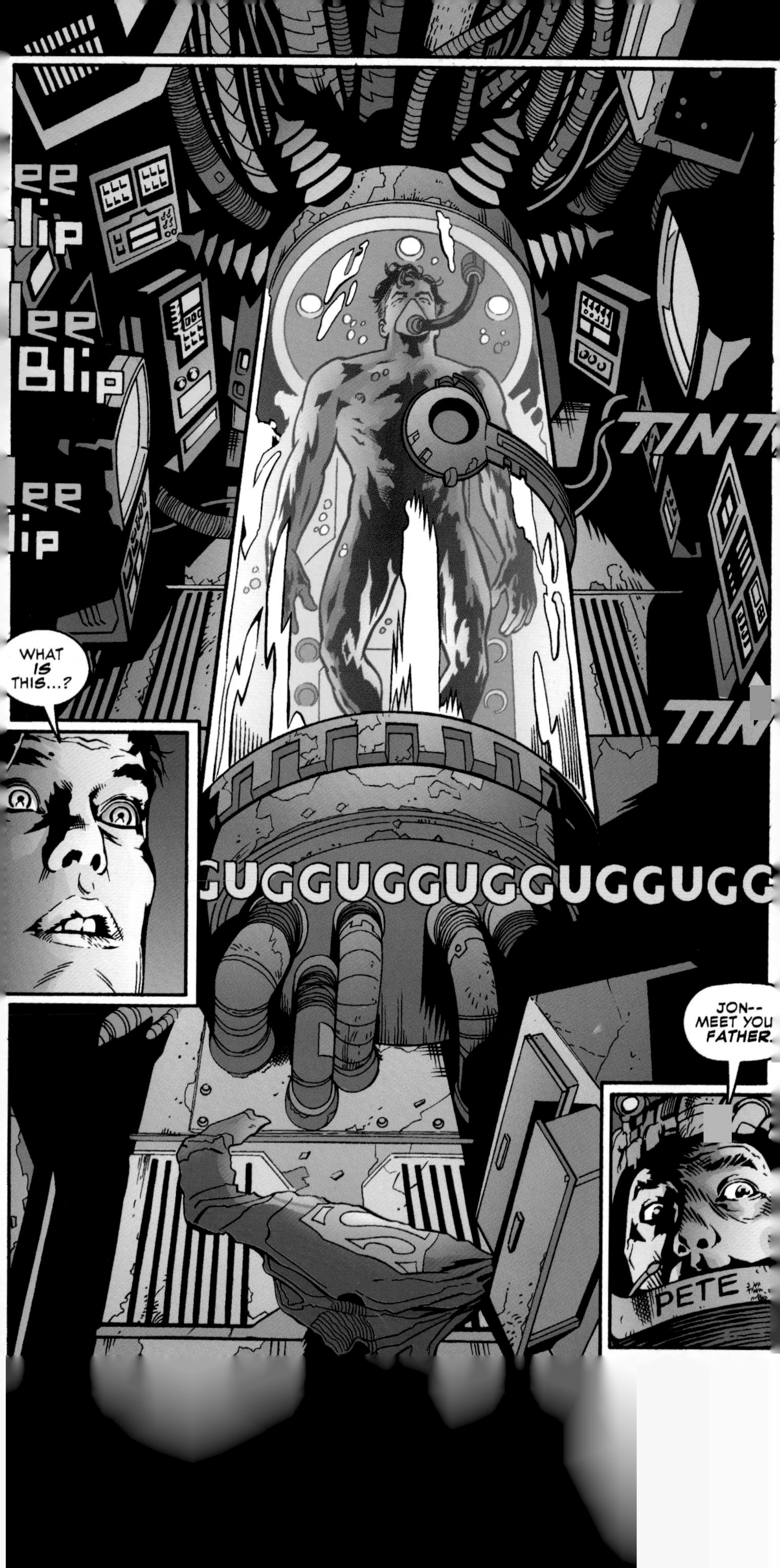
ee
lip
lee
Blip
ee
lip
TINT
TIN
WHAT IS THIS...?
GUGGUGGUGGUGG
JON--
MEET YOU
FATHER.
PETE

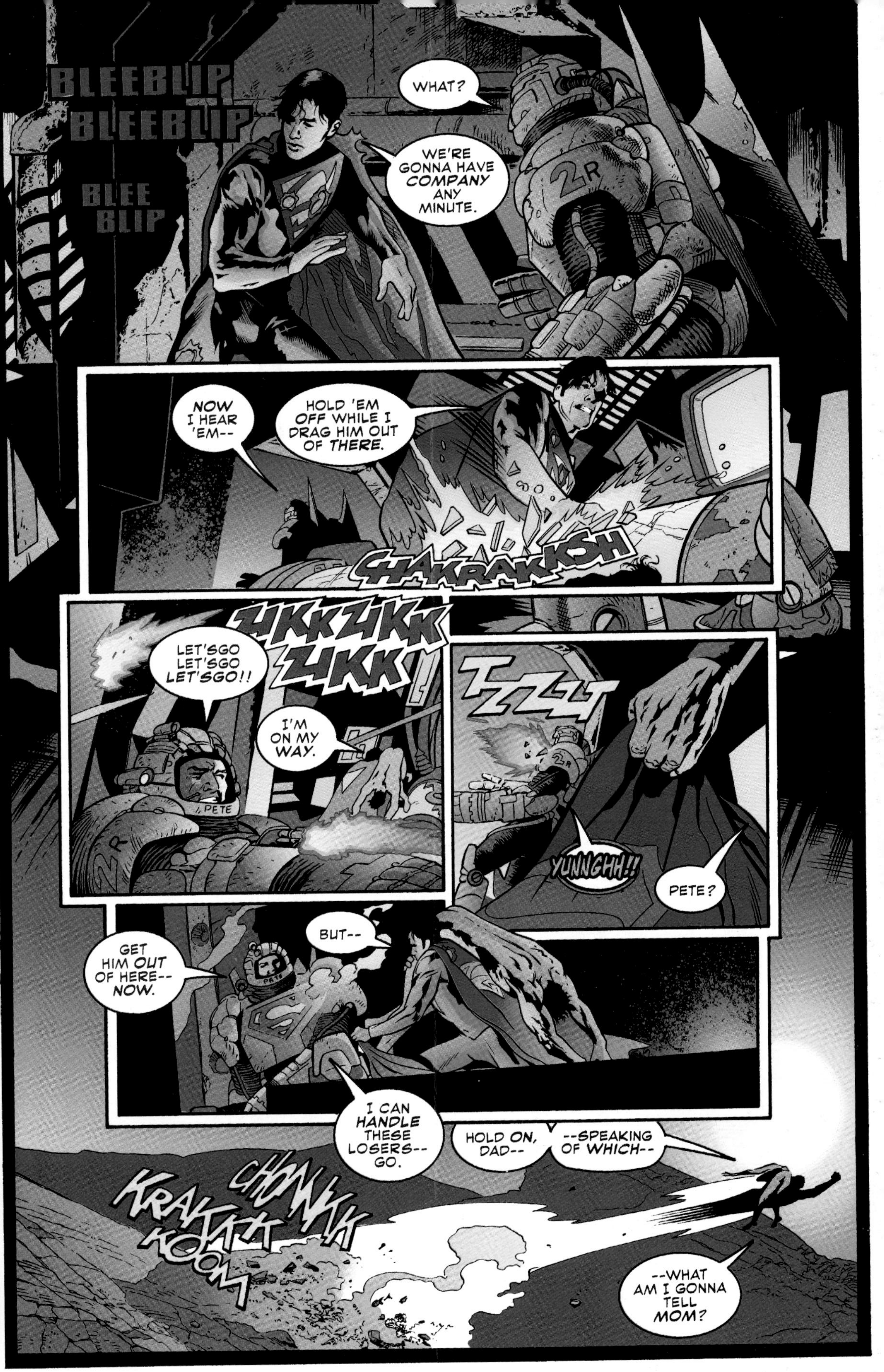
BLEEBLIP
BLEEBLIP
BLEE
BLIP
WHAT?
WE'RE GONNA HAVE COMPANY ANY MINUTE.
NOW I HEAR 'EM--
HOLD 'EM OFF WHILE I DRAG HIM OUT OF THERE.
CHAKRAKKKSH
ZUKKZUKK
ZUKK
LET'SGO LET'SGO LET'SGO!!
I'M ON MY WAY.
PETE
TZZZT
YUNNGHH!!
PETE?
GET HIM OUT OF HERE-- NOW.
BUT--
I CAN HANDLE THESE LOSERS-- GO.
HOLD ON, DAD--
--SPEAKING OF WHICH--
CHOWKKK
KRAKTAKK
KOOOM
--WHAT AM I GONNA TELL MOM?

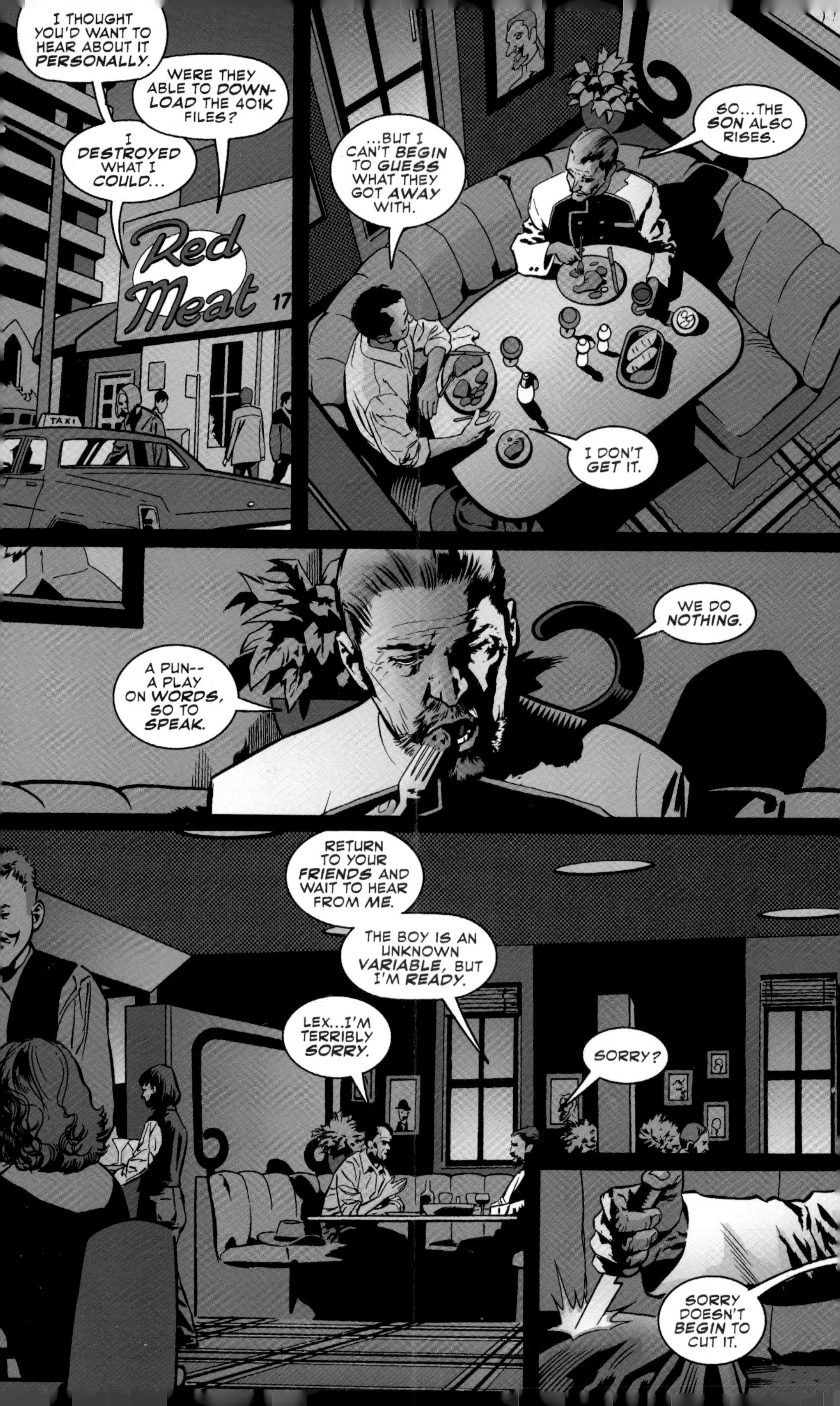
I THOUGHT YOU'D WANT TO HEAR ABOUT IT PERSONALLY.
WERE THEY ABLE TO DOWNLOAD THE 401K FILES?
I DESTROYED WHAT I COULD...
Red Meat
...BUT I CAN'T BEGIN TO GUESS WHAT THEY GOT AWAY WITH.
SO...THE SON ALSO RISES.
I DON'T GET IT.
A PUN--A PLAY ON WORDS, SO TO SPEAK.
WE DO NOTHING.
RETURN TO YOUR FRIENDS AND WAIT TO HEAR FROM ME.
THE BOY IS AN UNKNOWN VARIABLE, BUT I'M READY.
LEX...I'M TERRIBLY SORRY.
SORRY?
SORRY DOESN'T BEGIN TO CUT IT.

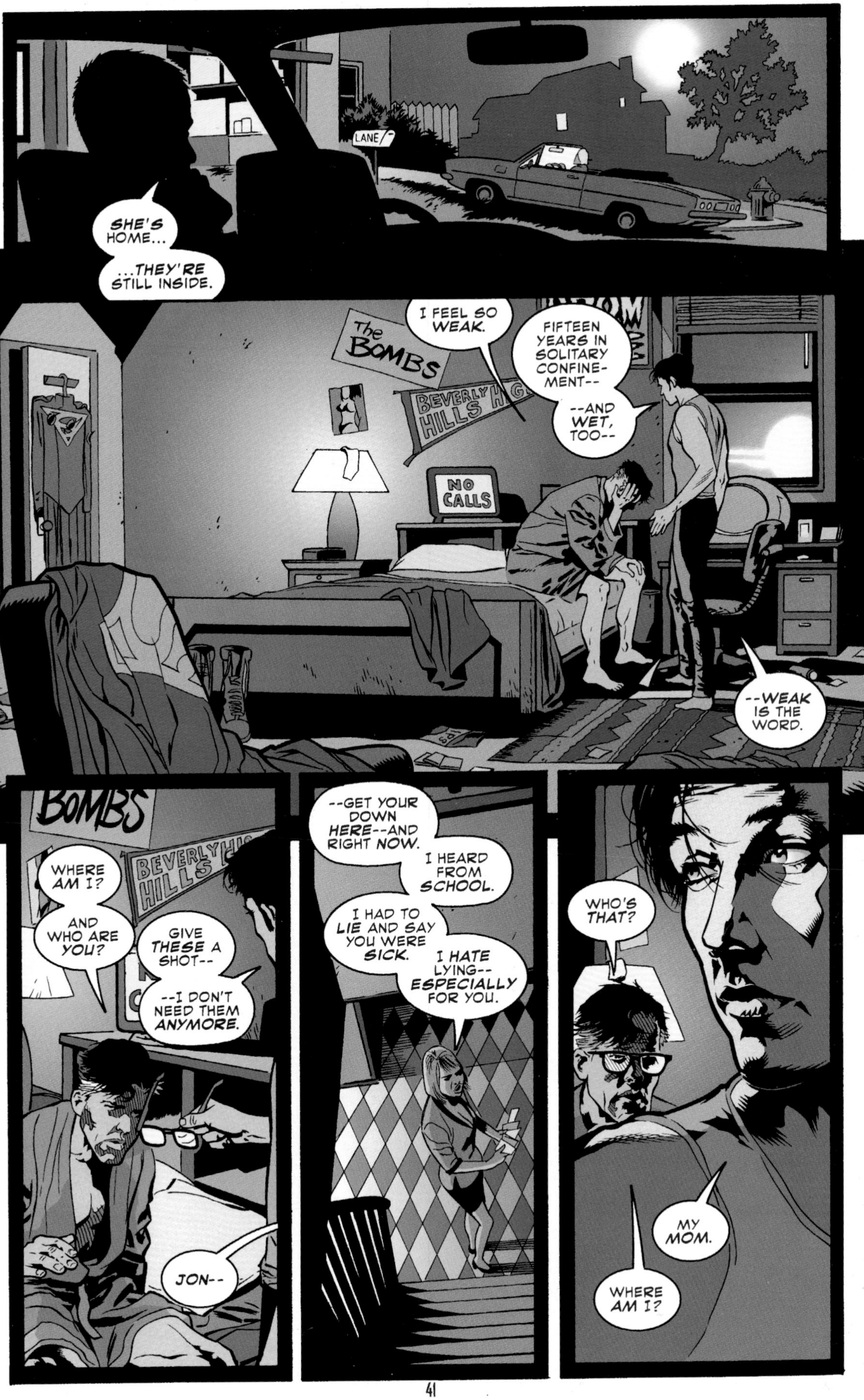
LANE
SHE'S HOME...
...THEY'RE STILL INSIDE.
The BOMBS
BEVERLY HILLS HIGH
NO CALLS
I FEEL SO WEAK.
FIFTEEN YEARS IN SOLITARY CONFINE-MENT--
--AND WET, TOO--
--WEAK IS THE WORD.
BOMBS
WHERE AM I?
AND WHO ARE YOU?
GIVE THESE A SHOT--
--I DON'T NEED THEM ANYMORE.
JON--
--GET YOUR DOWN HERE--AND RIGHT NOW.
I HEARD FROM SCHOOL.
I HAD TO LIE AND SAY YOU WERE SICK.
I HATE LYING--ESPECIALLY FOR YOU.
WHO'S THAT?
MY MOM.
WHERE AM I?

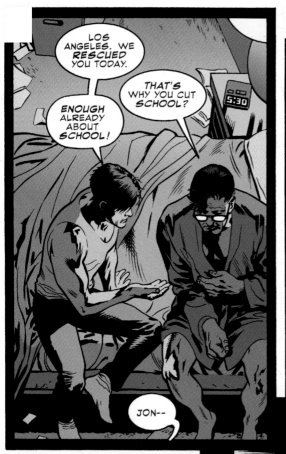

LOS ANGELES. WE *RESCUED* YOU TODAY.

THAT'S WHY YOU CUT SCHOOL?

ENOUGH ALREADY ABOUT SCHOOL!

JON--

I WAS IN EUROPE. THERE WAS A CIVIL WAR. ETHNIC CLEANSING--

--A NICE WAY TO SAY GENOCIDE.

THEY TOLD ME *NOT* TO GO, BUT I HAD TO...

DAMN IT, JON--

--I'M *TALKING* TO--

OH MY GOD.

LOIS.

CLARK.

NICE TO SEE YOU TWO CAN *STILL* FIND SOMETHING TO *SAY* AFTER ALL THESE YEARS.

TAKE IT *EASY,* HONEY--

--WE DID THE *BEST* WE COULD.

THE BEST YOU *COULD* --?!?!

YOU CALL LETTING *JON* TAKE *OFF* WITH HIM THE BEST YOU *COULD?*

BREEEP

DAMN!

ble to ecrypt-- lease try again.

THE ENCRYPTION'S IN *KRYPTONIAN.*

NONE OF THIS MAKES *SENSE.*

PARTICULARLY LETTING THE KID GET AWAY WITH *SUPERMAN.*

LANA...

WHAT IN GOD'S NAME WERE YOU *THINKING?*

YOU'LL NOTE I WAS *INJURED*--

THE *BENEFACTOR* DOESN'T GIVE A *DAMN* ABOUT *THAT* ANY MORE THAN I DO.

SO...?

WE SPOKE *TODAY*-- SHE *HAD* TO KNOW.

SO THIS CHANGES *EVERY-* THING.

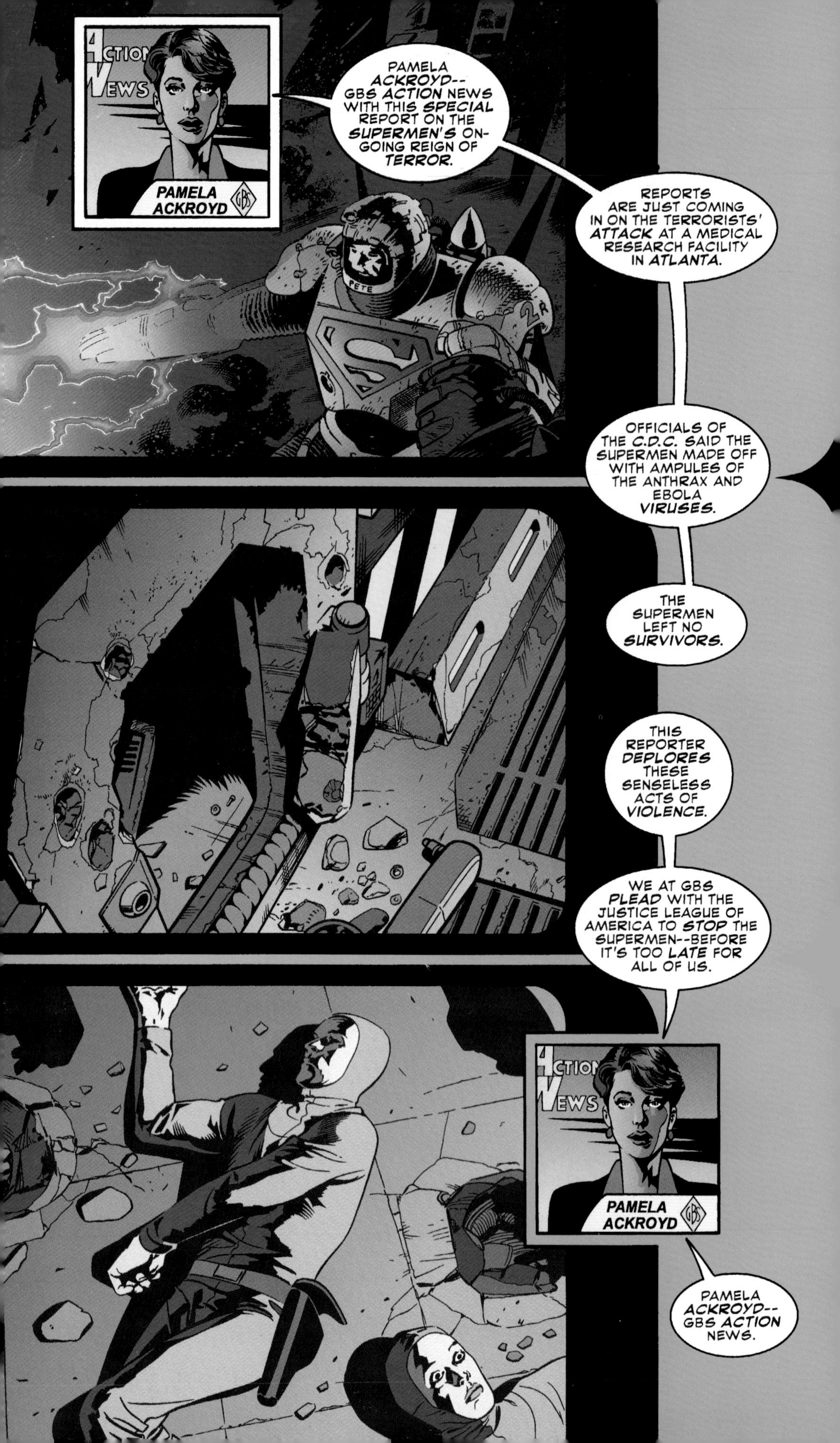
ACTION NEWS
PAMELA ACKROYD
GBS
PAMELA ACKROYD--GBS ACTION NEWS WITH THIS SPECIAL REPORT ON THE SUPERMEN'S ON-GOING REIGN OF TERROR.
REPORTS ARE JUST COMING IN ON THE TERRORISTS' ATTACK AT A MEDICAL RESEARCH FACILITY IN ATLANTA.
PETE
OFFICIALS OF THE C.D.C. SAID THE SUPERMEN MADE OFF WITH AMPULES OF THE ANTHRAX AND EBOLA VIRUSES.
THE SUPERMEN LEFT NO SURVIVORS.
THIS REPORTER DEPLORES THESE SENSELESS ACTS OF VIOLENCE.
WE AT GBS PLEAD WITH THE JUSTICE LEAGUE OF AMERICA TO STOP THE SUPERMEN--BEFORE IT'S TOO LATE FOR ALL OF US.
ACTION NEWS
PAMELA ACKROYD
GBS
PAMELA ACKROYD--GBS ACTION NEWS.

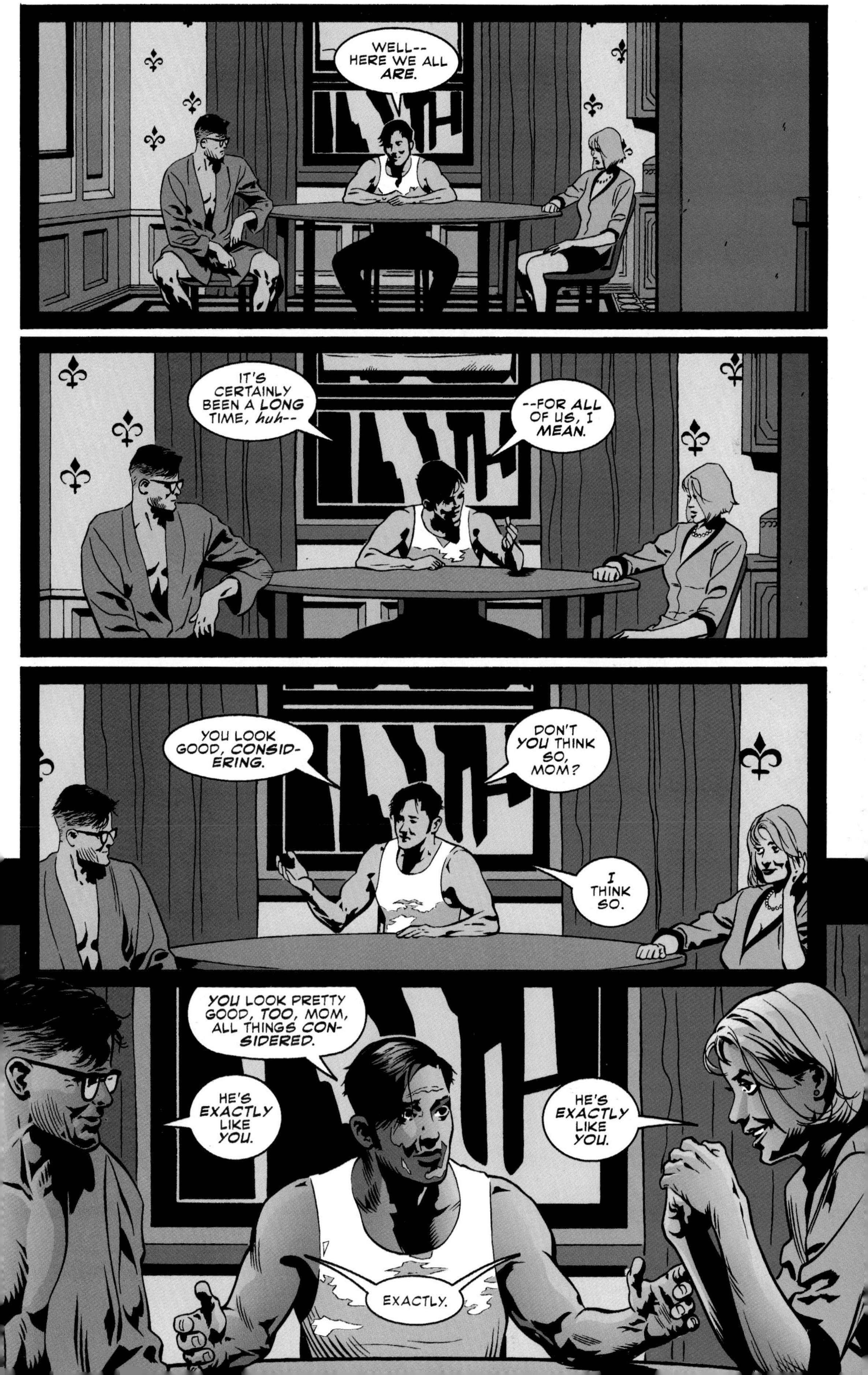
WELL-- HERE WE ALL ARE.
IT'S CERTAINLY BEEN A LONG TIME, huh--
--FOR ALL OF US, I MEAN.
YOU LOOK GOOD, CONSID-ERING.
DON'T YOU THINK SO, MOM?
I THINK SO.
YOU LOOK PRETTY GOOD, TOO, MOM, ALL THINGS CON-SIDERED.
HE'S EXACTLY LIKE YOU.
HE'S EXACTLY LIKE YOU.
EXACTLY.

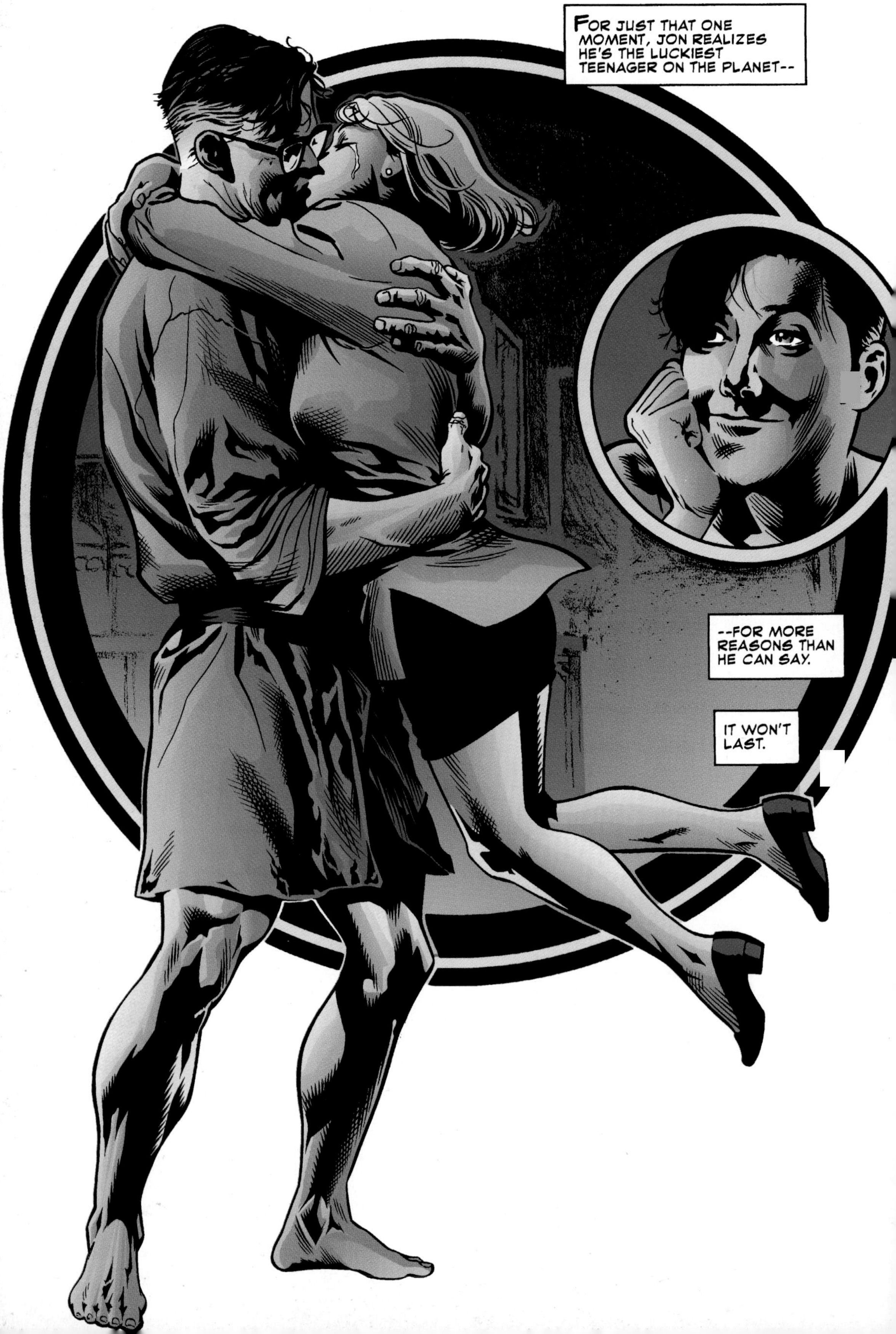
FOR JUST THAT ONE MOMENT, JON REALIZES HE'S THE LUCKIEST TEENAGER ON THE PLANET--
--FOR MORE REASONS THAN HE CAN SAY.
IT WON'T LAST.

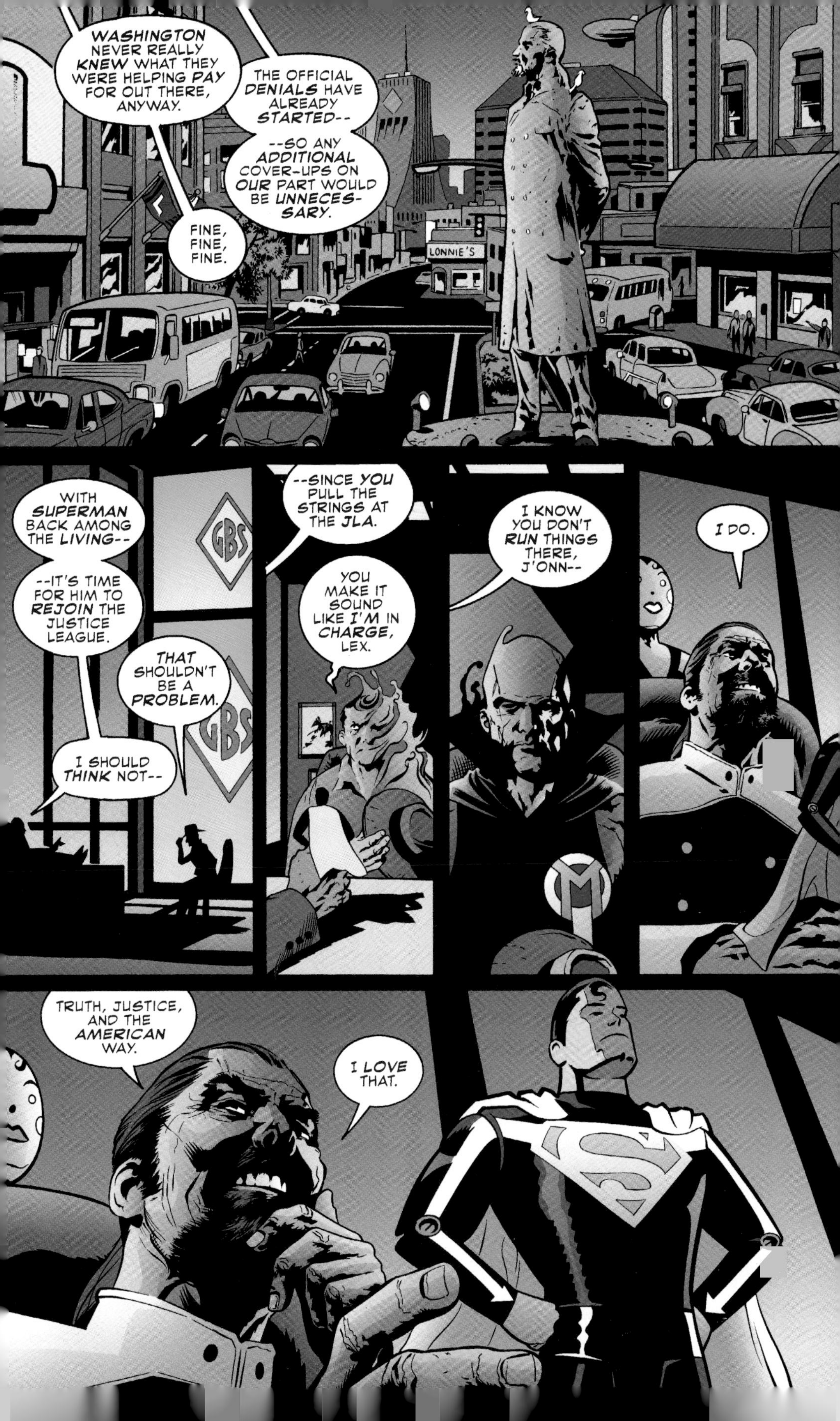
WASHINGTON NEVER REALLY KNEW WHAT THEY WERE HELPING PAY FOR OUT THERE, ANYWAY.
THE OFFICIAL DENIALS HAVE ALREADY STARTED--
--SO ANY ADDITIONAL COVER-UPS ON OUR PART WOULD BE UNNECES-SARY.
FINE, FINE, FINE.
LONNIE'S
WITH SUPERMAN BACK AMONG THE LIVING--
--IT'S TIME FOR HIM TO REJOIN THE JUSTICE LEAGUE.
THAT SHOULDN'T BE A PROBLEM.
I SHOULD THINK NOT--
--SINCE YOU PULL THE STRINGS AT THE JLA.
YOU MAKE IT SOUND LIKE I'M IN CHARGE, LEX.
I KNOW YOU DON'T RUN THINGS THERE, J'ONN--
I DO.
TRUTH, JUSTICE, AND THE AMERICAN WAY.
I LOVE THAT.

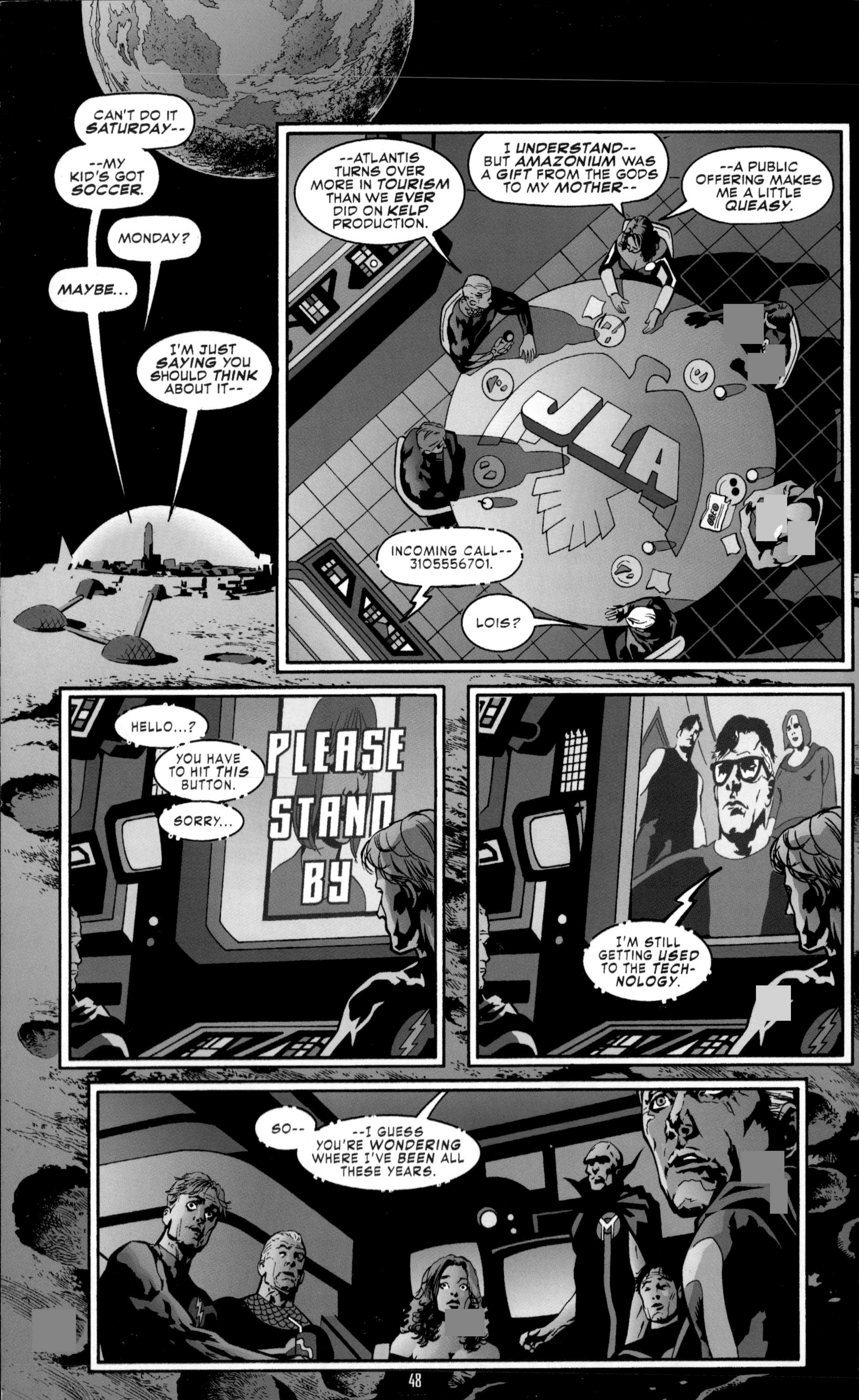
CAN'T DO IT SATURDAY--
--MY KID'S GOT SOCCER.
MONDAY?
MAYBE...
I'M JUST SAYING YOU SHOULD THINK ABOUT IT--
--ATLANTIS TURNS OVER MORE IN TOURISM THAN WE EVER DID ON KELP PRODUCTION.
I UNDERSTAND-- BUT AMAZONIUM WAS A GIFT FROM THE GODS TO MY MOTHER--
--A PUBLIC OFFERING MAKES ME A LITTLE QUEASY.
JLA
INCOMING CALL-- 3105556701.
LOIS?
HELLO...?
YOU HAVE TO HIT THIS BUTTON.
SORRY...
PLEASE STAND BY
I'M STILL GETTING USED TO THE TECH-NOLOGY.
SO--
--I GUESS YOU'RE WONDERING WHERE I'VE BEEN ALL THESE YEARS.

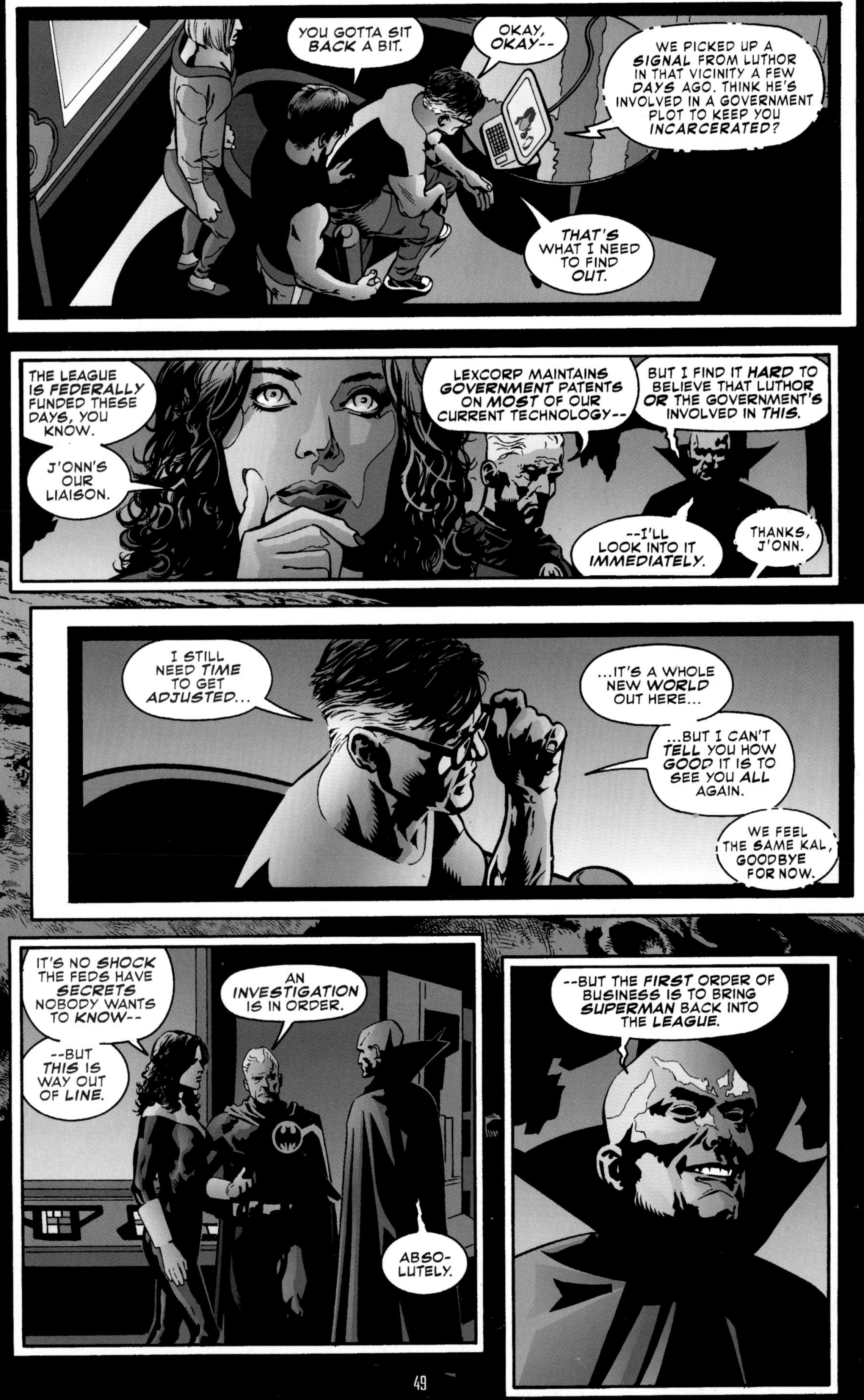
YOU GOTTA SIT BACK A BIT.
OKAY, OKAY--
WE PICKED UP A SIGNAL FROM LUTHOR IN THAT VICINITY A FEW DAYS AGO. THINK HE'S INVOLVED IN A GOVERNMENT PLOT TO KEEP YOU INCARCERATED?
THAT'S WHAT I NEED TO FIND OUT.
THE LEAGUE IS FEDERALLY FUNDED THESE DAYS, YOU KNOW.
J'ONN'S OUR LIAISON.
LEXCORP MAINTAINS GOVERNMENT PATENTS ON MOST OF OUR CURRENT TECHNOLOGY--
BUT I FIND IT HARD TO BELIEVE THAT LUTHOR OR THE GOVERNMENT'S INVOLVED IN THIS.
--I'LL LOOK INTO IT IMMEDIATELY.
THANKS, J'ONN.
I STILL NEED TIME TO GET ADJUSTED...
...IT'S A WHOLE NEW WORLD OUT HERE...
...BUT I CAN'T TELL YOU HOW GOOD IT IS TO SEE YOU ALL AGAIN.
WE FEEL THE SAME KAL, GOODBYE FOR NOW.
IT'S NO SHOCK THE FEDS HAVE SECRETS NOBODY WANTS TO KNOW--
--BUT THIS IS WAY OUT OF LINE.
AN INVESTIGATION IS IN ORDER.
ABSO-LUTELY.
--BUT THE FIRST ORDER OF BUSINESS IS TO BRING SUPERMAN BACK INTO THE LEAGUE.

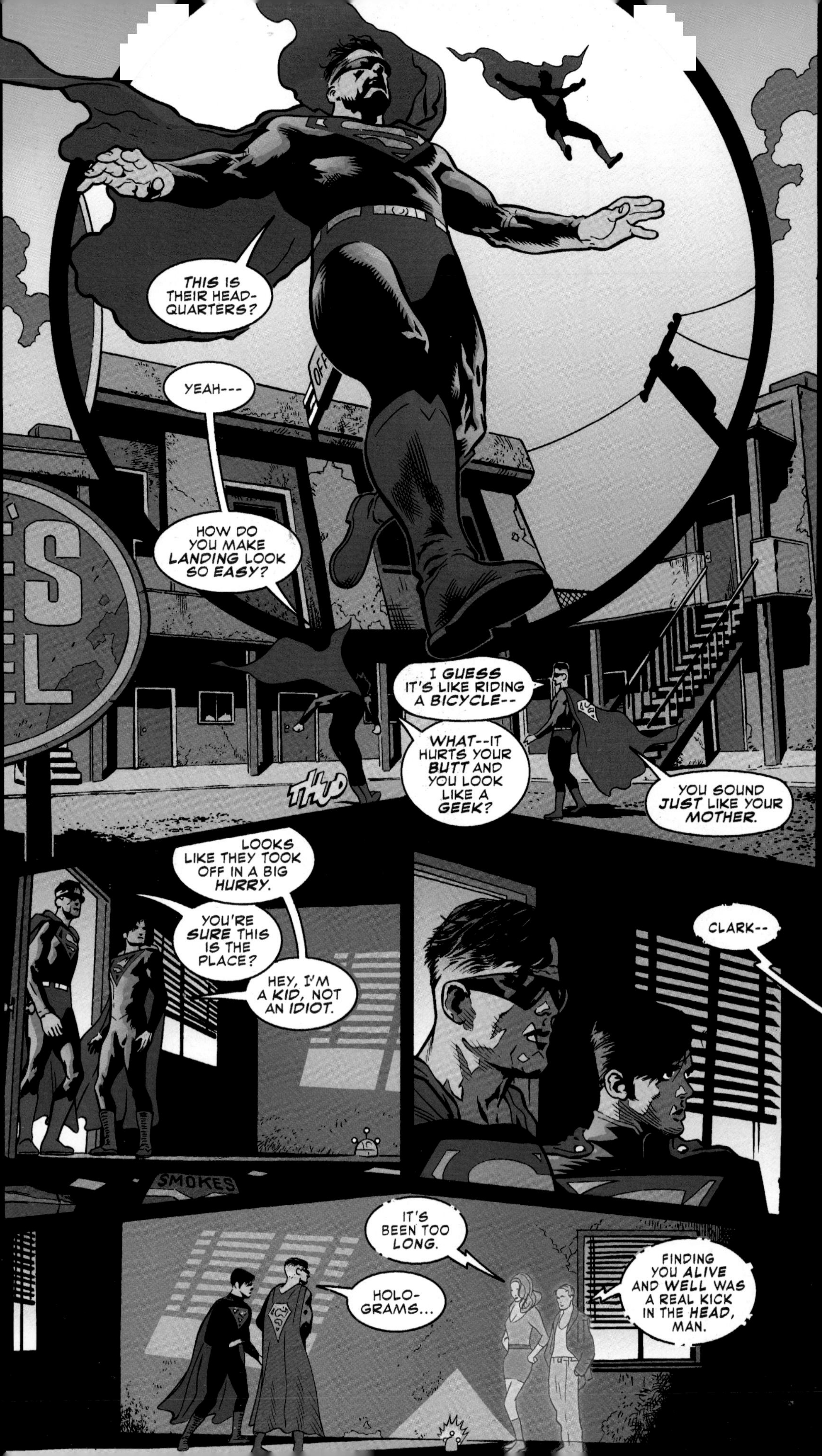

THIS IS THEIR HEAD-QUARTERS?
YEAH---
HOW DO YOU MAKE LANDING LOOK SO EASY?
I GUESS IT'S LIKE RIDING A BICYCLE--
WHAT--IT HURTS YOUR BUTT AND YOU LOOK LIKE A GEEK?
YOU SOUND JUST LIKE YOUR MOTHER.
THUD
LOOKS LIKE THEY TOOK OFF IN A BIG HURRY.
YOU'RE SURE THIS IS THE PLACE?
HEY, I'M A KID, NOT AN IDIOT.
CLARK--
SMOKES
IT'S BEEN TOO LONG.
HOLO-GRAMS...
FINDING YOU ALIVE AND WELL WAS A REAL KICK IN THE HEAD, MAN.

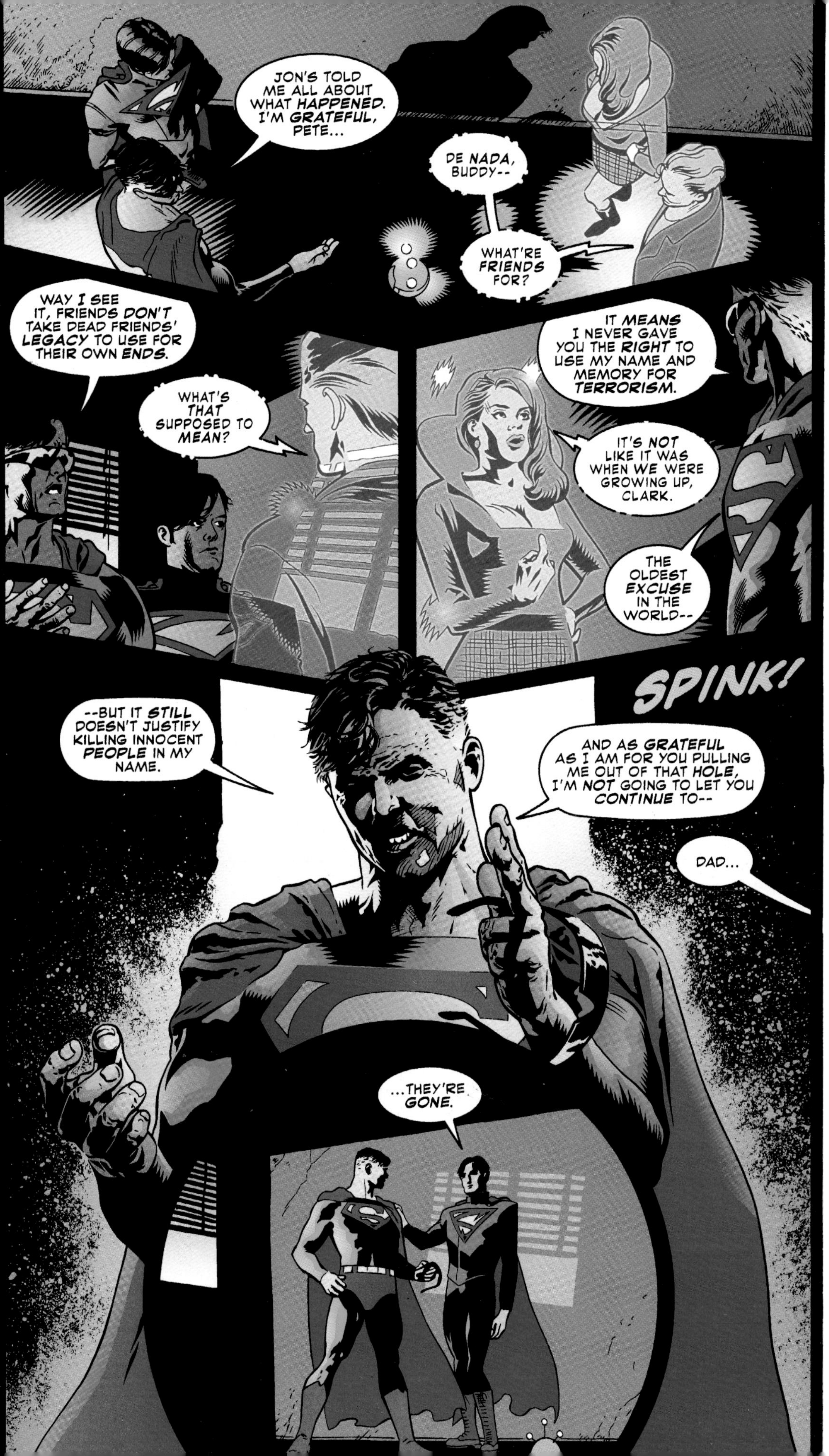
JON'S TOLD ME ALL ABOUT WHAT HAPPENED. I'M GRATEFUL, PETE...
DE NADA, BUDDY--
WHAT'RE FRIENDS FOR?
WAY I SEE IT, FRIENDS DON'T TAKE DEAD FRIENDS' LEGACY TO USE FOR THEIR OWN ENDS.
WHAT'S THAT SUPPOSED TO MEAN?
IT MEANS I NEVER GAVE YOU THE RIGHT TO USE MY NAME AND MEMORY FOR TERRORISM.
IT'S NOT LIKE IT WAS WHEN WE WERE GROWING UP, CLARK.
THE OLDEST EXCUSE IN THE WORLD--
--BUT IT STILL DOESN'T JUSTIFY KILLING INNOCENT PEOPLE IN MY NAME.
AND AS GRATEFUL AS I AM FOR YOU PULLING ME OUT OF THAT HOLE, I'M NOT GOING TO LET YOU CONTINUE TO--
SPINK!
DAD...
...THEY'RE GONE.

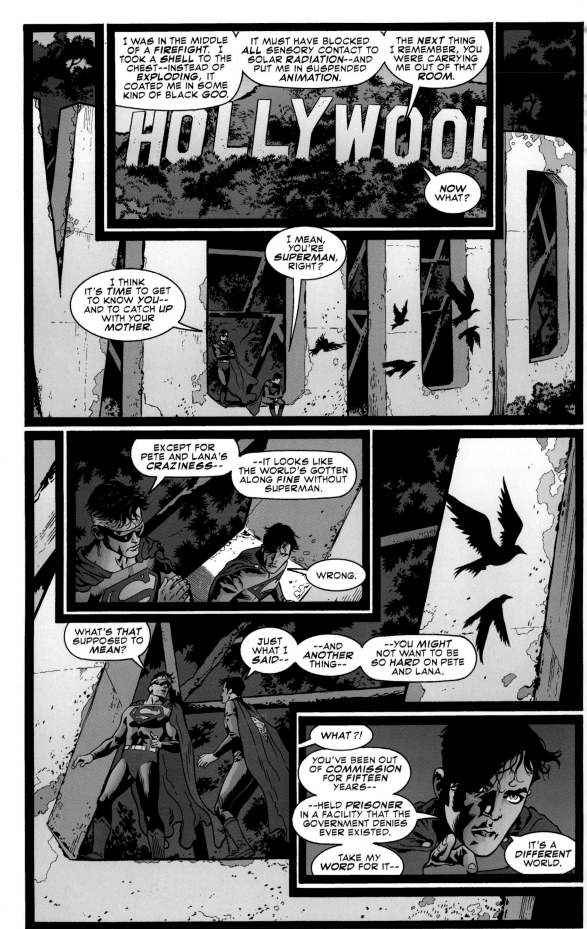

I WAS IN THE MIDDLE OF A *FIREFIGHT*. I TOOK A *SHELL* TO THE CHEST--INSTEAD OF *EXPLODING*, IT COATED ME IN SOME KIND OF BLACK *GOO*.

IT MUST HAVE BLOCKED *ALL* SENSORY CONTACT TO SOLAR *RADIATION*--AND PUT ME IN SUSPENDED *ANIMATION*.

THE *NEXT* THING I REMEMBER, YOU WERE CARRYING ME OUT OF THAT *ROOM*.

NOW WHAT?

I THINK IT'S *TIME* TO GET TO KNOW *YOU*-- AND TO CATCH *UP* WITH YOUR MOTHER.

I MEAN, YOU'RE *SUPERMAN*, RIGHT?

EXCEPT FOR PETE AND LANA'S *CRAZINESS*--

--IT LOOKS LIKE THE WORLD'S GOTTEN ALONG *FINE* WITHOUT SUPERMAN.

WRONG.

WHAT'S *THAT* SUPPOSED TO MEAN?

JUST WHAT I *SAID*--

--AND *ANOTHER* THING--

--YOU *MIGHT* NOT WANT TO BE SO *HARD* ON PETE AND LANA.

WHAT?!

YOU'VE BEEN OUT OF *COMMISSION* FOR FIFTEEN YEARS--

--HELD *PRISONER* IN A FACILITY THAT THE GOVERNMENT DENIES EVER EXISTED.

TAKE MY *WORD* FOR IT--

IT'S A *DIFFERENT* WORLD.

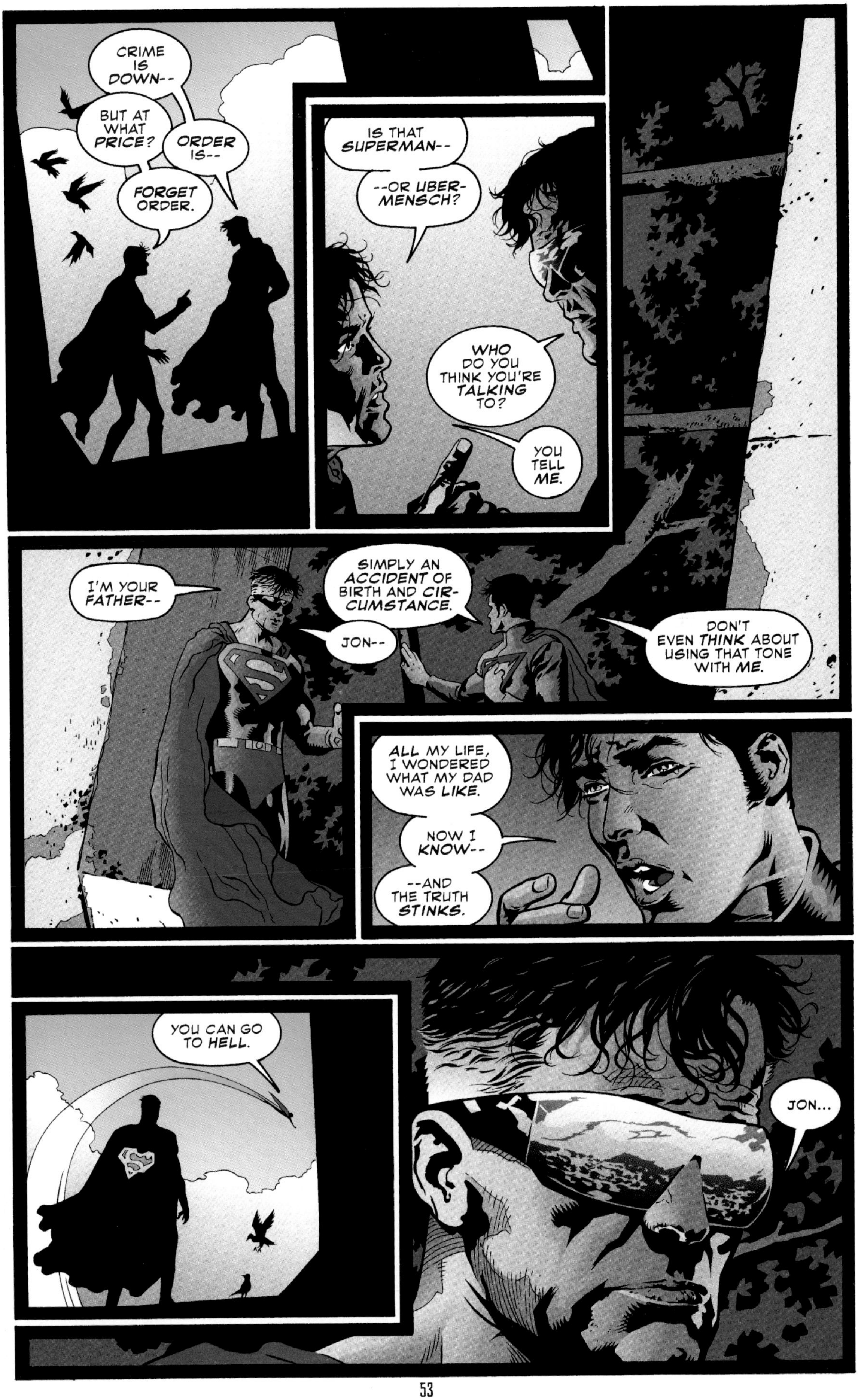
CRIME IS DOWN--
BUT AT WHAT PRICE?
ORDER IS--
FORGET ORDER.
IS THAT SUPERMAN--
--OR UBER-MENSCH?
WHO DO YOU THINK YOU'RE TALKING TO?
YOU TELL ME.
I'M YOUR FATHER--
JON--
SIMPLY AN ACCIDENT OF BIRTH AND CIR-CUMSTANCE.
DON'T EVEN THINK ABOUT USING THAT TONE WITH ME.
ALL MY LIFE, I WONDERED WHAT MY DAD WAS LIKE.
NOW I KNOW--
--AND THE TRUTH STINKS.
YOU CAN GO TO HELL.
JON...

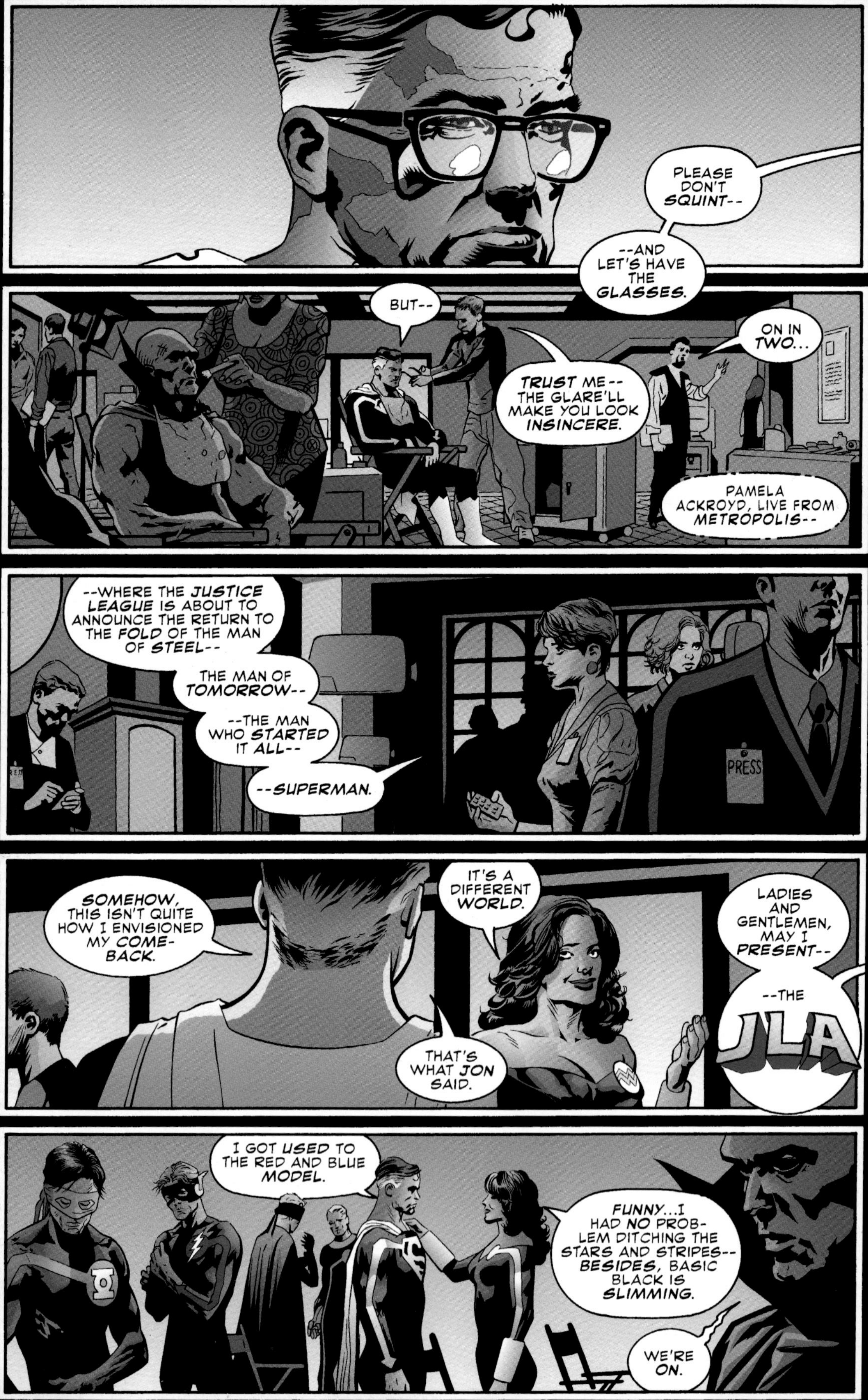

PLEASE DON'T SQUINT--
--AND LET'S HAVE THE GLASSES.
BUT--
TRUST ME-- THE GLARE'LL MAKE YOU LOOK INSINCERE.
ON IN TWO...
PAMELA ACKROYD, LIVE FROM METROPOLIS--
--WHERE THE JUSTICE LEAGUE IS ABOUT TO ANNOUNCE THE RETURN TO THE FOLD OF THE MAN OF STEEL--
THE MAN OF TOMORROW--
--THE MAN WHO STARTED IT ALL--
--SUPERMAN.
PRESS
SOMEHOW, THIS ISN'T QUITE HOW I ENVISIONED MY COME-BACK.
IT'S A DIFFERENT WORLD.
THAT'S WHAT JON SAID.
LADIES AND GENTLEMEN, MAY I PRESENT--
--THE
JLA
I GOT USED TO THE RED AND BLUE MODEL.
FUNNY...I HAD NO PROB-LEM DITCHING THE STARS AND STRIPES-- BESIDES, BASIC BLACK IS SLIMMING.
WE'RE ON.

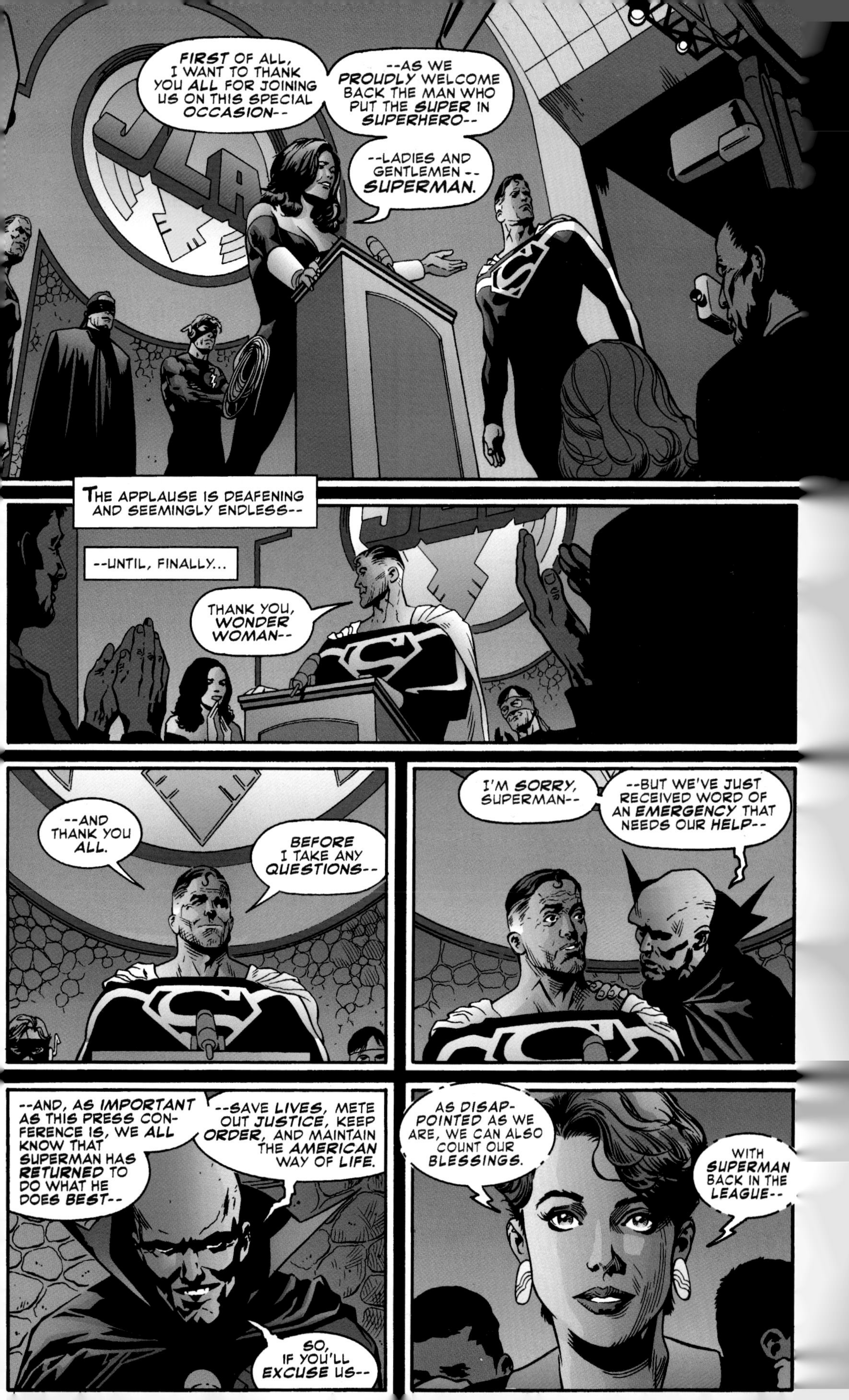
FIRST OF ALL, I WANT TO THANK YOU ALL FOR JOINING US ON THIS SPECIAL OCCASION--
--AS WE PROUDLY WELCOME BACK THE MAN WHO PUT THE SUPER IN SUPERHERO--
--LADIES AND GENTLEMEN -- SUPERMAN.
THE APPLAUSE IS DEAFENING AND SEEMINGLY ENDLESS--
--UNTIL, FINALLY...
THANK YOU, WONDER WOMAN--
--AND THANK YOU ALL.
BEFORE I TAKE ANY QUESTIONS--
I'M SORRY, SUPERMAN--
--BUT WE'VE JUST RECEIVED WORD OF AN EMERGENCY THAT NEEDS OUR HELP--
--AND, AS IMPORTANT AS THIS PRESS CONFERENCE IS, WE ALL KNOW THAT SUPERMAN HAS RETURNED TO DO WHAT HE DOES BEST--
--SAVE LIVES, METE OUT JUSTICE, KEEP ORDER, AND MAINTAIN THE AMERICAN WAY OF LIFE.
SO, IF YOU'LL EXCUSE US--
AS DISAPPOINTED AS WE ARE, WE CAN ALSO COUNT OUR BLESSINGS.
WITH SUPERMAN BACK IN THE LEAGUE--

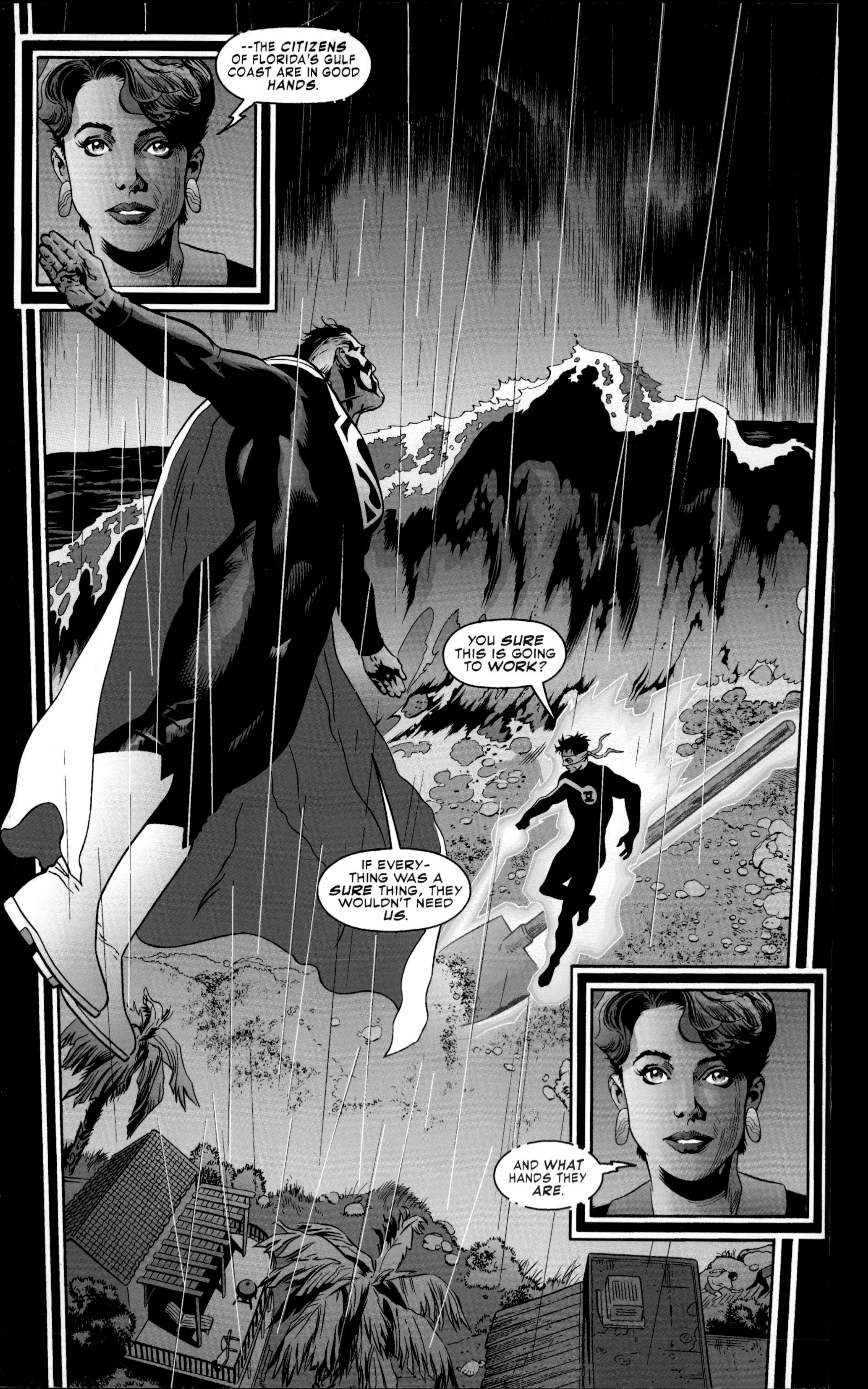
--THE CITIZENS OF FLORIDA'S GULF COAST ARE IN GOOD HANDS.
YOU SURE THIS IS GOING TO WORK?
IF EVERY-THING WAS A SURE THING, THEY WOULDN'T NEED US.
AND WHAT HANDS THEY ARE.

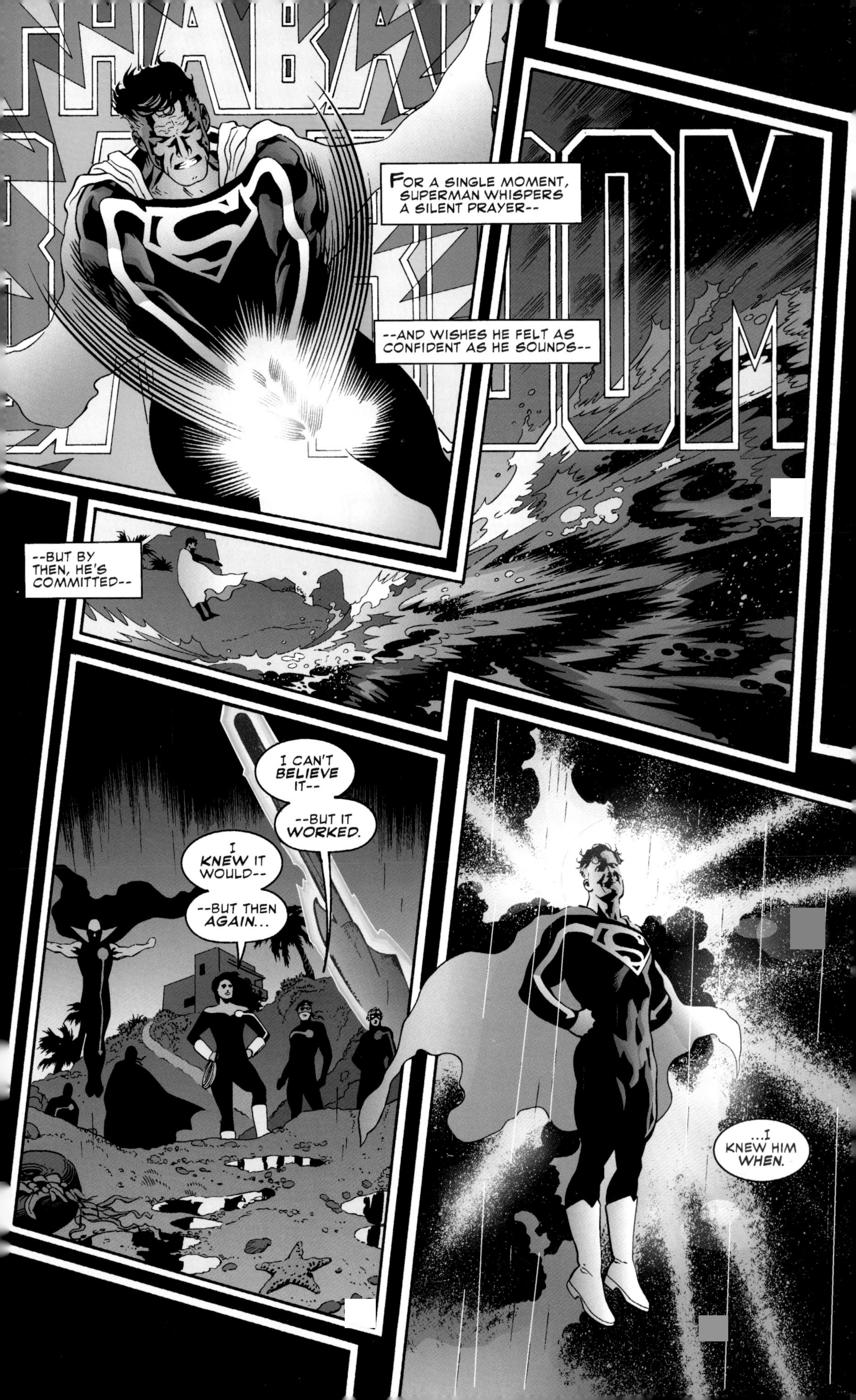

FOR A SINGLE MOMENT, SUPERMAN WHISPERS A SILENT PRAYER--
--AND WISHES HE FELT AS CONFIDENT AS HE SOUNDS--
--BUT BY THEN, HE'S COMMITTED--
I CAN'T BELIEVE IT--
--BUT IT WORKED.
I KNEW IT WOULD--
--BUT THEN AGAIN...
...I KNEW HIM WHEN.

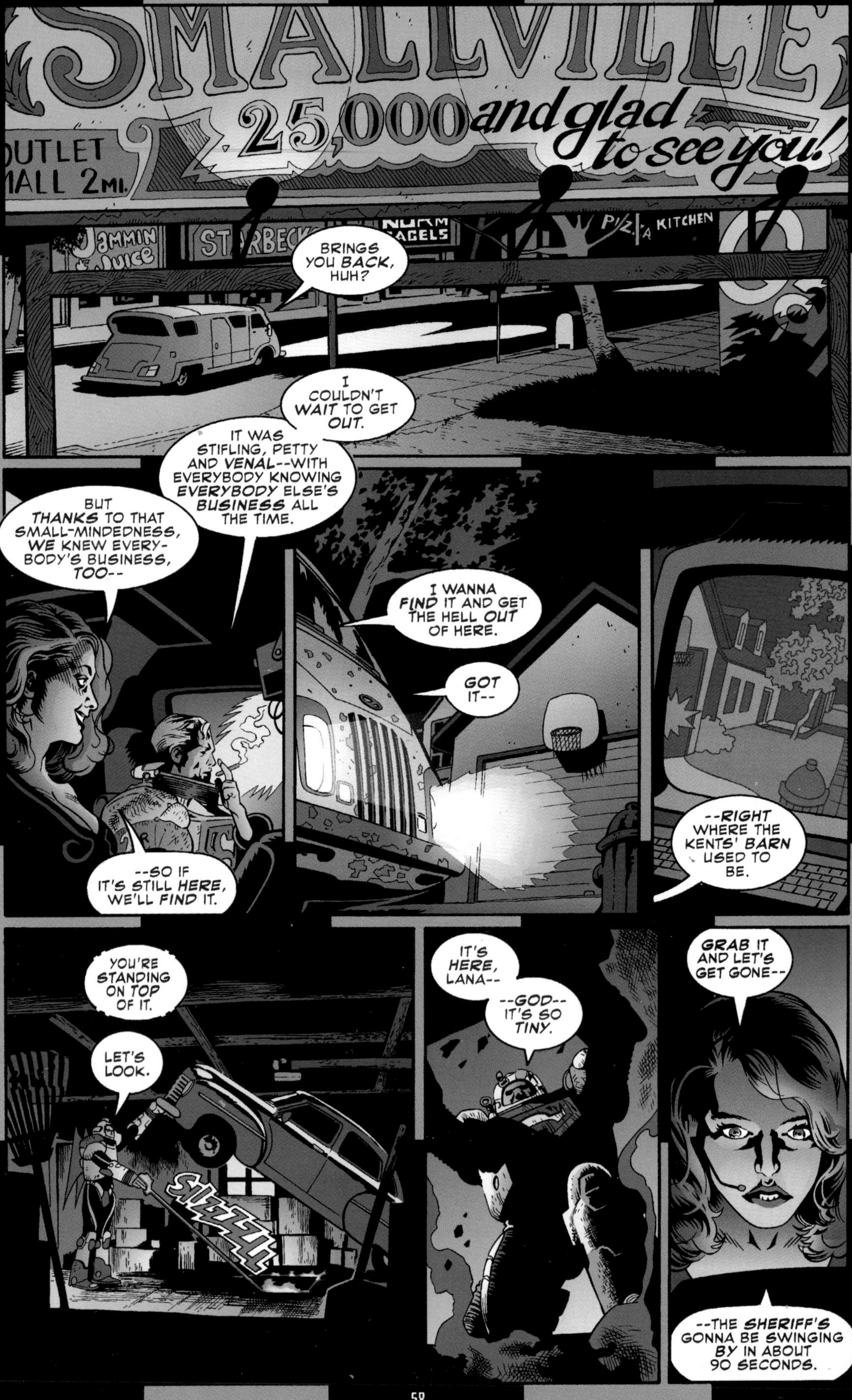
SMALLVILLE
25,000 and glad to see you!
OUTLET MALL 2MI.
Jammin Juice
STARBECK
NORM BAGELS
PIZZA KITCHEN
BRINGS YOU BACK, HUH?
I COULDN'T WAIT TO GET OUT.
IT WAS STIFLING, PETTY AND VENAL--WITH EVERYBODY KNOWING EVERYBODY ELSE'S BUSINESS ALL THE TIME.
BUT THANKS TO THAT SMALL-MINDEDNESS, WE KNEW EVERY-BODY'S BUSINESS, TOO--
--SO IF IT'S STILL HERE, WE'LL FIND IT.
I WANNA FIND IT AND GET THE HELL OUT OF HERE.
GOT IT--
--RIGHT WHERE THE KENTS' BARN USED TO BE.
YOU'RE STANDING ON TOP OF IT.
LET'S LOOK.
SHZZZT
IT'S HERE, LANA--
--GOD-- IT'S SO TINY.
GRAB IT AND LET'S GET GONE--
--THE SHERIFF'S GONNA BE SWINGING BY IN ABOUT 90 SECONDS.

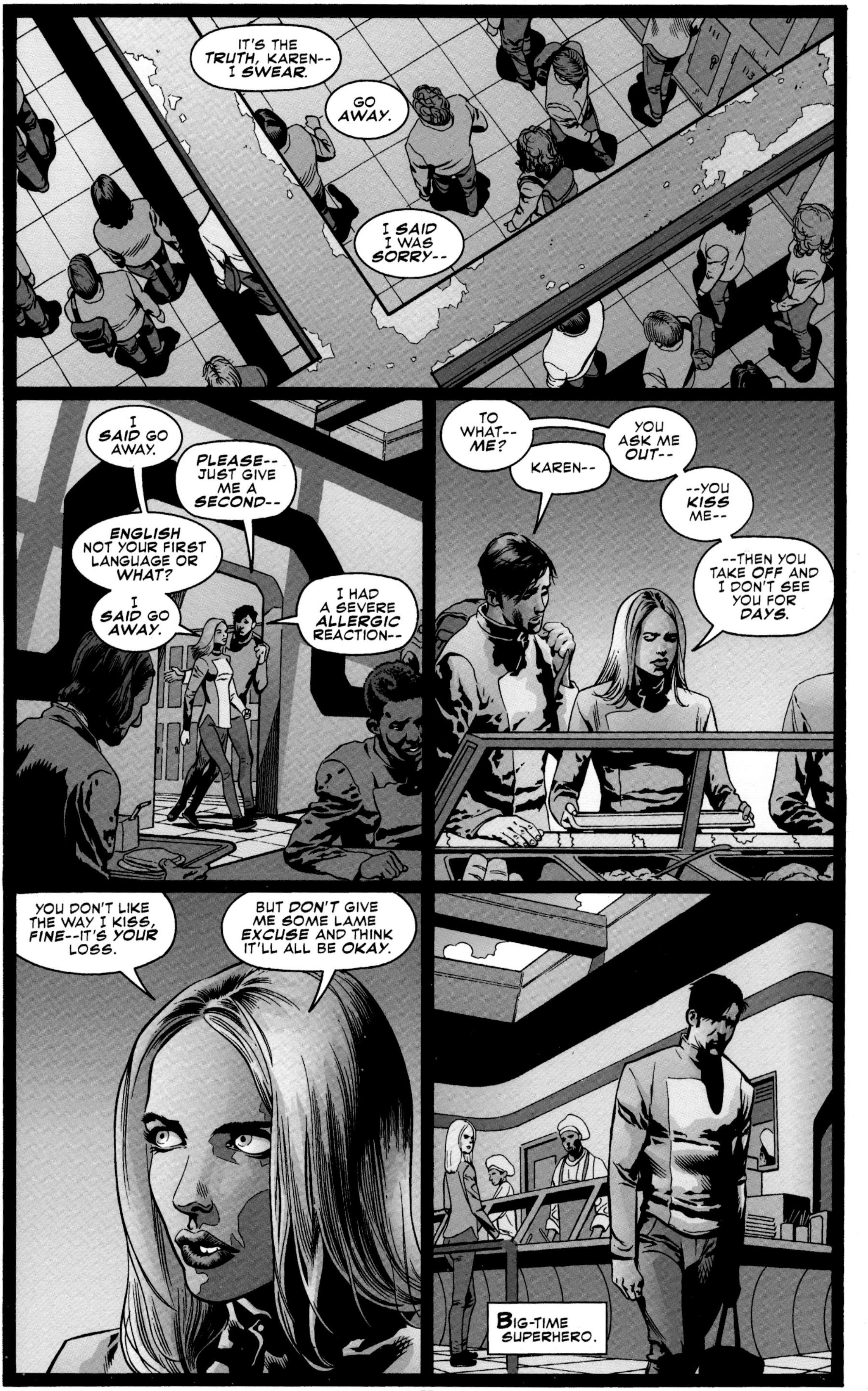
IT'S THE TRUTH, KAREN-- I SWEAR.
GO AWAY.
I SAID I WAS SORRY--
I SAID GO AWAY.
PLEASE-- JUST GIVE ME A SECOND--
ENGLISH NOT YOUR FIRST LANGUAGE OR WHAT?
I SAID GO AWAY.
I HAD A SEVERE ALLERGIC REACTION--
TO WHAT-- ME?
YOU ASK ME OUT--
KAREN--
--YOU KISS ME--
--THEN YOU TAKE OFF AND I DON'T SEE YOU FOR DAYS.
YOU DON'T LIKE THE WAY I KISS, FINE--IT'S YOUR LOSS.
BUT DON'T GIVE ME SOME LAME EXCUSE AND THINK IT'LL ALL BE OKAY.
BIG-TIME SUPERHERO.

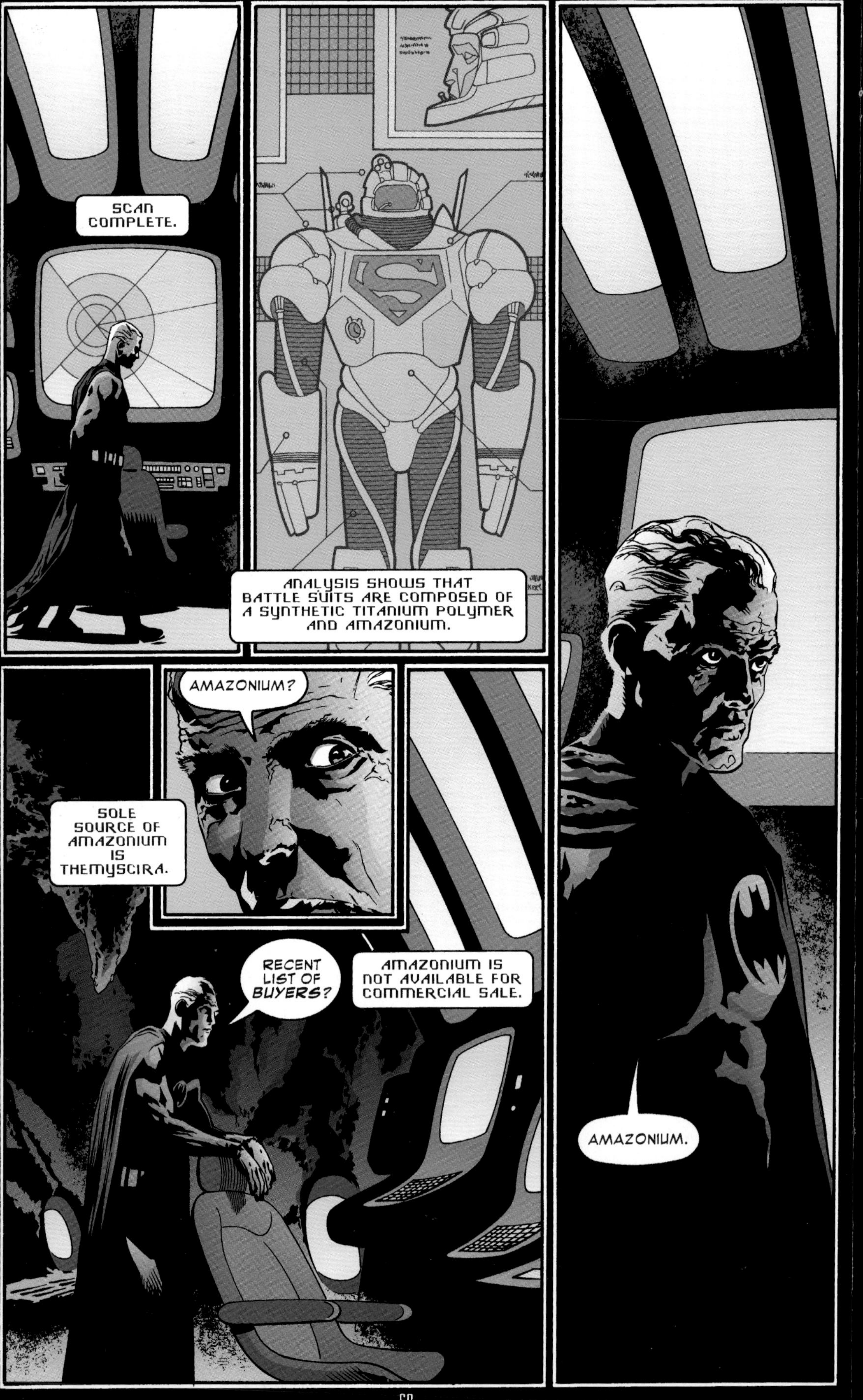
SCAN COMPLETE.
ANALYSIS SHOWS THAT BATTLE SUITS ARE COMPOSED OF A SYNTHETIC TITANIUM POLYMER AND AMAZONIUM.
AMAZONIUM?
SOLE SOURCE OF AMAZONIUM IS THEMYSCIRA.
RECENT LIST OF BUYERS?
AMAZONIUM IS NOT AVAILABLE FOR COMMERCIAL SALE.
AMAZONIUM.

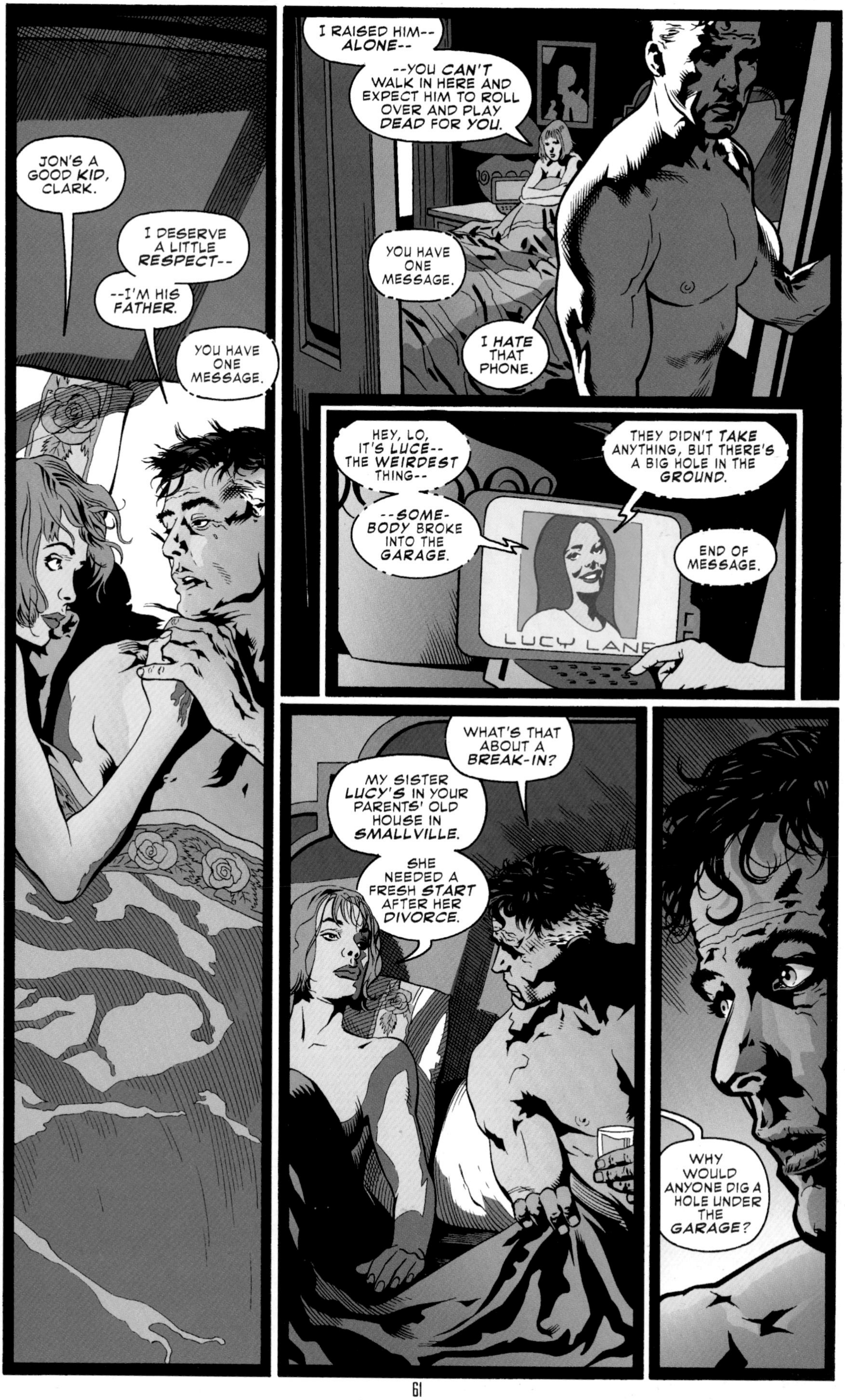
JON'S A GOOD KID, CLARK.
I DESERVE A LITTLE RESPECT--
--I'M HIS FATHER.
YOU HAVE ONE MESSAGE.
I RAISED HIM-- ALONE--
--YOU CAN'T WALK IN HERE AND EXPECT HIM TO ROLL OVER AND PLAY DEAD FOR YOU.
YOU HAVE ONE MESSAGE.
I HATE THAT PHONE.
HEY, LO, IT'S LUCE-- THE WEIRDEST THING--
--SOME-BODY BROKE INTO THE GARAGE.
THEY DIDN'T TAKE ANYTHING, BUT THERE'S A BIG HOLE IN THE GROUND.
END OF MESSAGE.
LUCY LANE
WHAT'S THAT ABOUT A BREAK-IN?
MY SISTER LUCY'S IN YOUR PARENTS' OLD HOUSE IN SMALLVILLE.
SHE NEEDED A FRESH START AFTER HER DIVORCE.
WHY WOULD ANYONE DIG A HOLE UNDER THE GARAGE?

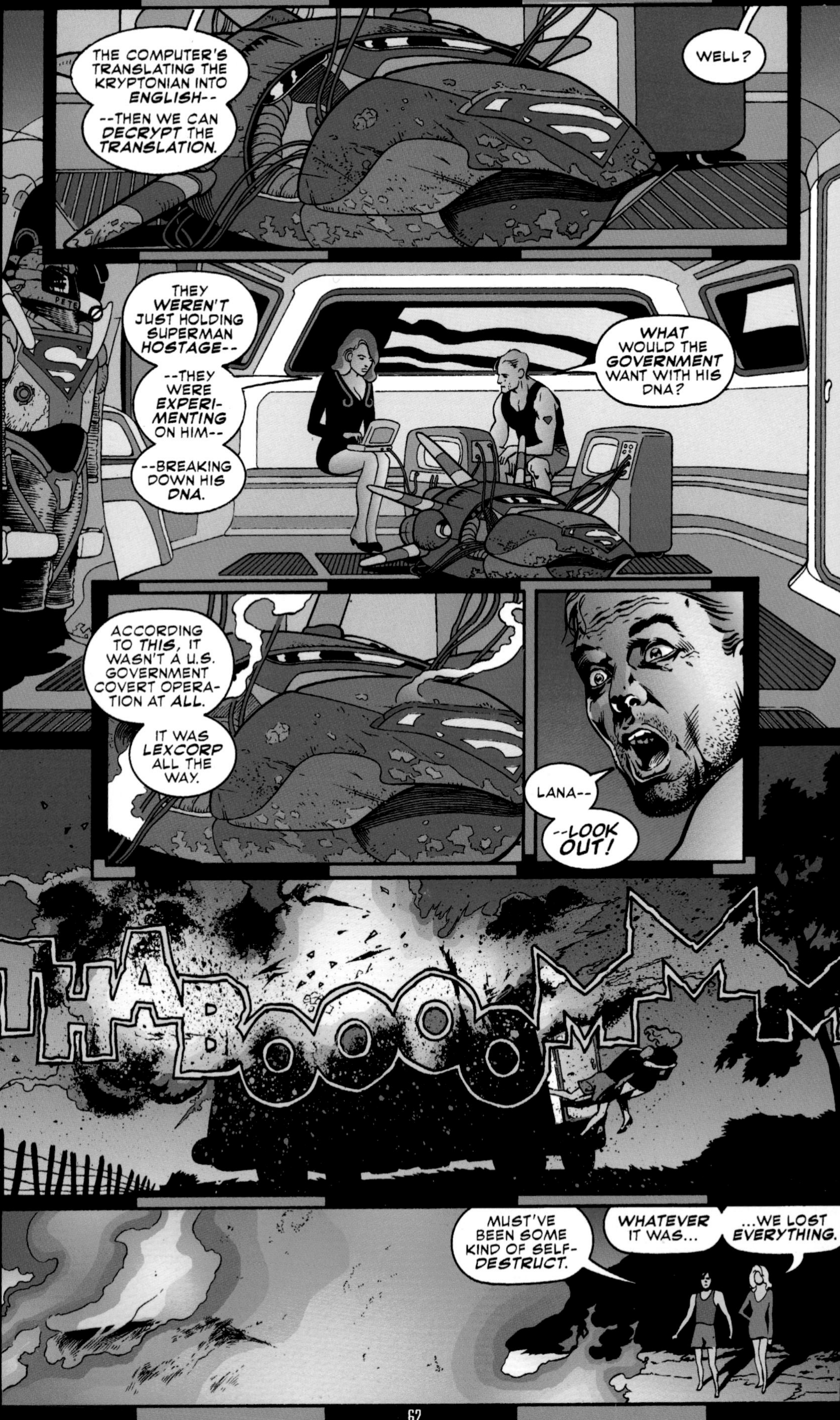
THE COMPUTER'S TRANSLATING THE KRYPTONIAN INTO ENGLISH--
--THEN WE CAN DECRYPT THE TRANSLATION.
WELL?
THEY WEREN'T JUST HOLDING SUPERMAN HOSTAGE--
--THEY WERE EXPERIMENTING ON HIM--
--BREAKING DOWN HIS DNA.
WHAT WOULD THE GOVERNMENT WANT WITH HIS DNA?
PETE
ACCORDING TO THIS, IT WASN'T A U.S. GOVERNMENT COVERT OPERATION AT ALL.
IT WAS LEXCORP ALL THE WAY.
LANA--
--LOOK OUT!
THABOOOOMMMM
MUST'VE BEEN SOME KIND OF SELF-DESTRUCT.
WHATEVER IT WAS...
...WE LOST EVERYTHING.

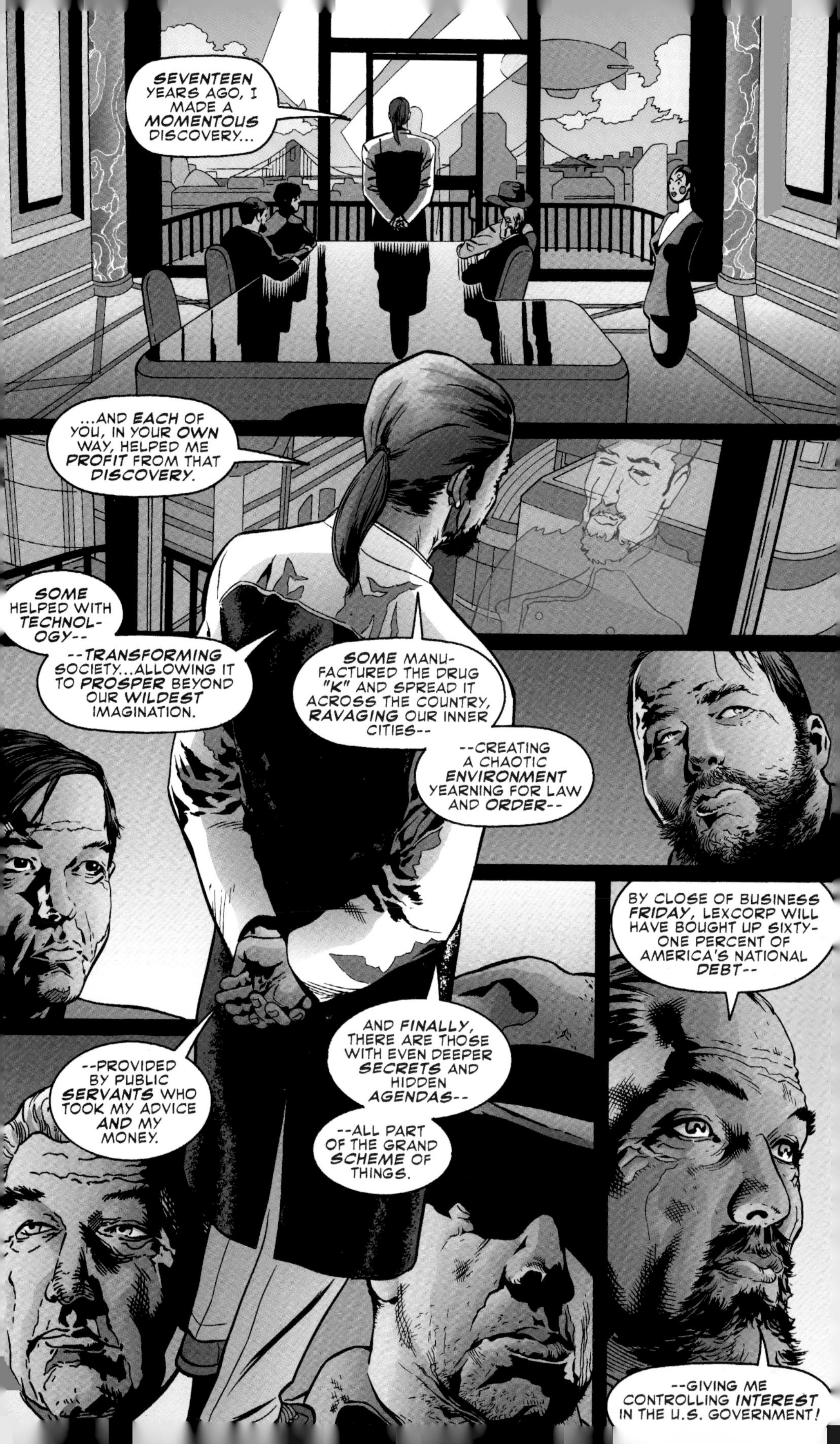
SEVENTEEN YEARS AGO, I MADE A MOMENTOUS DISCOVERY...
...AND EACH OF YOU, IN YOUR OWN WAY, HELPED ME PROFIT FROM THAT DISCOVERY.
SOME HELPED WITH TECHNOL-OGY--
--TRANSFORMING SOCIETY...ALLOWING IT TO PROSPER BEYOND OUR WILDEST IMAGINATION.
SOME MANU-FACTURED THE DRUG "K" AND SPREAD IT ACROSS THE COUNTRY, RAVAGING OUR INNER CITIES--
--CREATING A CHAOTIC ENVIRONMENT YEARNING FOR LAW AND ORDER--
--PROVIDED BY PUBLIC SERVANTS WHO TOOK MY ADVICE AND MY MONEY.
AND FINALLY, THERE ARE THOSE WITH EVEN DEEPER SECRETS AND HIDDEN AGENDAS--
--ALL PART OF THE GRAND SCHEME OF THINGS.
BY CLOSE OF BUSINESS FRIDAY, LEXCORP WILL HAVE BOUGHT UP SIXTY-ONE PERCENT OF AMERICA'S NATIONAL DEBT--
--GIVING ME CONTROLLING INTEREST IN THE U.S. GOVERNMENT!

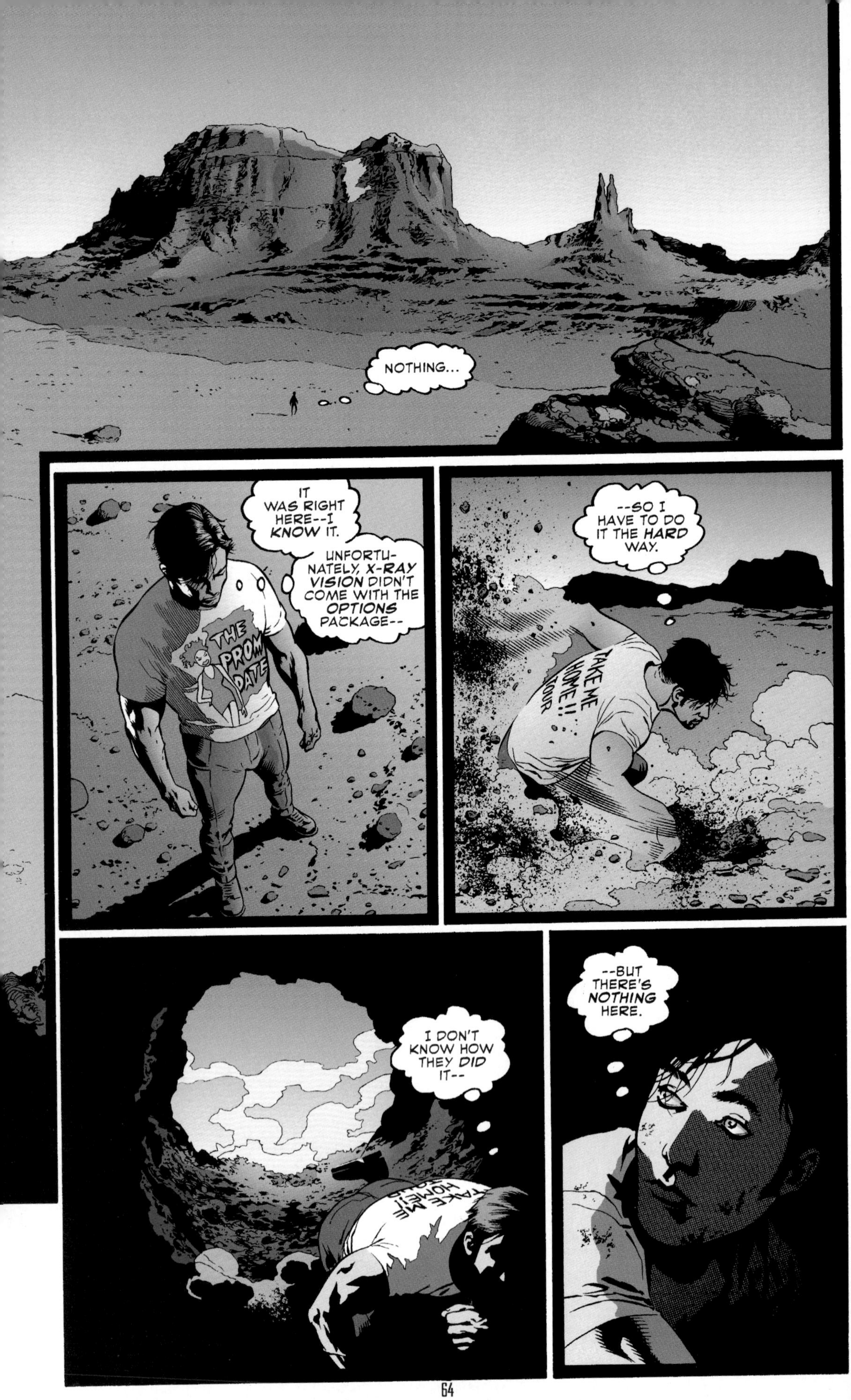
NOTHING...
IT WAS RIGHT HERE--I KNOW IT.
UNFORTU-NATELY, X-RAY VISION DIDN'T COME WITH THE OPTIONS PACKAGE--
THE PROM DATE
--SO I HAVE TO DO IT THE HARD WAY.
TAKE ME HOME!! TOUR
I DON'T KNOW HOW THEY DID IT--
--BUT THERE'S NOTHING HERE.

GREEN LANTERN, FLASH, AQUAMAN--

--THEY'VE ALL GOTTEN SO COMFORTABLE.

WHO'D'VE THOUGHT I'D LIVE TO SEE THE 9-TO-5 BUREAUCRATIC SUPERHERO.

I WONDER HOW BRUCE FEELS ABOUT THIS.

EVERYTHING ELSE HAS GONE TOTALLY TO HELL--

--I HOPE THE KEY STILL WORKS.

!!?!

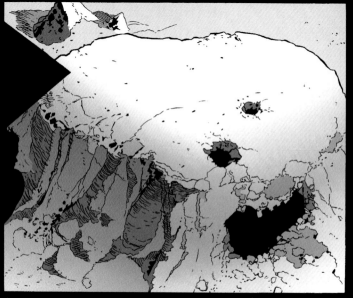

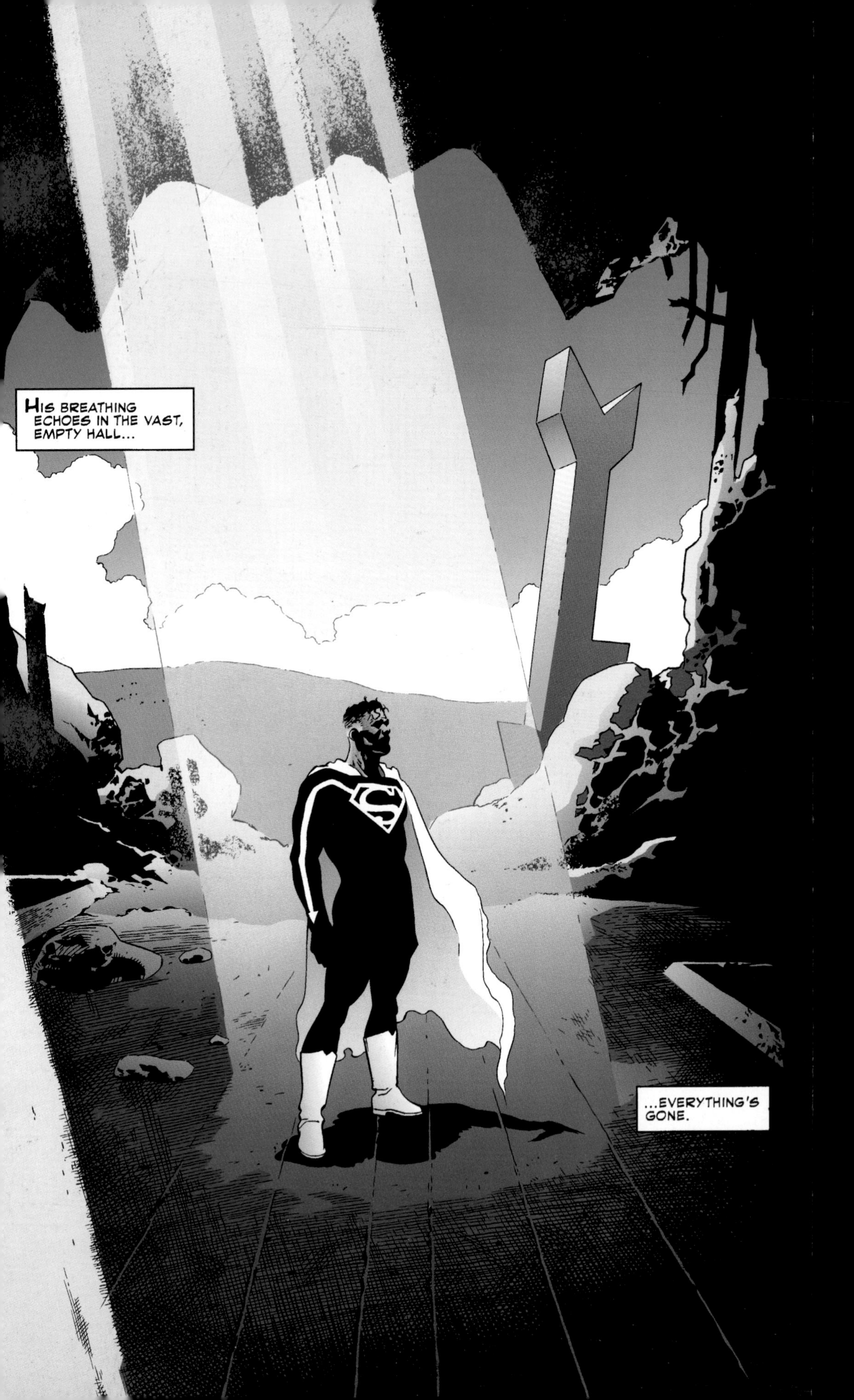
HIS BREATHING ECHOES IN THE VAST, EMPTY HALL...
...EVERYTHING'S GONE.

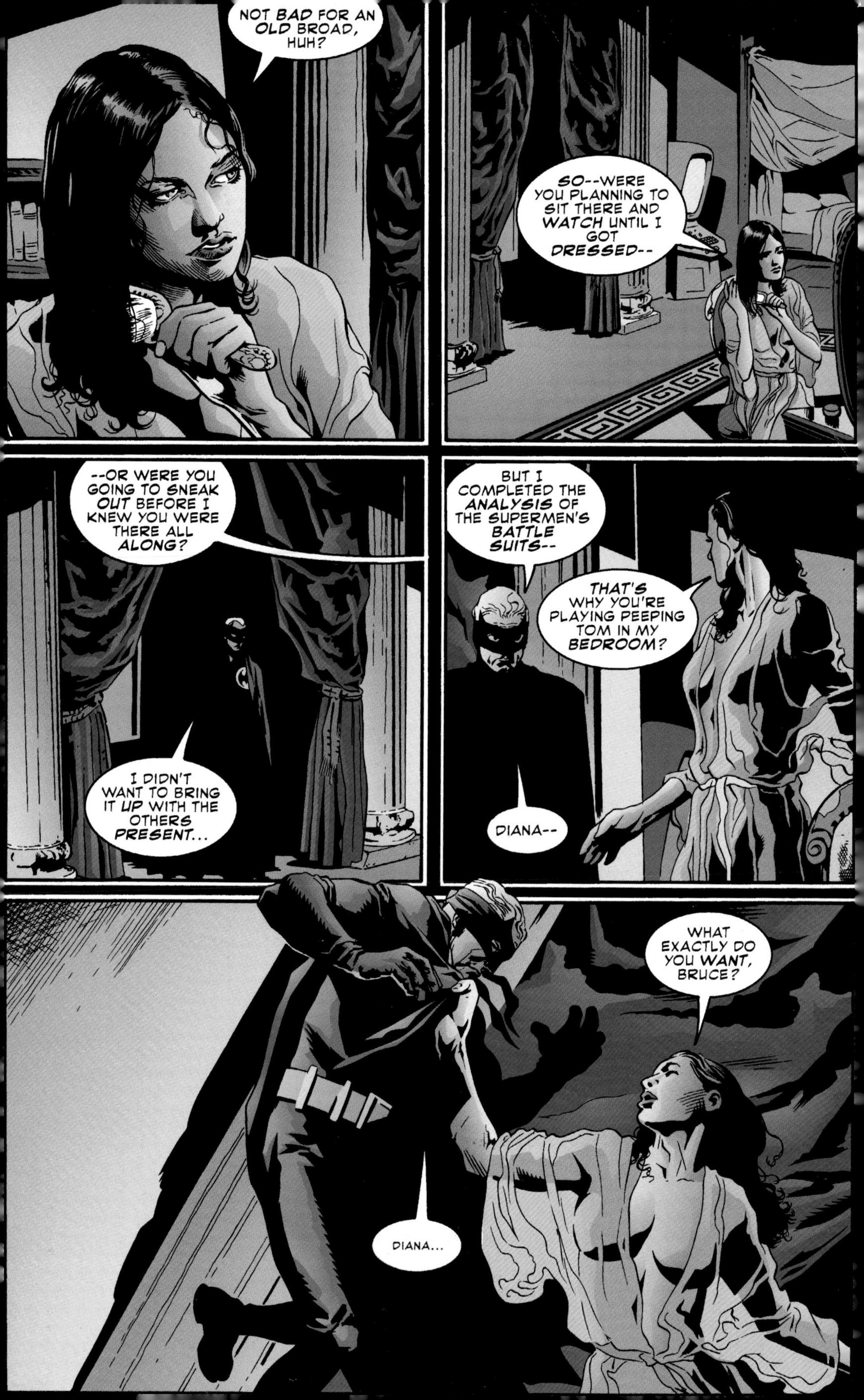
NOT BAD FOR AN OLD BROAD, HUH?
SO--WERE YOU PLANNING TO SIT THERE AND WATCH UNTIL I GOT DRESSED--
--OR WERE YOU GOING TO SNEAK OUT BEFORE I KNEW YOU WERE THERE ALL ALONG?
I DIDN'T WANT TO BRING IT UP WITH THE OTHERS PRESENT...
BUT I COMPLETED THE ANALYSIS OF THE SUPERMEN'S BATTLE SUITS--
THAT'S WHY YOU'RE PLAYING PEEPING TOM IN MY BEDROOM?
DIANA--
WHAT EXACTLY DO YOU WANT, BRUCE?
DIANA...

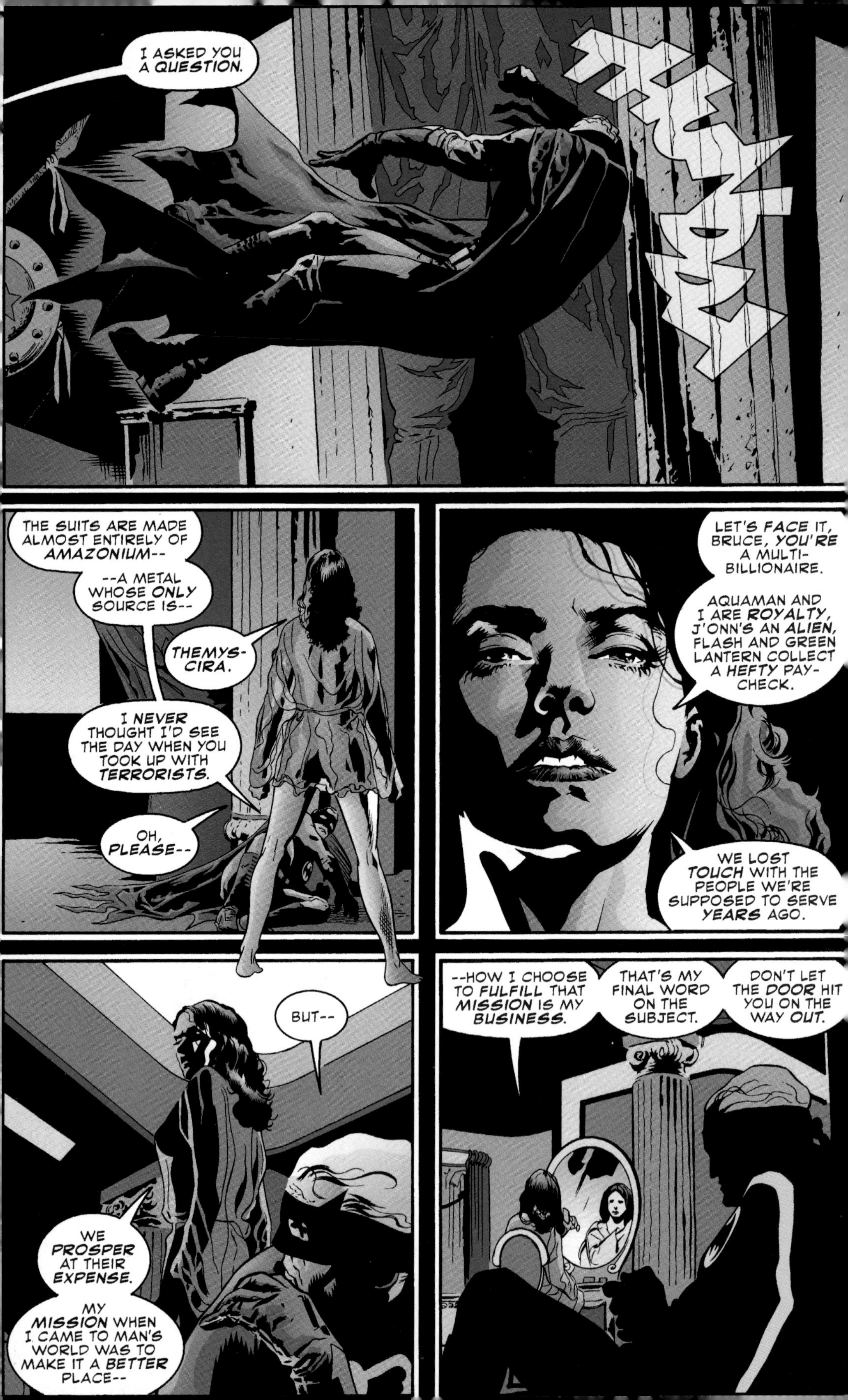
I ASKED YOU A QUESTION.
THE SUITS ARE MADE ALMOST ENTIRELY OF AMAZONIUM--
--A METAL WHOSE ONLY SOURCE IS--
THEMYS-CIRA.
I NEVER THOUGHT I'D SEE THE DAY WHEN YOU TOOK UP WITH TERRORISTS.
OH, PLEASE--
LET'S FACE IT, BRUCE, YOU'RE A MULTI-BILLIONAIRE.
AQUAMAN AND I ARE ROYALTY, J'ONN'S AN ALIEN, FLASH AND GREEN LANTERN COLLECT A HEFTY PAY-CHECK.
WE LOST TOUCH WITH THE PEOPLE WE'RE SUPPOSED TO SERVE YEARS AGO.
BUT--
WE PROSPER AT THEIR EXPENSE.
MY MISSION WHEN I CAME TO MAN'S WORLD WAS TO MAKE IT A BETTER PLACE--
--HOW I CHOOSE TO FULFILL THAT MISSION IS MY BUSINESS.
THAT'S MY FINAL WORD ON THE SUBJECT.
DON'T LET THE DOOR HIT YOU ON THE WAY OUT.

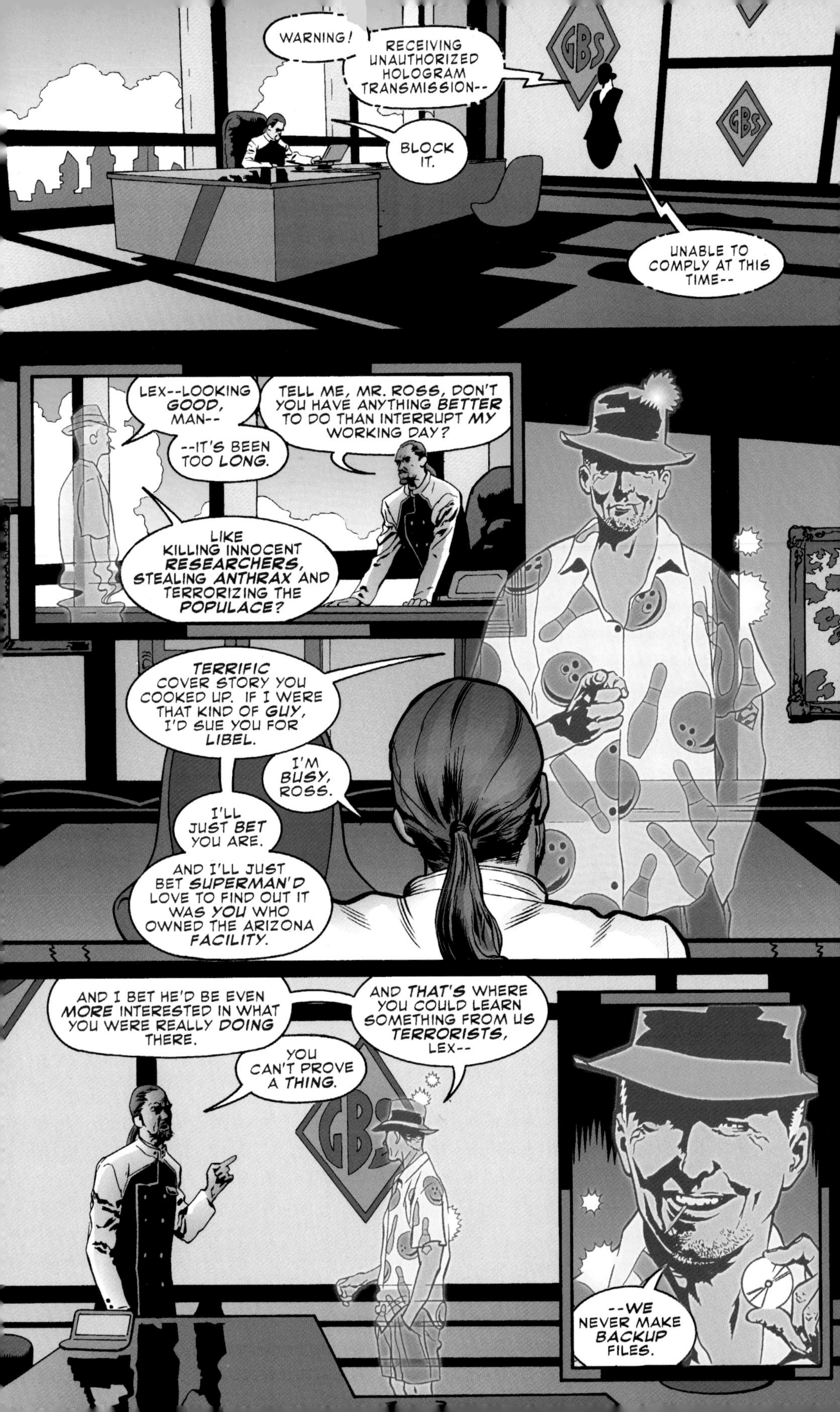
WARNING!
RECEIVING UNAUTHORIZED HOLOGRAM TRANSMISSION--
BLOCK IT.
UNABLE TO COMPLY AT THIS TIME--
LEX--LOOKING GOOD, MAN--
--IT'S BEEN TOO LONG.
TELL ME, MR. ROSS, DON'T YOU HAVE ANYTHING BETTER TO DO THAN INTERRUPT MY WORKING DAY?
LIKE KILLING INNOCENT RESEARCHERS, STEALING ANTHRAX AND TERRORIZING THE POPULACE?
TERRIFIC COVER STORY YOU COOKED UP. IF I WERE THAT KIND OF GUY, I'D SUE YOU FOR LIBEL.
I'M BUSY, ROSS.
I'LL JUST BET YOU ARE.
AND I'LL JUST BET SUPERMAN'D LOVE TO FIND OUT IT WAS YOU WHO OWNED THE ARIZONA FACILITY.
AND I BET HE'D BE EVEN MORE INTERESTED IN WHAT YOU WERE REALLY DOING THERE.
YOU CAN'T PROVE A THING.
AND THAT'S WHERE YOU COULD LEARN SOMETHING FROM US TERRORISTS, LEX--
--WE NEVER MAKE BACKUP FILES.

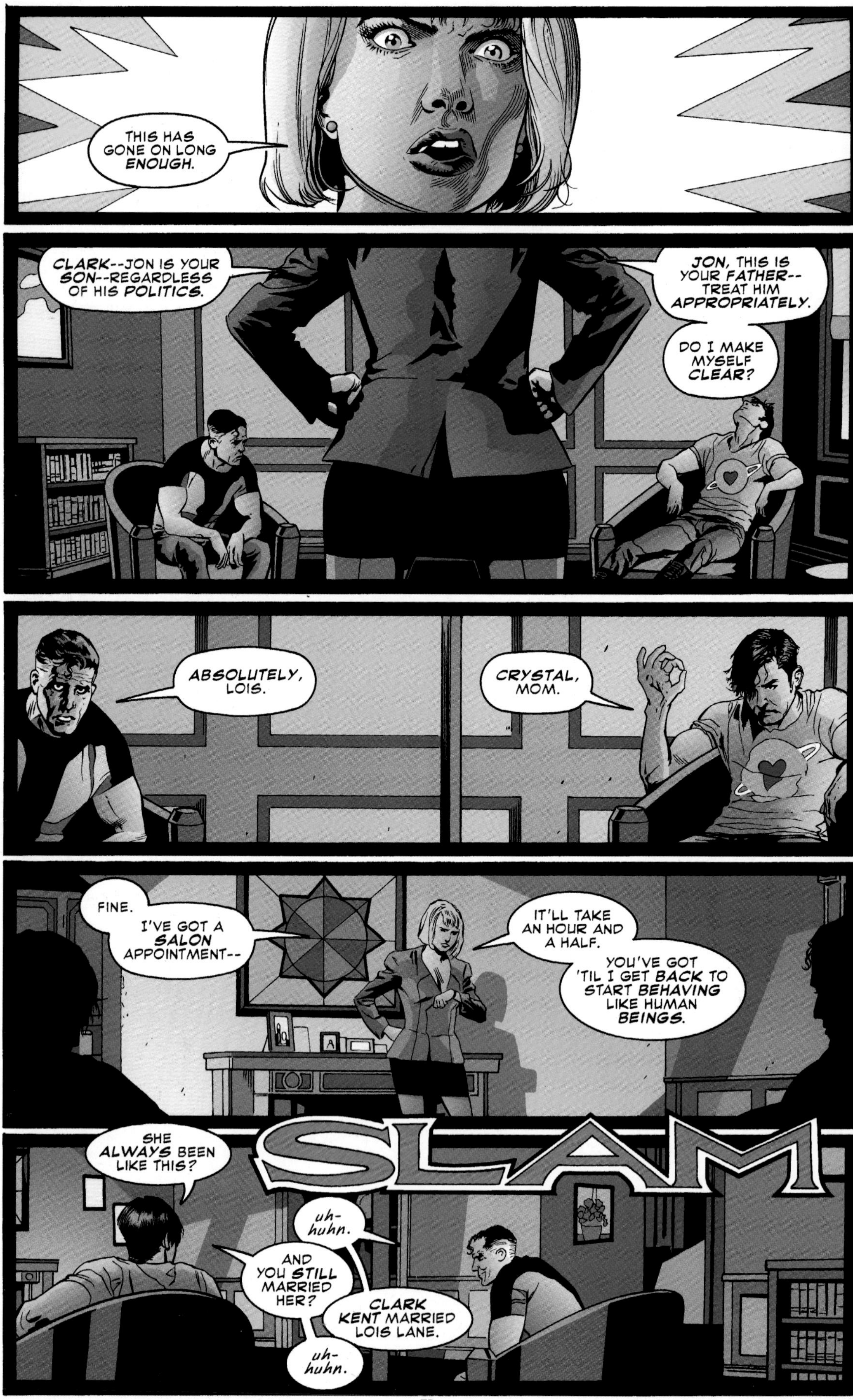
THIS HAS GONE ON LONG ENOUGH.
CLARK--JON IS YOUR SON--REGARDLESS OF HIS POLITICS.
JON, THIS IS YOUR FATHER--TREAT HIM APPROPRIATELY.
DO I MAKE MYSELF CLEAR?
ABSOLUTELY, LOIS.
CRYSTAL, MOM.
FINE.
I'VE GOT A SALON APPOINTMENT--
IT'LL TAKE AN HOUR AND A HALF.
YOU'VE GOT 'TIL I GET BACK TO START BEHAVING LIKE HUMAN BEINGS.
SLAM
SHE ALWAYS BEEN LIKE THIS?
uh-huhn.
AND YOU STILL MARRIED HER?
CLARK KENT MARRIED LOIS LANE.
uh-huhn.

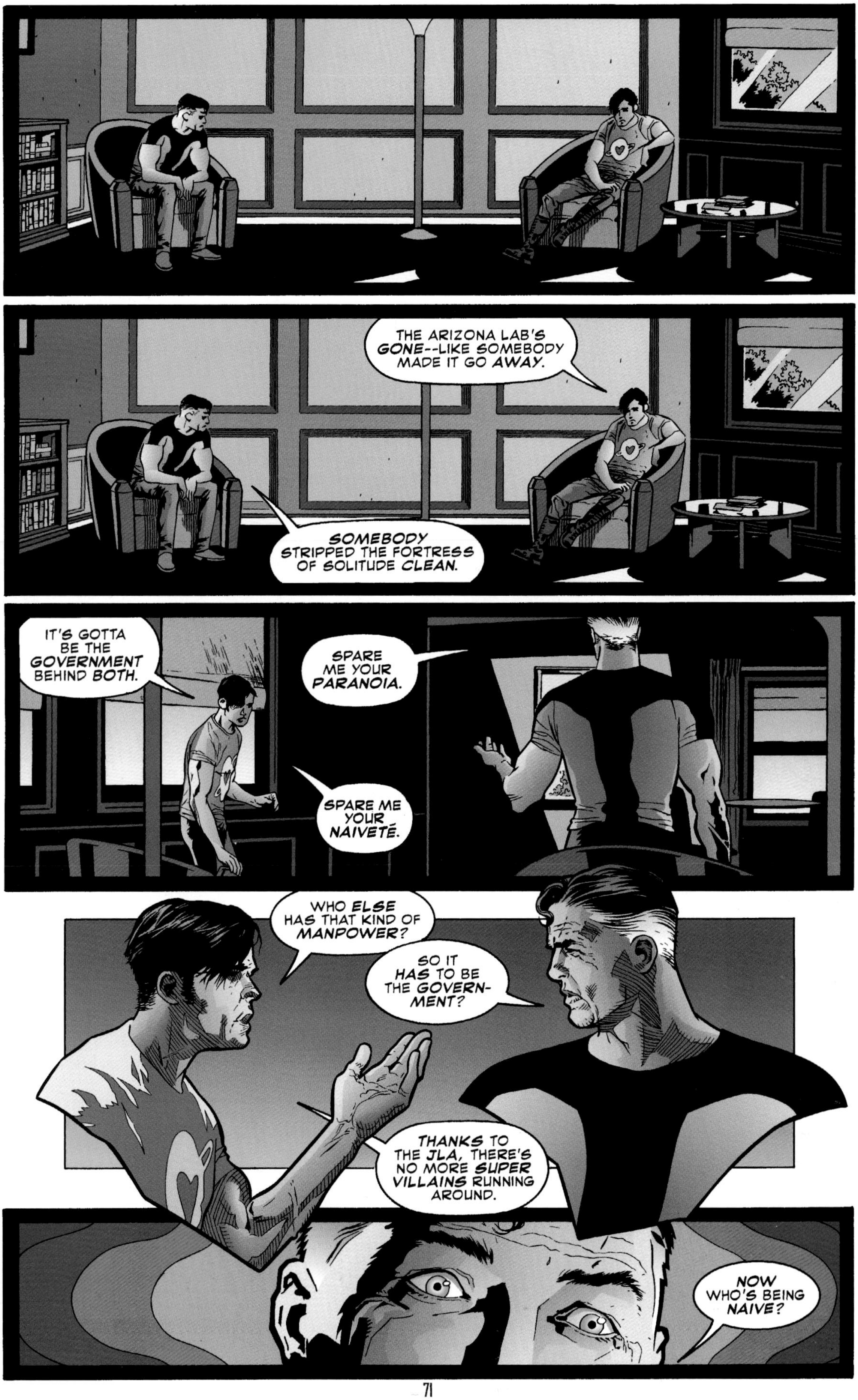
THE ARIZONA LAB'S GONE--LIKE SOMEBODY MADE IT GO AWAY.
SOMEBODY STRIPPED THE FORTRESS OF SOLITUDE CLEAN.
IT'S GOTTA BE THE GOVERNMENT BEHIND BOTH.
SPARE ME YOUR PARANOIA.
SPARE ME YOUR NAIVETÉ.
WHO ELSE HAS THAT KIND OF MANPOWER?
SO IT HAS TO BE THE GOVERNMENT?
THANKS TO THE JLA, THERE'S NO MORE SUPER VILLAINS RUNNING AROUND.
NOW WHO'S BEING NAIVE?

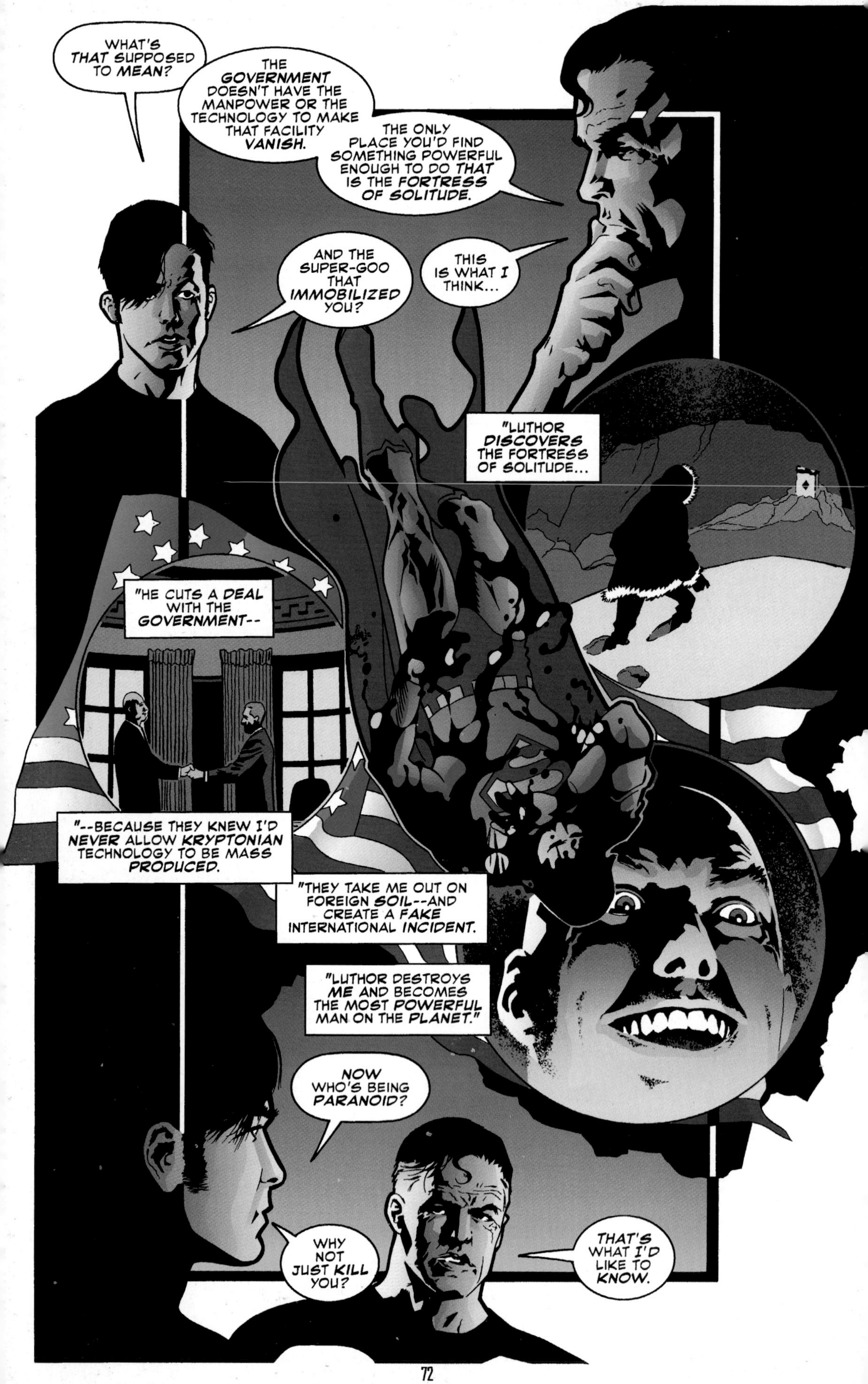
WHAT'S THAT SUPPOSED TO MEAN?
THE GOVERNMENT DOESN'T HAVE THE MANPOWER OR THE TECHNOLOGY TO MAKE THAT FACILITY VANISH.
THE ONLY PLACE YOU'D FIND SOMETHING POWERFUL ENOUGH TO DO THAT IS THE FORTRESS OF SOLITUDE.
AND THE SUPER-GOO THAT IMMOBILIZED YOU?
THIS IS WHAT I THINK...
"LUTHOR DISCOVERS THE FORTRESS OF SOLITUDE...
"HE CUTS A DEAL WITH THE GOVERNMENT--
"--BECAUSE THEY KNEW I'D NEVER ALLOW KRYPTONIAN TECHNOLOGY TO BE MASS PRODUCED.
"THEY TAKE ME OUT ON FOREIGN SOIL--AND CREATE A FAKE INTERNATIONAL INCIDENT.
"LUTHOR DESTROYS ME AND BECOMES THE MOST POWERFUL MAN ON THE PLANET."
NOW WHO'S BEING PARANOID?
WHY NOT JUST KILL YOU?
THAT'S WHAT I'D LIKE TO KNOW.

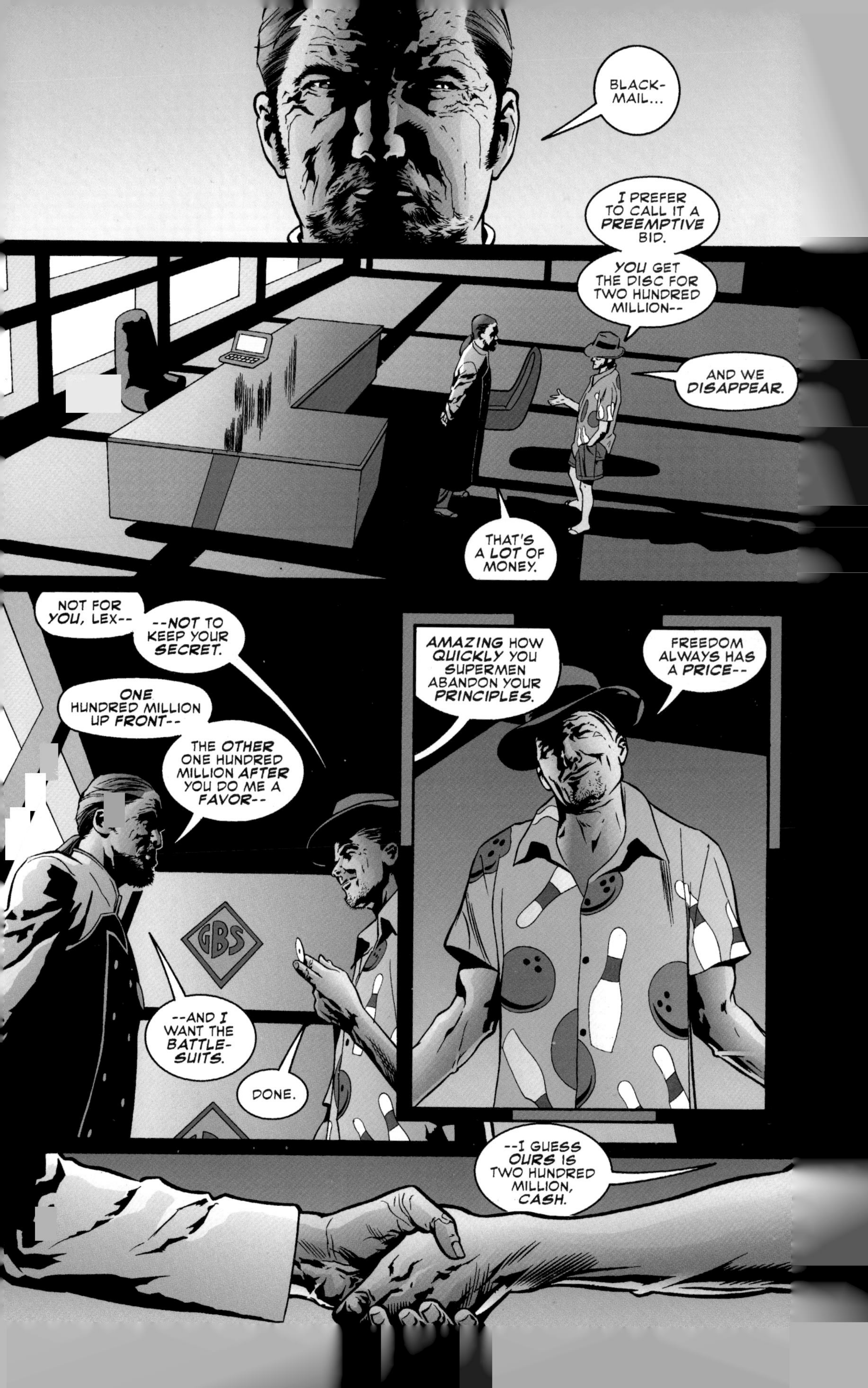
BLACK-MAIL...
I PREFER TO CALL IT A PREEMPTIVE BID.
YOU GET THE DISC FOR TWO HUNDRED MILLION--
AND WE DISAPPEAR.
THAT'S A LOT OF MONEY.
NOT FOR YOU, LEX--
--NOT TO KEEP YOUR SECRET.
ONE HUNDRED MILLION UP FRONT--
THE OTHER ONE HUNDRED MILLION AFTER YOU DO ME A FAVOR--
--AND I WANT THE BATTLE-SUITS.
DONE.
AMAZING HOW QUICKLY YOU SUPERMEN ABANDON YOUR PRINCIPLES.
FREEDOM ALWAYS HAS A PRICE--
--I GUESS OURS IS TWO HUNDRED MILLION, CASH.
GBS

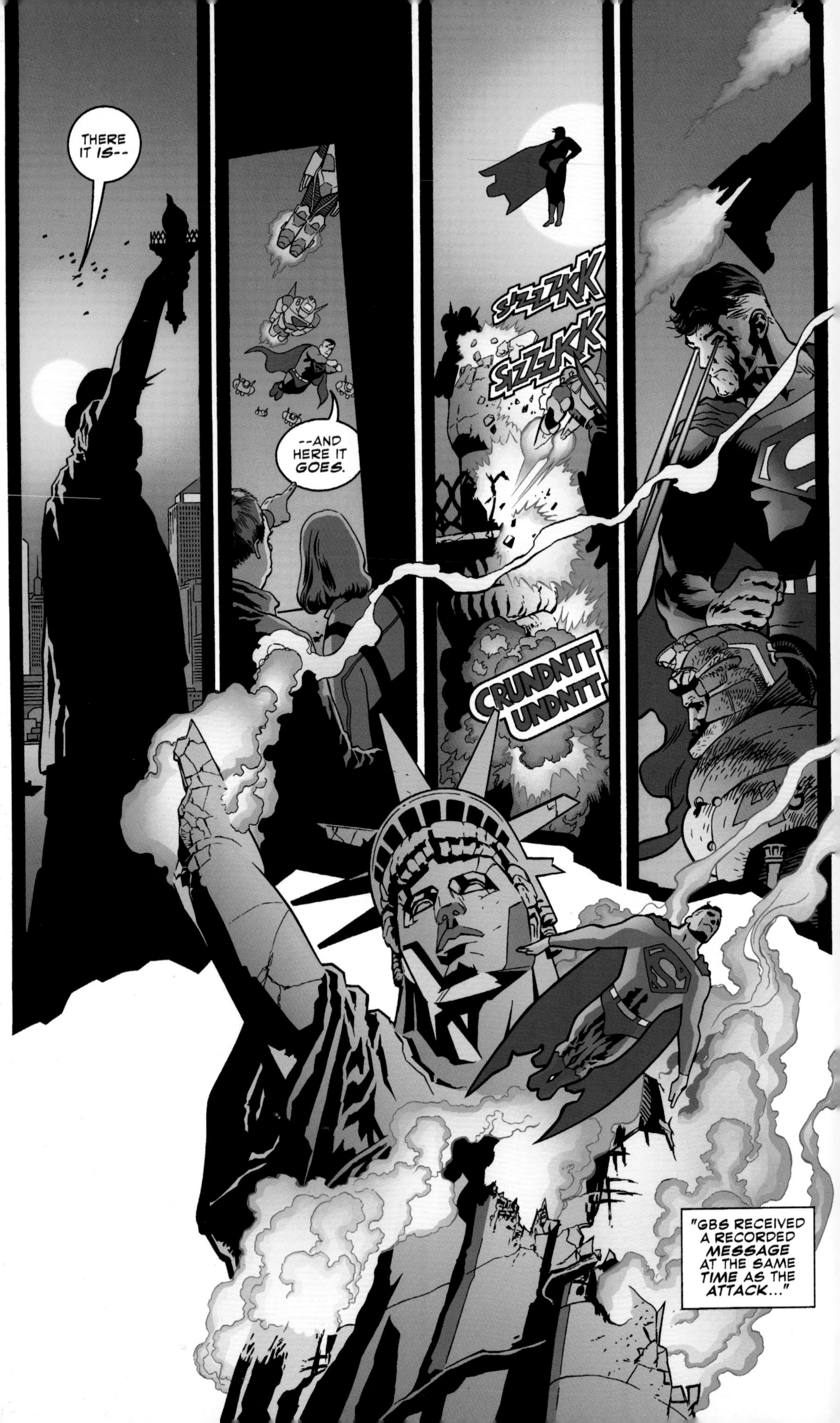
THERE IT IS--
--AND HERE IT GOES.
SIZZZKK
SIZZZKK
CRUNDNTT UNDNTT
"GBS RECEIVED A RECORDED MESSAGE AT THE SAME TIME AS THE ATTACK..."

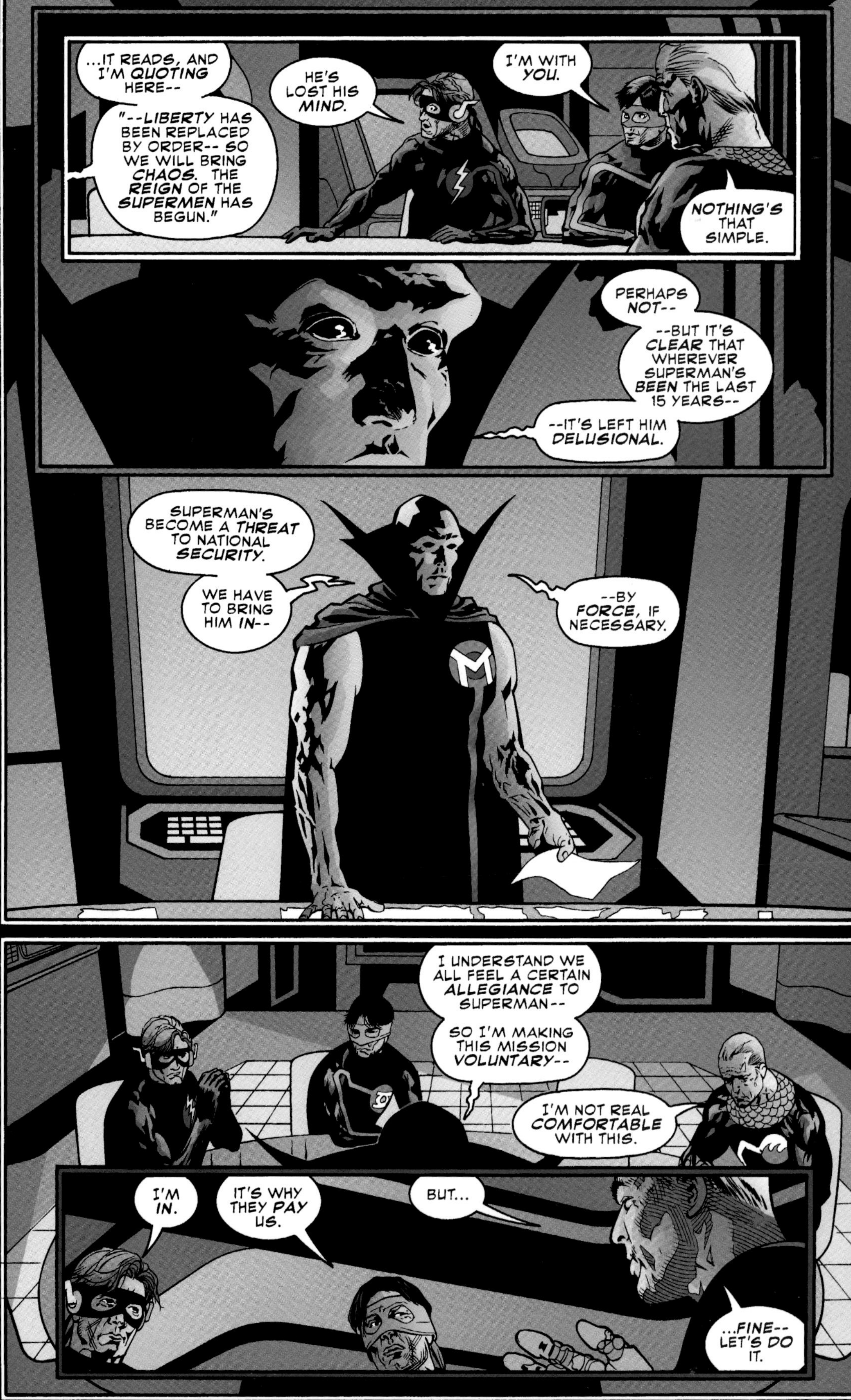

...IT READS, AND I'M QUOTING HERE--
"--LIBERTY HAS BEEN REPLACED BY ORDER-- SO WE WILL BRING CHAOS. THE REIGN OF THE SUPERMEN HAS BEGUN."
HE'S LOST HIS MIND.
I'M WITH YOU.
NOTHING'S THAT SIMPLE.
PERHAPS NOT--
--BUT IT'S CLEAR THAT WHEREVER SUPERMAN'S BEEN THE LAST 15 YEARS--
--IT'S LEFT HIM DELUSIONAL.
SUPERMAN'S BECOME A THREAT TO NATIONAL SECURITY.
WE HAVE TO BRING HIM IN--
--BY FORCE, IF NECESSARY.
I UNDERSTAND WE ALL FEEL A CERTAIN ALLEGIANCE TO SUPERMAN--
SO I'M MAKING THIS MISSION VOLUNTARY--
I'M NOT REAL COMFORTABLE WITH THIS.
I'M IN.
IT'S WHY THEY PAY US.
BUT...
...FINE-- LET'S DO IT.

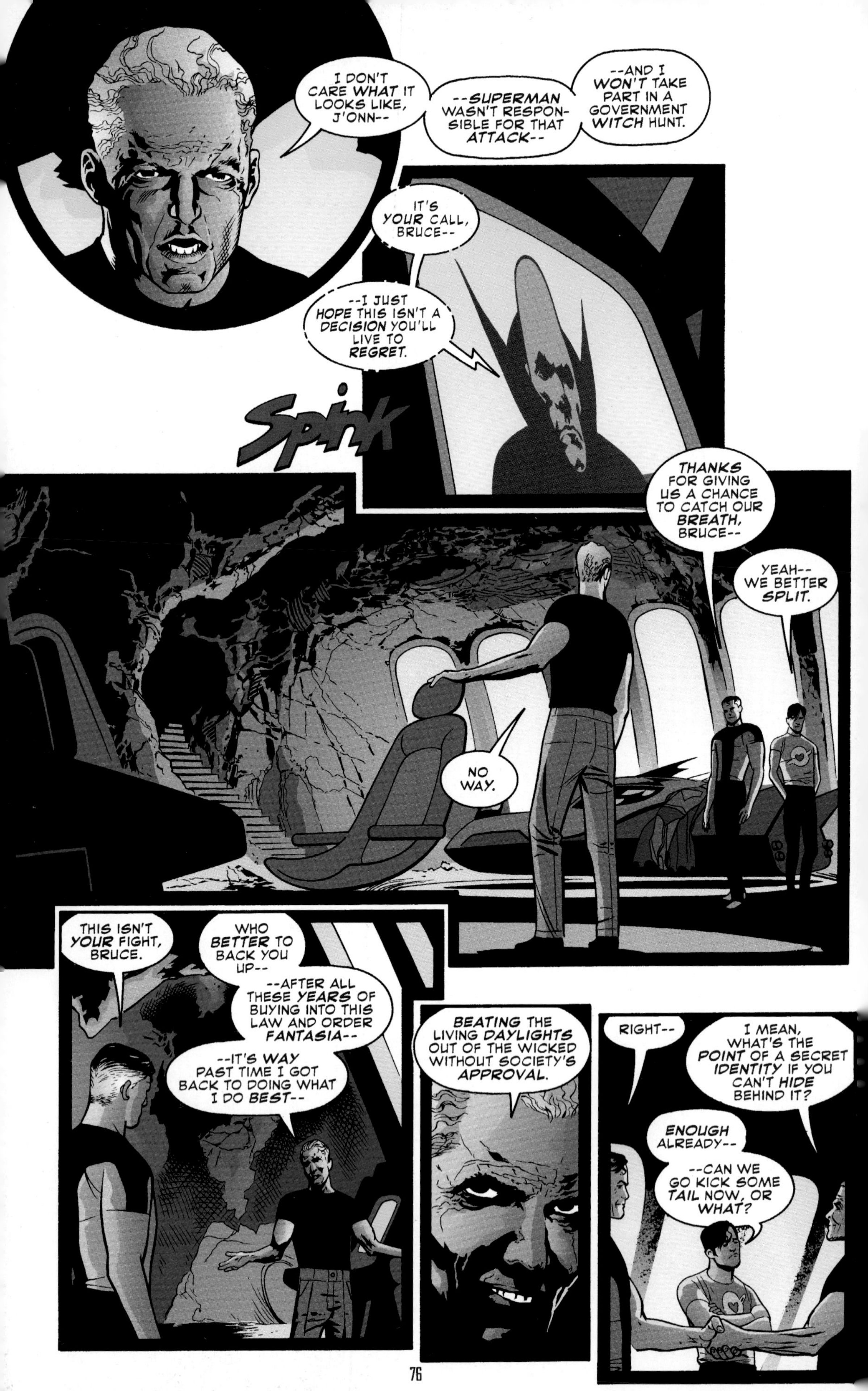

I DON'T CARE WHAT IT LOOKS LIKE, J'ONN--
--SUPERMAN WASN'T RESPONSIBLE FOR THAT ATTACK--
--AND I WON'T TAKE PART IN A GOVERNMENT WITCH HUNT.
IT'S YOUR CALL, BRUCE--
--I JUST HOPE THIS ISN'T A DECISION YOU'LL LIVE TO REGRET.
Spink
THANKS FOR GIVING US A CHANCE TO CATCH OUR BREATH, BRUCE--
YEAH-- WE BETTER SPLIT.
NO WAY.
THIS ISN'T YOUR FIGHT, BRUCE.
WHO BETTER TO BACK YOU UP--
--AFTER ALL THESE YEARS OF BUYING INTO THIS LAW AND ORDER FANTASIA--
--IT'S WAY PAST TIME I GOT BACK TO DOING WHAT I DO BEST--
BEATING THE LIVING DAYLIGHTS OUT OF THE WICKED WITHOUT SOCIETY'S APPROVAL.
RIGHT--
I MEAN, WHAT'S THE POINT OF A SECRET IDENTITY IF YOU CAN'T HIDE BEHIND IT?
ENOUGH ALREADY--
--CAN WE GO KICK SOME TAIL NOW, OR WHAT?

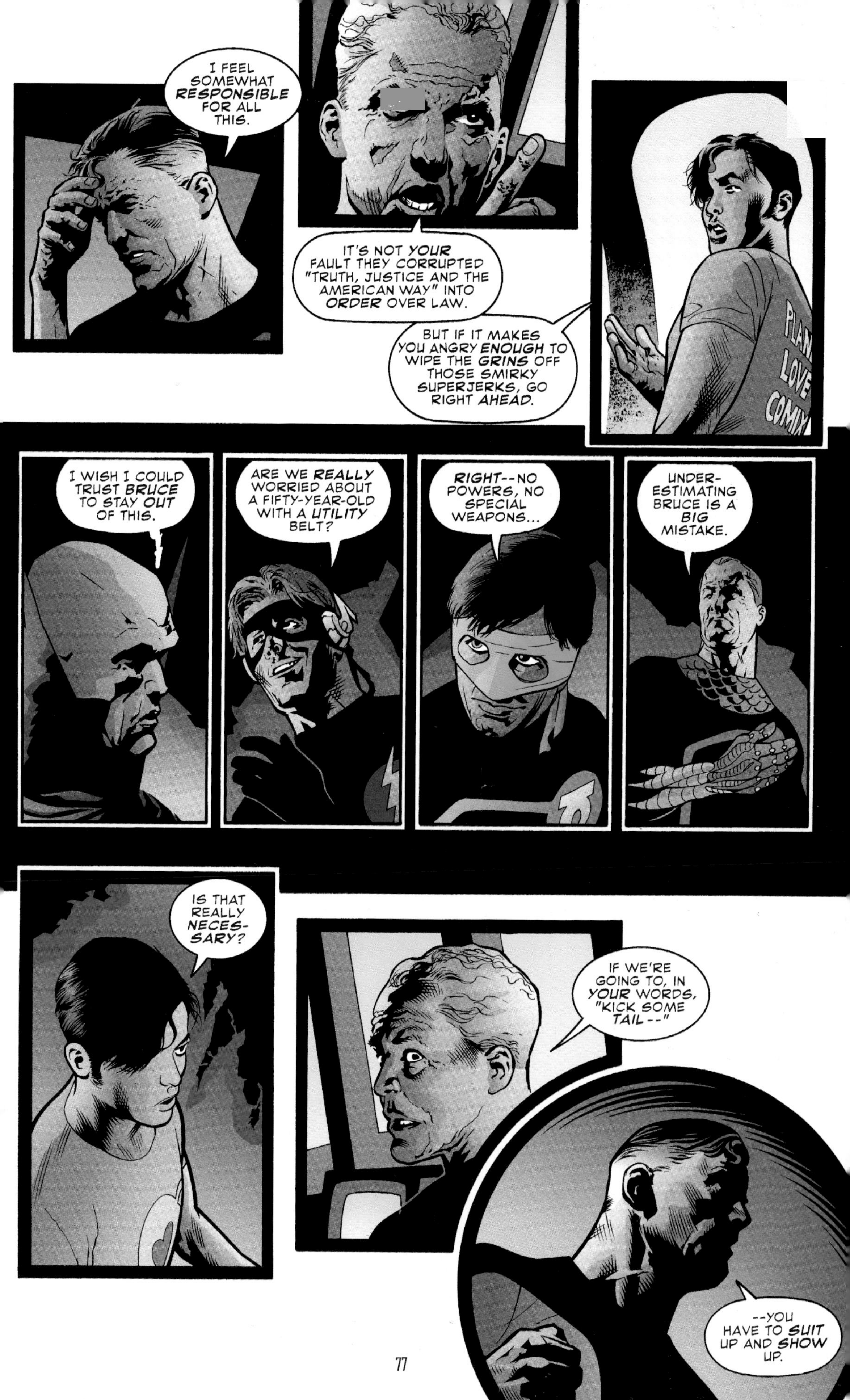
I FEEL SOMEWHAT RESPONSIBLE FOR ALL THIS.
IT'S NOT YOUR FAULT THEY CORRUPTED "TRUTH, JUSTICE AND THE AMERICAN WAY" INTO ORDER OVER LAW.
BUT IF IT MAKES YOU ANGRY ENOUGH TO WIPE THE GRINS OFF THOSE SMIRKY SUPERJERKS, GO RIGHT AHEAD.
PLAN LOVE COMIX
I WISH I COULD TRUST BRUCE TO STAY OUT OF THIS.
ARE WE REALLY WORRIED ABOUT A FIFTY-YEAR-OLD WITH A UTILITY BELT?
RIGHT--NO POWERS, NO SPECIAL WEAPONS...
UNDER-ESTIMATING BRUCE IS A BIG MISTAKE.
IS THAT REALLY NECES-SARY?
IF WE'RE GOING TO, IN YOUR WORDS, "KICK SOME TAIL--"
--YOU HAVE TO SUIT UP AND SHOW UP.

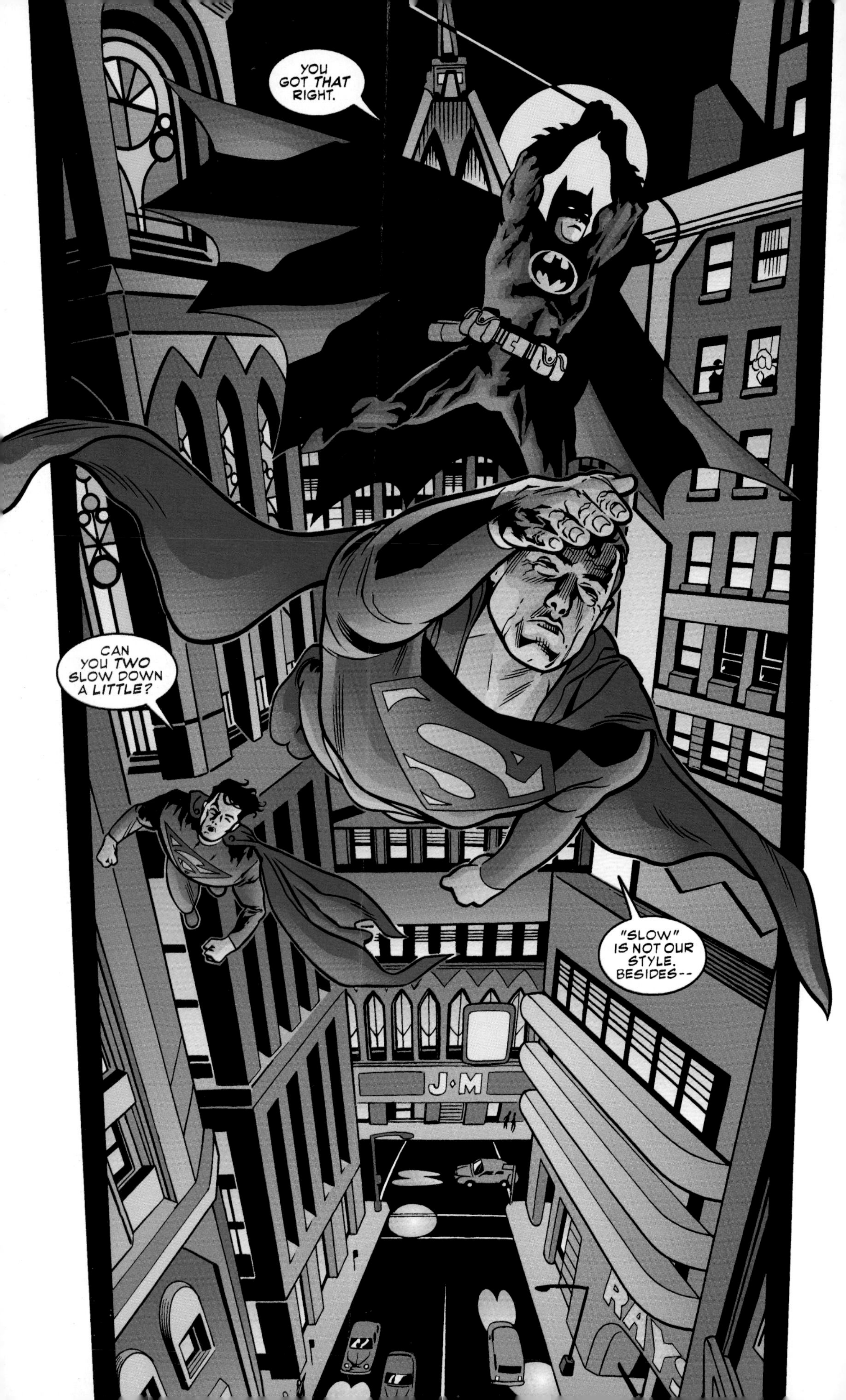
YOU GOT THAT RIGHT.
CAN YOU TWO SLOW DOWN A LITTLE?
"SLOW" IS NOT OUR STYLE. BESIDES--
J·M

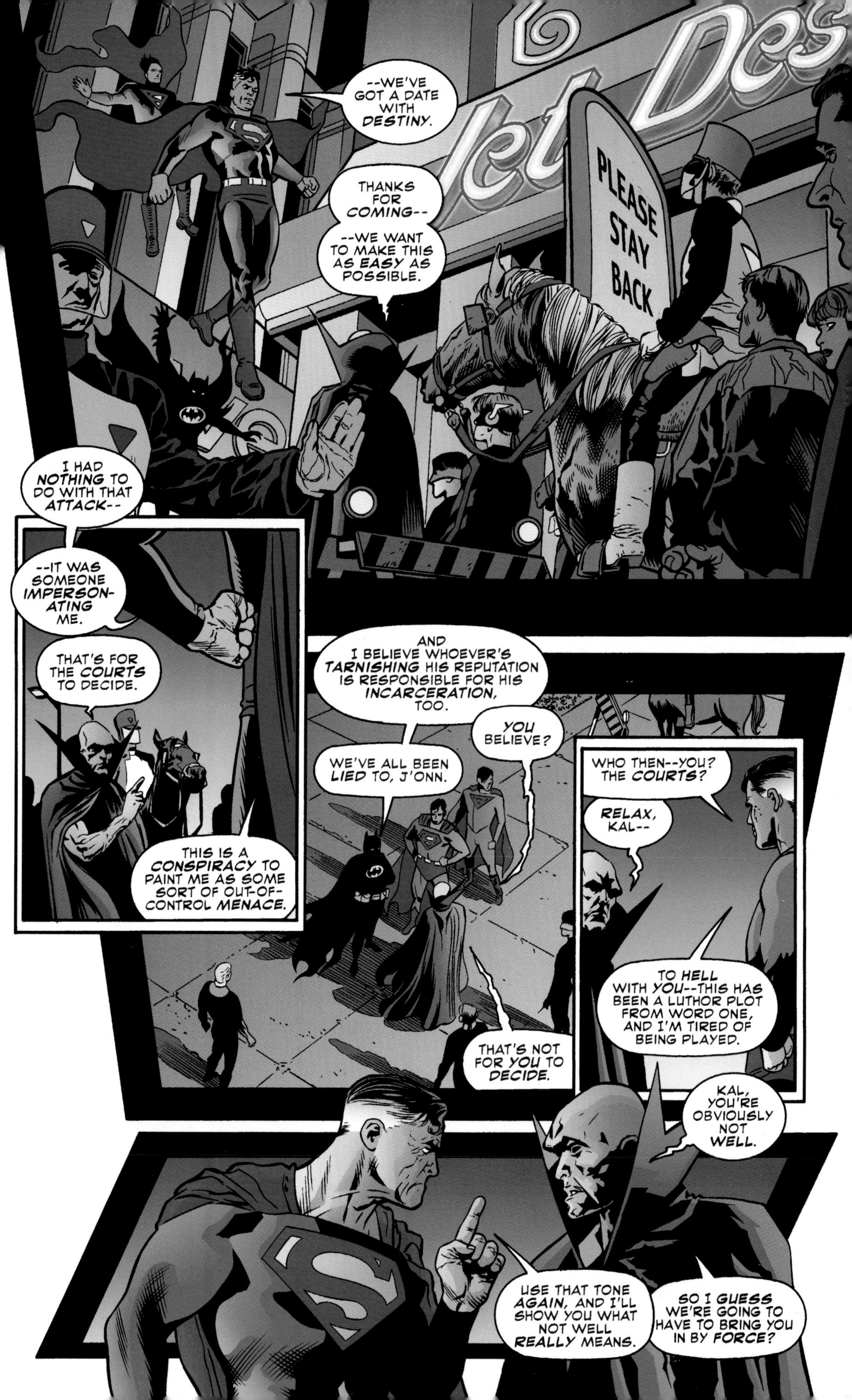

--WE'VE GOT A DATE WITH DESTINY.
THANKS FOR COMING--
--WE WANT TO MAKE THIS AS EASY AS POSSIBLE.
PLEASE STAY BACK
I HAD NOTHING TO DO WITH THAT ATTACK--
--IT WAS SOMEONE IMPERSON-ATING ME.
THAT'S FOR THE COURTS TO DECIDE.
THIS IS A CONSPIRACY TO PAINT ME AS SOME SORT OF OUT-OF-CONTROL MENACE.
AND I BELIEVE WHOEVER'S TARNISHING HIS REPUTATION IS RESPONSIBLE FOR HIS INCARCERATION, TOO.
YOU BELIEVE?
WE'VE ALL BEEN LIED TO, J'ONN.
THAT'S NOT FOR YOU TO DECIDE.
WHO THEN--YOU? THE COURTS?
RELAX, KAL--
TO HELL WITH YOU--THIS HAS BEEN A LUTHOR PLOT FROM WORD ONE, AND I'M TIRED OF BEING PLAYED.
KAL, YOU'RE OBVIOUSLY NOT WELL.
USE THAT TONE AGAIN, AND I'LL SHOW YOU WHAT NOT WELL REALLY MEANS.
SO I GUESS WE'RE GOING TO HAVE TO BRING YOU IN BY FORCE?

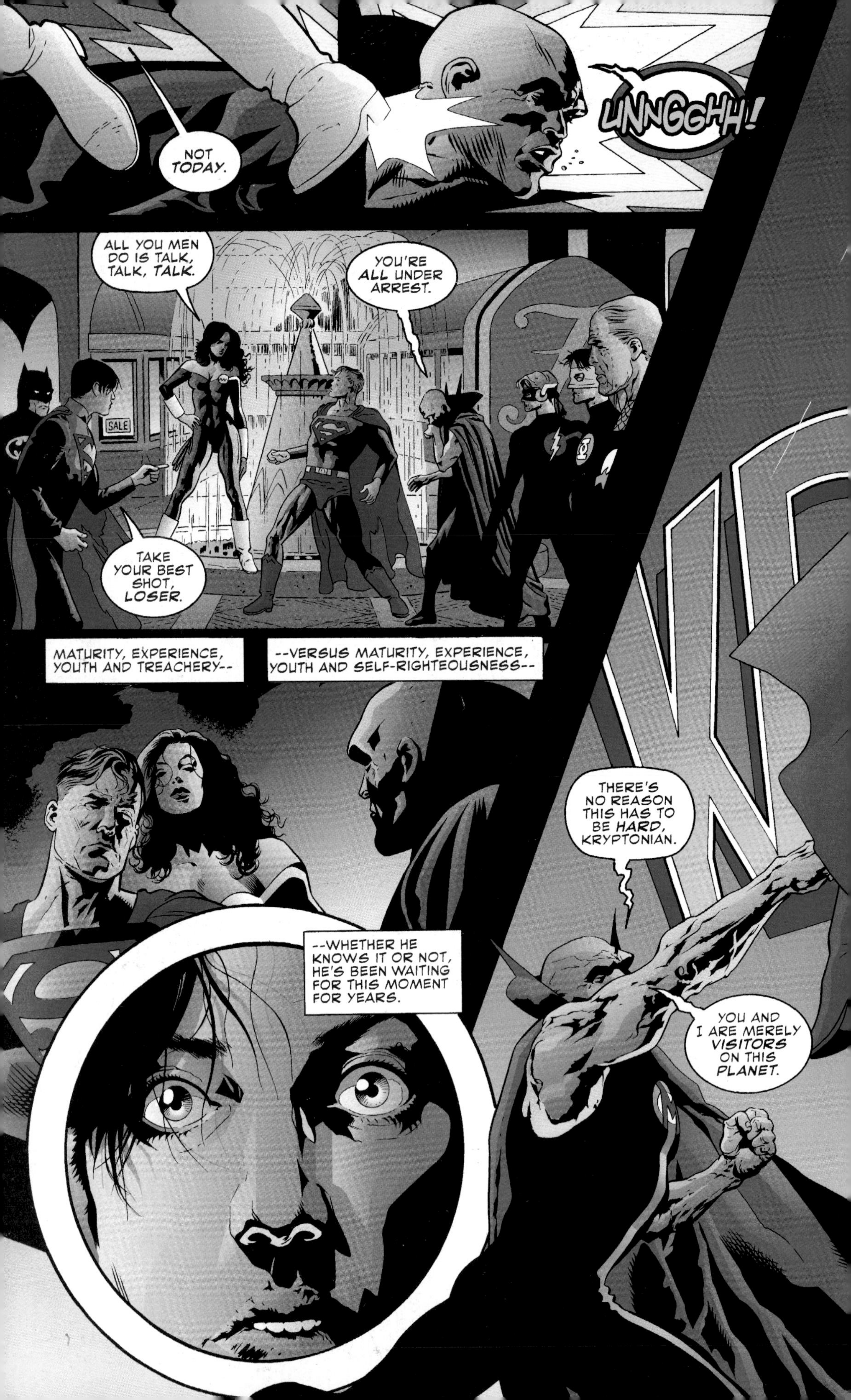
NOT TODAY.
UNNGGHH!
ALL YOU MEN DO IS TALK, TALK, TALK.
YOU'RE ALL UNDER ARREST.
SALE
TAKE YOUR BEST SHOT, LOSER.
MATURITY, EXPERIENCE, YOUTH AND TREACHERY--
--VERSUS MATURITY, EXPERIENCE, YOUTH AND SELF-RIGHTEOUSNESS--
THERE'S NO REASON THIS HAS TO BE HARD, KRYPTONIAN.
--WHETHER HE KNOWS IT OR NOT, HE'S BEEN WAITING FOR THIS MOMENT FOR YEARS.
YOU AND I ARE MERELY VISITORS ON THIS PLANET.

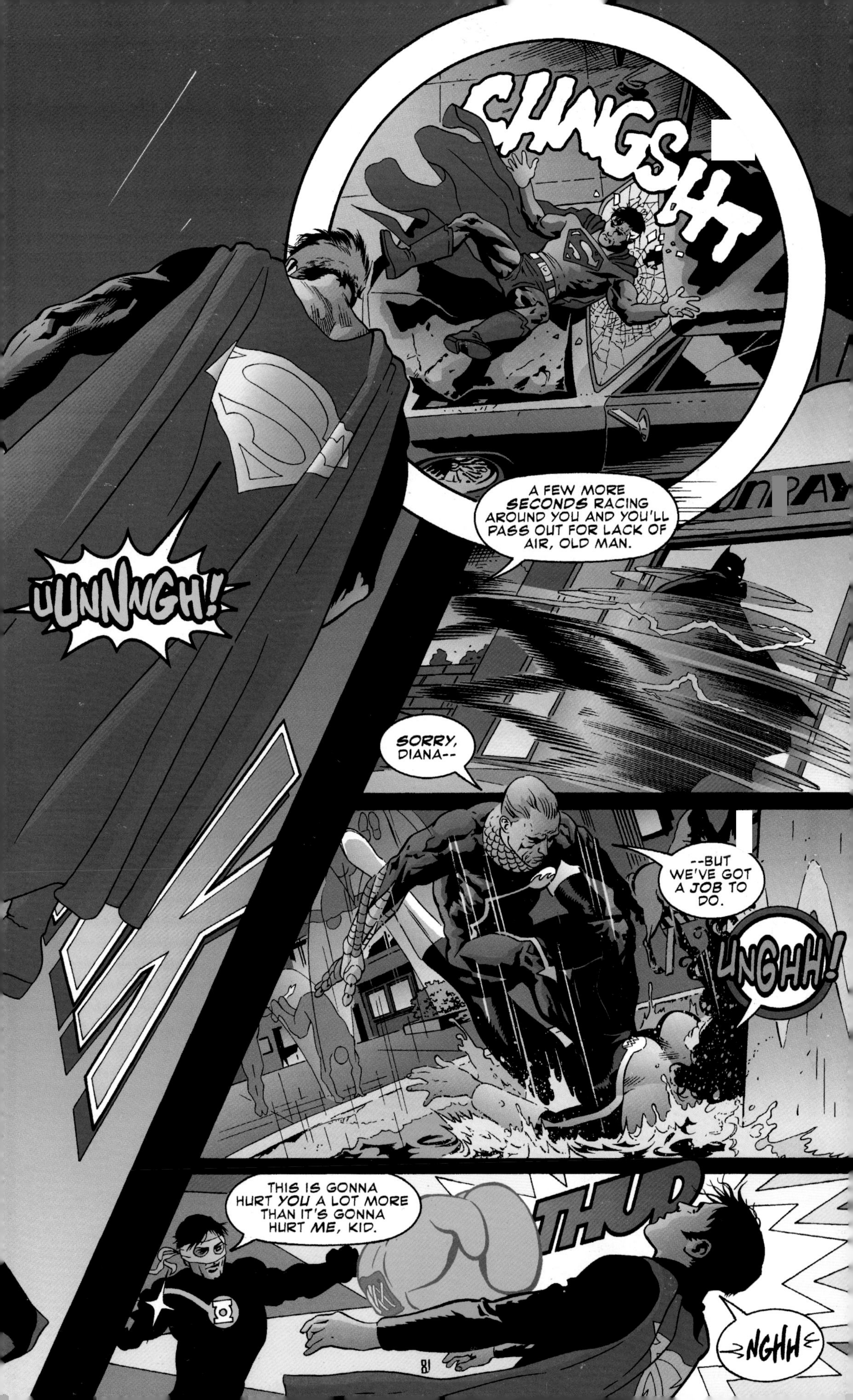
CHNGSHT
UUNNNGH!
A FEW MORE SECONDS RACING AROUND YOU AND YOU'LL PASS OUT FOR LACK OF AIR, OLD MAN.
SORRY, DIANA--
--BUT WE'VE GOT A JOB TO DO.
UNGHH!
THIS IS GONNA HURT YOU A LOT MORE THAN IT'S GONNA HURT ME, KID.
NGHH

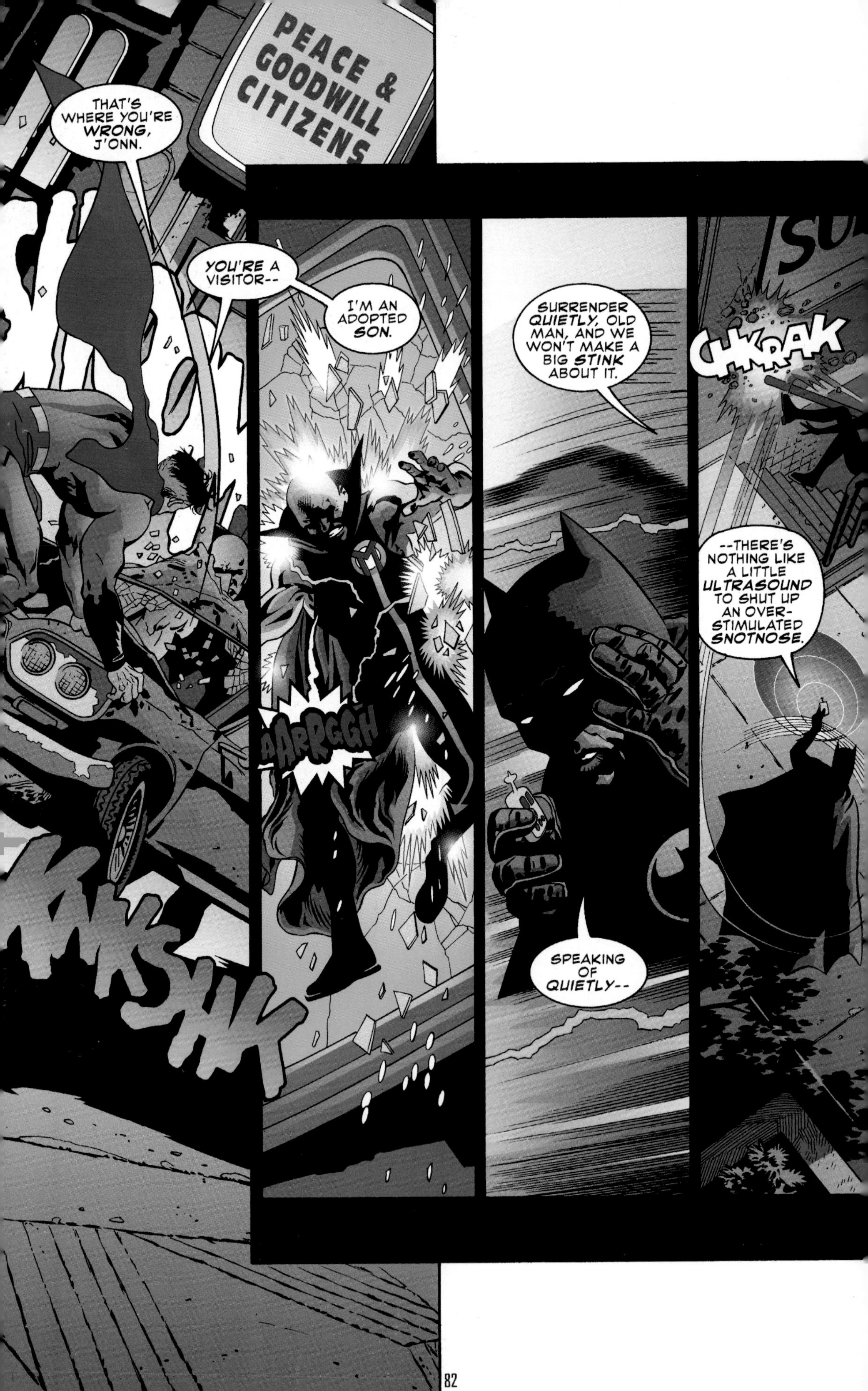
PEACE & GOODWILL CITIZENS
THAT'S WHERE YOU'RE WRONG, J'ONN.
YOU'RE A VISITOR--
I'M AN ADOPTED SON.
AARRGGH
SURRENDER QUIETLY, OLD MAN, AND WE WON'T MAKE A BIG STINK ABOUT IT.
SPEAKING OF QUIETLY--
CHKRAK
--THERE'S NOTHING LIKE A LITTLE ULTRASOUND TO SHUT UP AN OVER-STIMULATED SNOTNOSE.

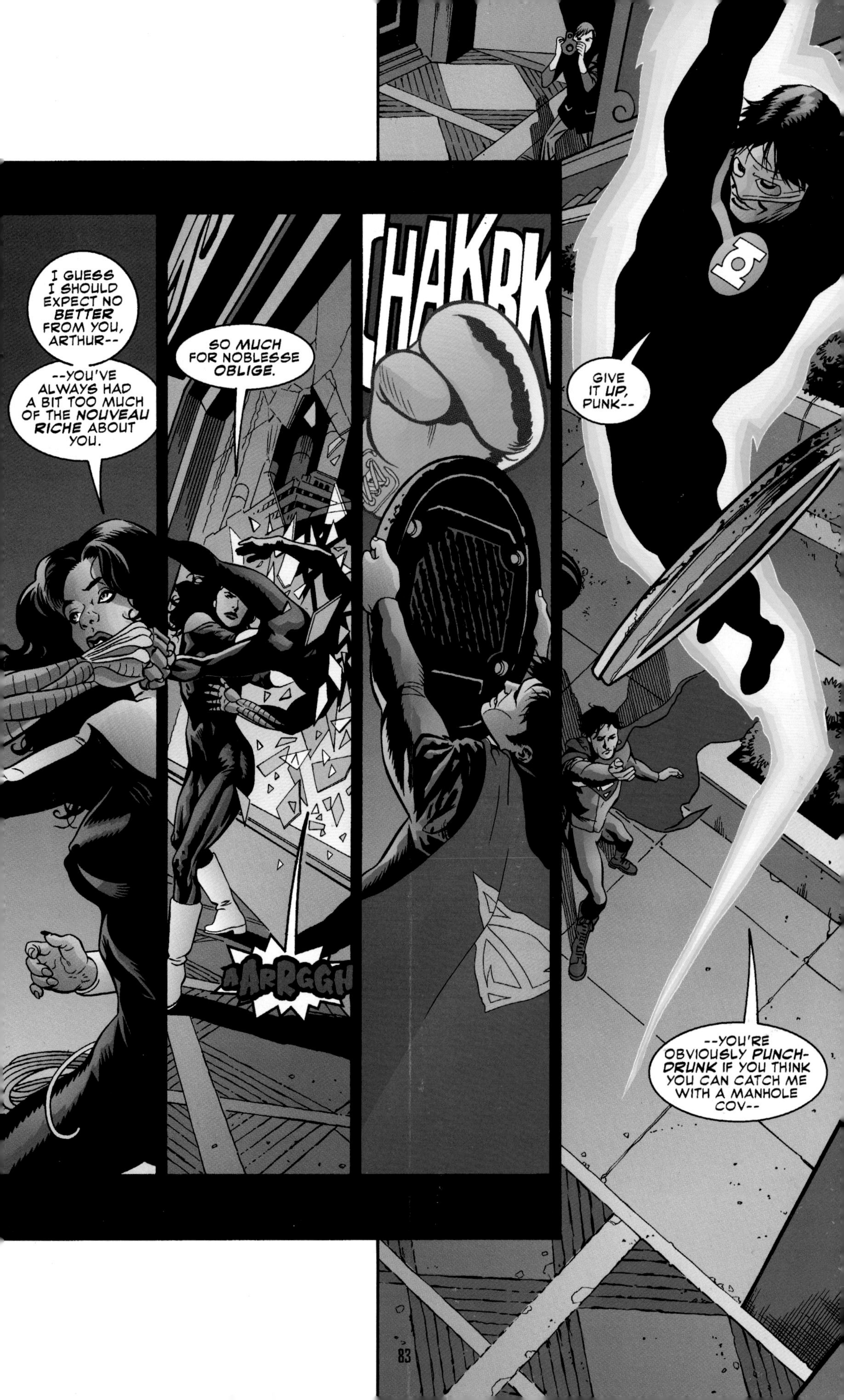
I GUESS I SHOULD EXPECT NO BETTER FROM YOU, ARTHUR--
--YOU'VE ALWAYS HAD A BIT TOO MUCH OF THE NOUVEAU RICHE ABOUT YOU.
SO MUCH FOR NOBLESSE OBLIGE.
AARGGH
HAKRK
GIVE IT UP, PUNK--
--YOU'RE OBVIOUSLY PUNCH-DRUNK IF YOU THINK YOU CAN CATCH ME WITH A MANHOLE COV--

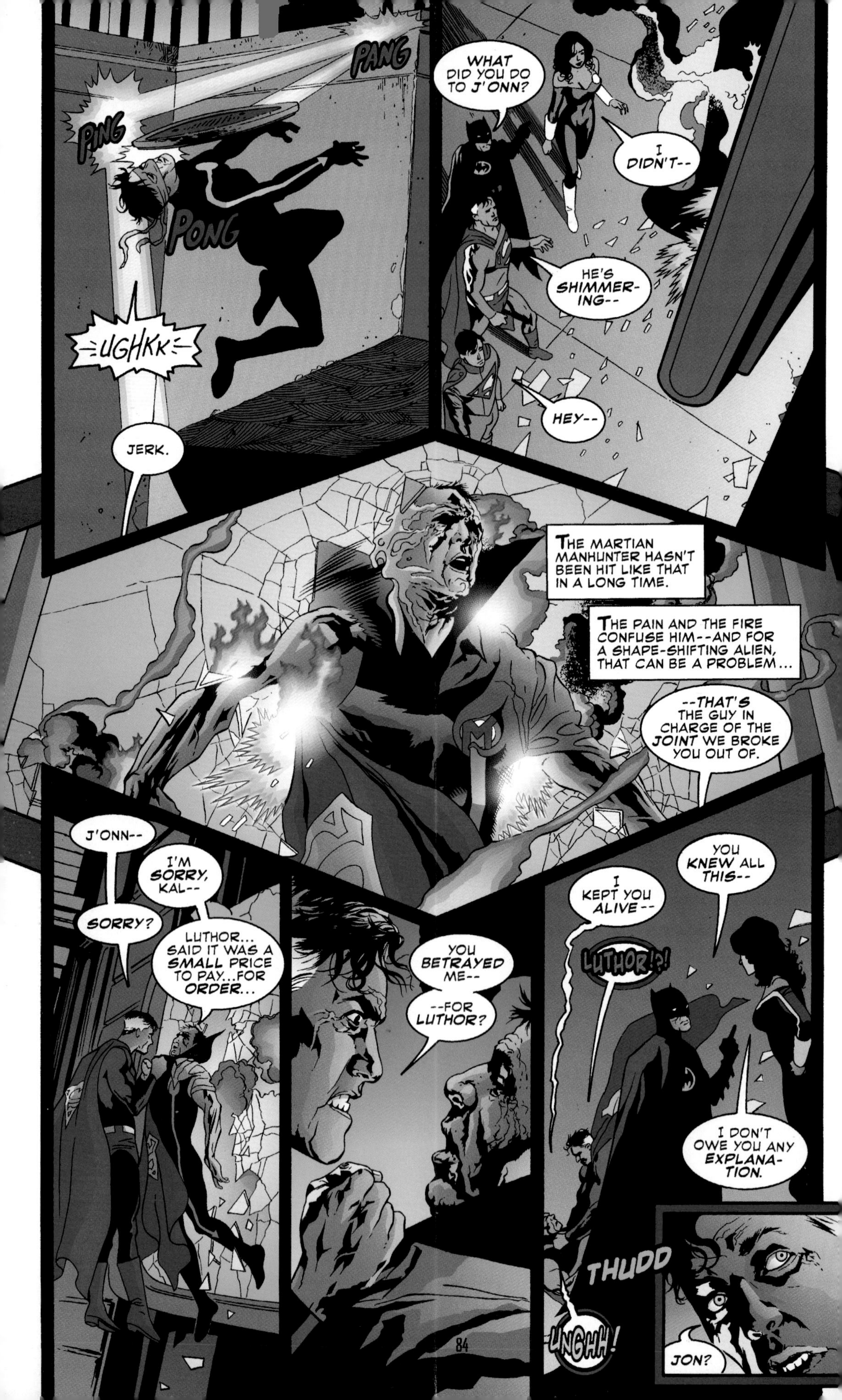
PANG
PING
PONG
UGHKK
JERK.
WHAT DID YOU DO TO J'ONN?
I DIDN'T--
HE'S SHIMMERING--
HEY--
THE MARTIAN MANHUNTER HASN'T BEEN HIT LIKE THAT IN A LONG TIME.
THE PAIN AND THE FIRE CONFUSE HIM--AND FOR A SHAPE-SHIFTING ALIEN, THAT CAN BE A PROBLEM...
--THAT'S THE GUY IN CHARGE OF THE JOINT WE BROKE YOU OUT OF.
J'ONN--
I'M SORRY, KAL--
SORRY?
LUTHOR... SAID IT WAS A SMALL PRICE TO PAY...FOR ORDER...
YOU BETRAYED ME--
--FOR LUTHOR?
YOU KNEW ALL THIS--
I KEPT YOU ALIVE--
LUTHOR!?!
I DON'T OWE YOU ANY EXPLANATION.
THUDD
UNGHH!
JON?

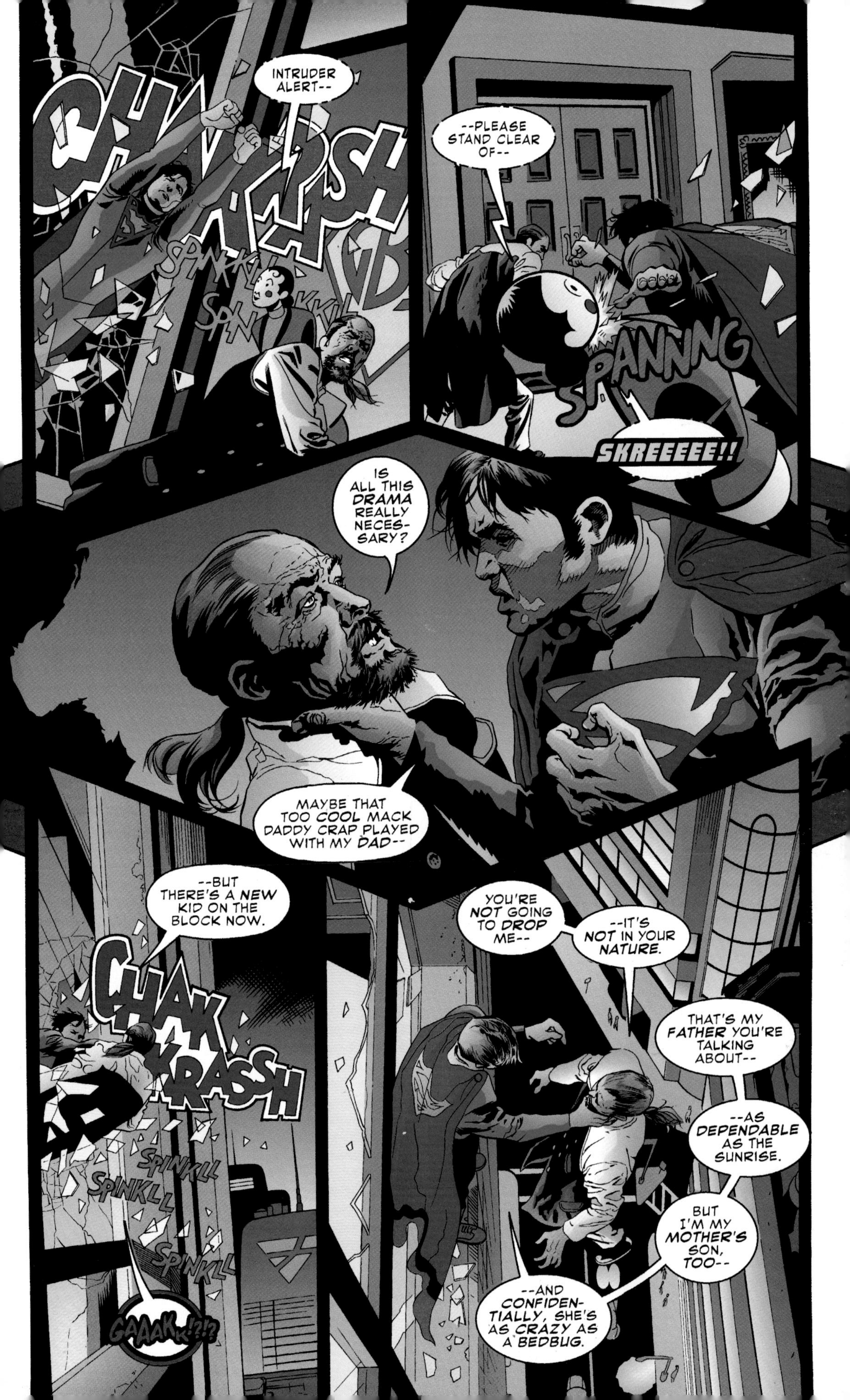

INTRUDER ALERT--
CHHHH
SPINKLL
SPINKKLL
--PLEASE STAND CLEAR OF--
SPANNNG
SKREEEEE!!
IS ALL THIS DRAMA REALLY NECES-SARY?
MAYBE THAT TOO COOL MACK DADDY CRAP PLAYED WITH MY DAD--
--BUT THERE'S A NEW KID ON THE BLOCK NOW.
CHAK KRASSH
SPINKLL
SPINKLL
SPINKLL
GAAAKk!?!?
YOU'RE NOT GOING TO DROP ME--
--IT'S NOT IN YOUR NATURE.
THAT'S MY FATHER YOU'RE TALKING ABOUT--
--AS DEPENDABLE AS THE SUNRISE.
BUT I'M MY MOTHER'S SON, TOO--
--AND CONFIDEN-TIALLY, SHE'S AS CRAZY AS A BEDBUG.

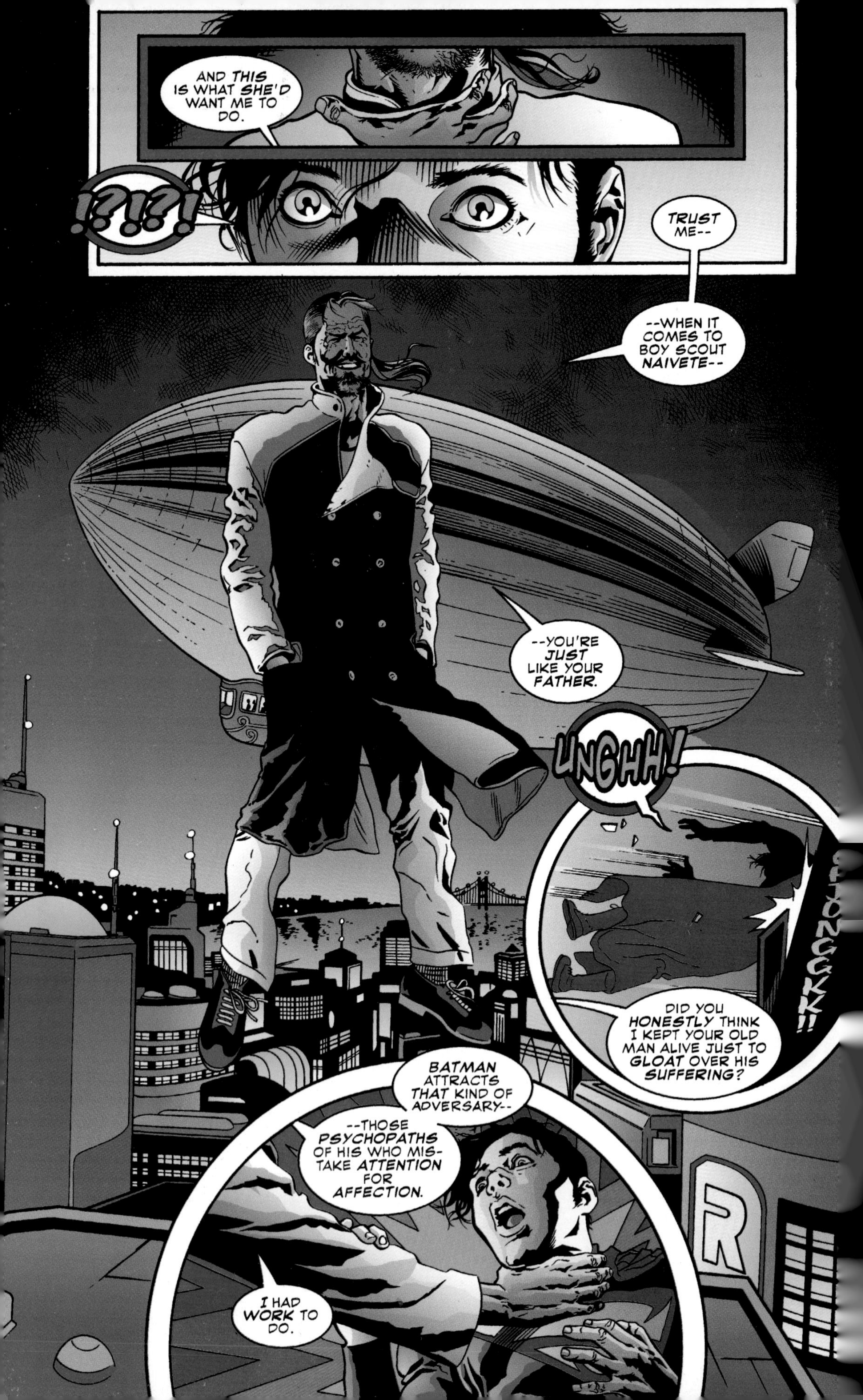
AND THIS IS WHAT SHE'D WANT ME TO DO.
!?!?!
TRUST ME--
--WHEN IT COMES TO BOY SCOUT NAIVETE--
--YOU'RE JUST LIKE YOUR FATHER.
UNGHH!
DID YOU HONESTLY THINK I KEPT YOUR OLD MAN ALIVE JUST TO GLOAT OVER HIS SUFFERING?
BATMAN ATTRACTS THAT KIND OF ADVERSARY--
--THOSE PSYCHOPATHS OF HIS WHO MIS-TAKE ATTENTION FOR AFFECTION.
I HAD WORK TO DO.

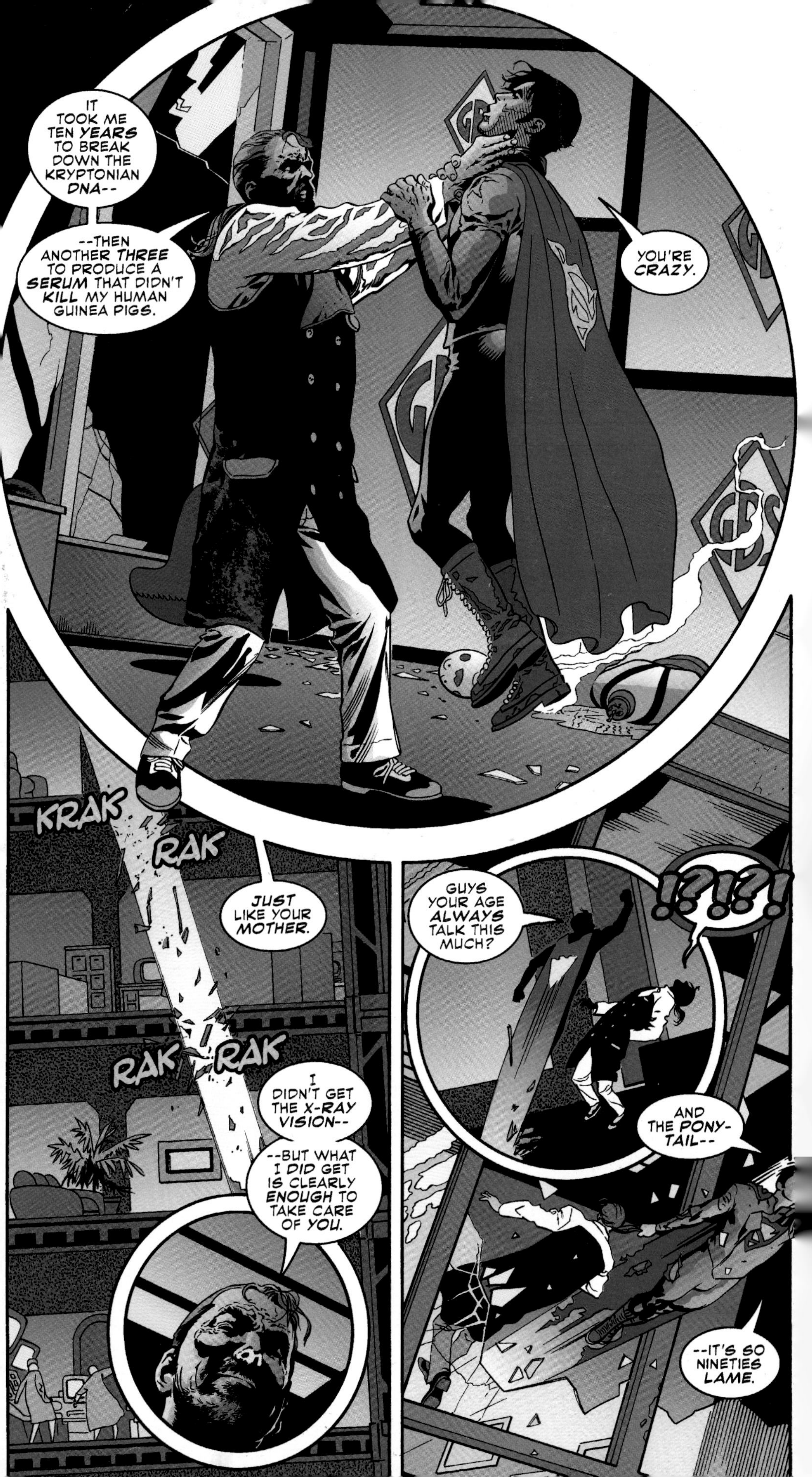
IT TOOK ME TEN YEARS TO BREAK DOWN THE KRYPTONIAN DNA--
--THEN ANOTHER THREE TO PRODUCE A SERUM THAT DIDN'T KILL MY HUMAN GUINEA PIGS.
YOU'RE CRAZY.
KRAK
RAK
JUST LIKE YOUR MOTHER.
RAK
RAK
I DIDN'T GET THE X-RAY VISION--
--BUT WHAT I DID GET IS CLEARLY ENOUGH TO TAKE CARE OF YOU.
GUYS YOUR AGE ALWAYS TALK THIS MUCH?
!?!?!
AND THE PONY-TAIL--
--IT'S SO NINETIES LAME.

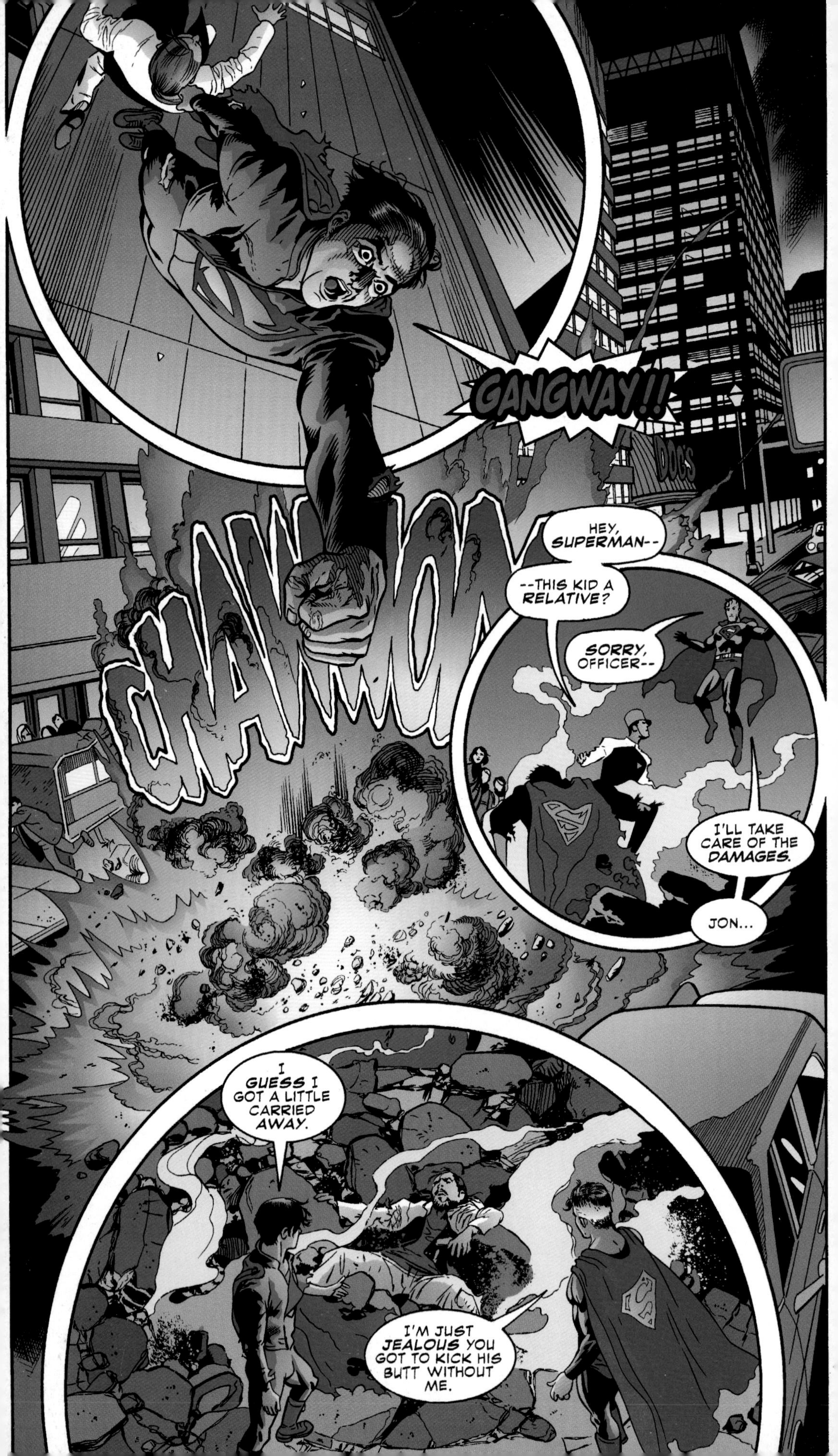
GANGWAY!!
CHAWOOM
HEY, SUPERMAN--
--THIS KID A RELATIVE?
SORRY, OFFICER--
I'LL TAKE CARE OF THE DAMAGES.
JON...
I GUESS I GOT A LITTLE CARRIED AWAY.
I'M JUST JEALOUS YOU GOT TO KICK HIS BUTT WITHOUT ME.

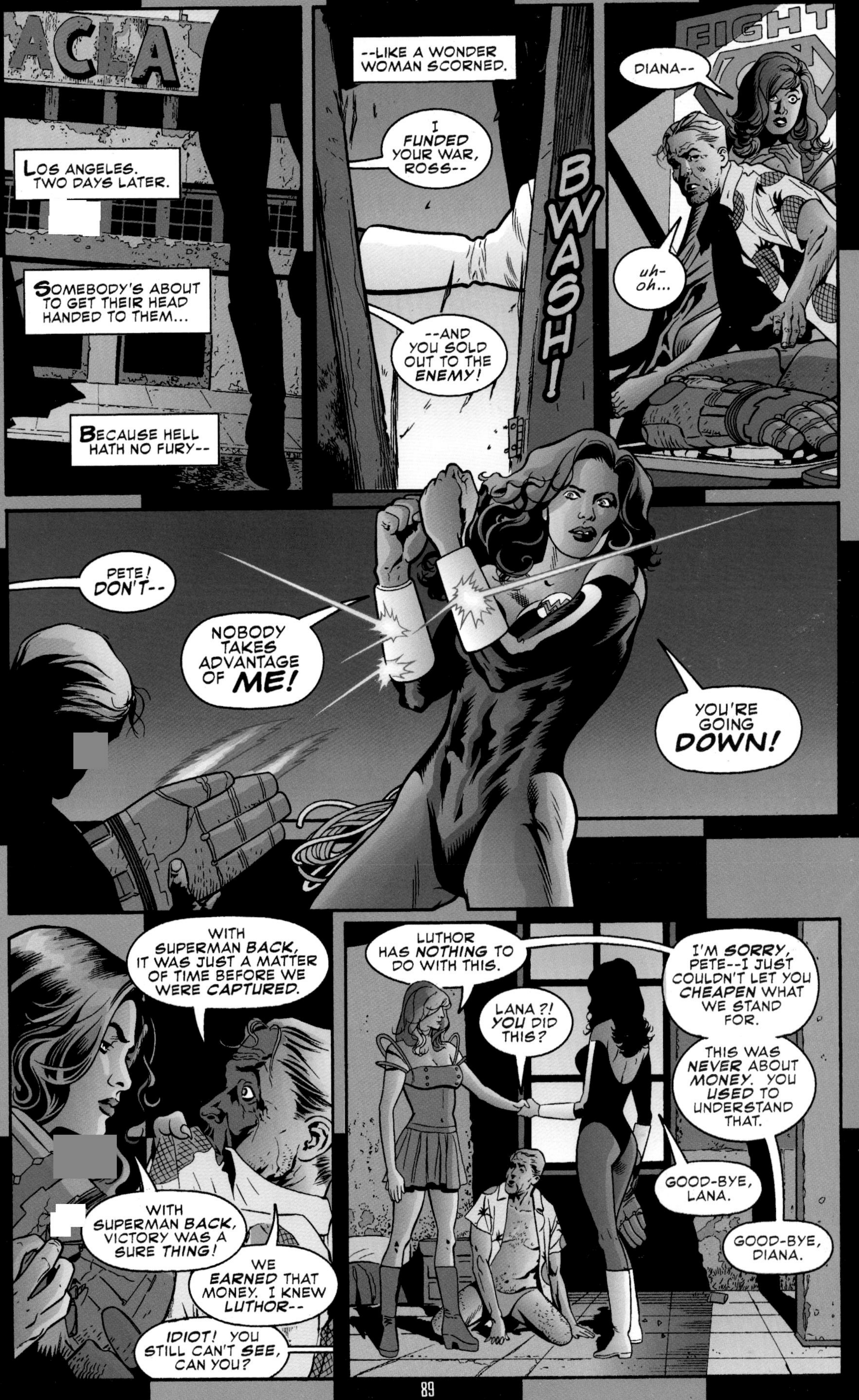
ACLA
LOS ANGELES. TWO DAYS LATER.
SOMEBODY'S ABOUT TO GET THEIR HEAD HANDED TO THEM...
BECAUSE HELL HATH NO FURY--
--LIKE A WONDER WOMAN SCORNED.
I FUNDED YOUR WAR, ROSS--
--AND YOU SOLD OUT TO THE ENEMY!
BWASH!
FIGHT
DIANA--
uh-oh...
PETE! DON'T--
NOBODY TAKES ADVANTAGE OF ME!
YOU'RE GOING DOWN!
WITH SUPERMAN BACK, IT WAS JUST A MATTER OF TIME BEFORE WE WERE CAPTURED.
WITH SUPERMAN BACK, VICTORY WAS A SURE THING!
WE EARNED THAT MONEY. I KNEW LUTHOR--
IDIOT! YOU STILL CAN'T SEE, CAN YOU?
LUTHOR HAS NOTHING TO DO WITH THIS.
LANA?! YOU DID THIS?
I'M SORRY, PETE--I JUST COULDN'T LET YOU CHEAPEN WHAT WE STAND FOR.
THIS WAS NEVER ABOUT MONEY. YOU USED TO UNDERSTAND THAT.
GOOD-BYE, LANA.
GOOD-BYE, DIANA.

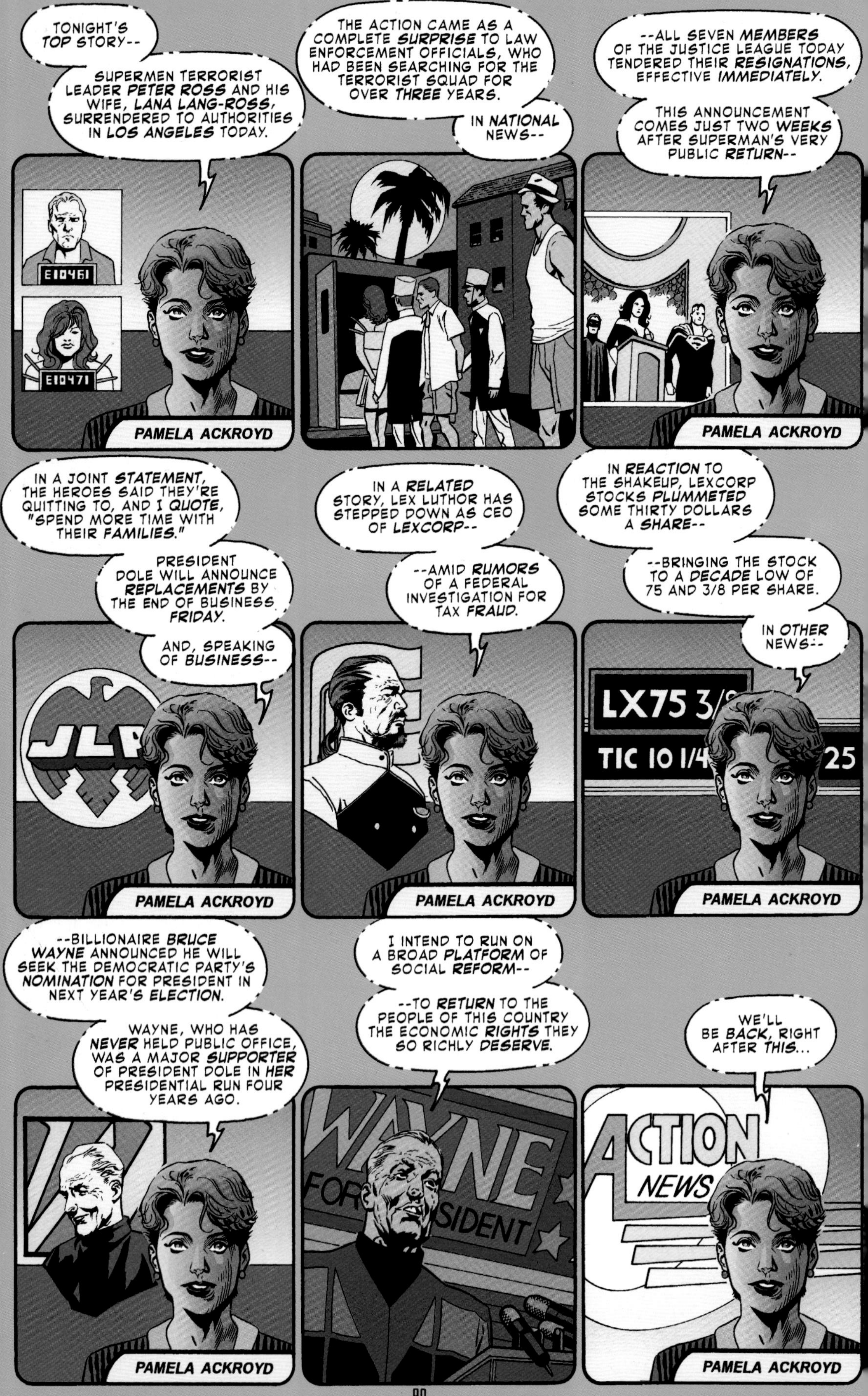

TONIGHT'S TOP STORY--
SUPERMEN TERRORIST LEADER PETER ROSS AND HIS WIFE, LANA LANG-ROSS, SURRENDERED TO AUTHORITIES IN LOS ANGELES TODAY.
E10461
E10471
PAMELA ACKROYD
THE ACTION CAME AS A COMPLETE SURPRISE TO LAW ENFORCEMENT OFFICIALS, WHO HAD BEEN SEARCHING FOR THE TERRORIST SQUAD FOR OVER THREE YEARS.
IN NATIONAL NEWS--
--ALL SEVEN MEMBERS OF THE JUSTICE LEAGUE TODAY TENDERED THEIR RESIGNATIONS, EFFECTIVE IMMEDIATELY.
THIS ANNOUNCEMENT COMES JUST TWO WEEKS AFTER SUPERMAN'S VERY PUBLIC RETURN--
PAMELA ACKROYD
IN A JOINT STATEMENT, THE HEROES SAID THEY'RE QUITTING TO, AND I QUOTE, "SPEND MORE TIME WITH THEIR FAMILIES."
PRESIDENT DOLE WILL ANNOUNCE REPLACEMENTS BY THE END OF BUSINESS FRIDAY.
AND, SPEAKING OF BUSINESS--
JLA
PAMELA ACKROYD
IN A RELATED STORY, LEX LUTHOR HAS STEPPED DOWN AS CEO OF LEXCORP--
--AMID RUMORS OF A FEDERAL INVESTIGATION FOR TAX FRAUD.
PAMELA ACKROYD
IN REACTION TO THE SHAKEUP, LEXCORP STOCKS PLUMMETED SOME THIRTY DOLLARS A SHARE--
--BRINGING THE STOCK TO A DECADE LOW OF 75 AND 3/8 PER SHARE.
IN OTHER NEWS--
LX75 3/
TIC 10 1/4
25
PAMELA ACKROYD
--BILLIONAIRE BRUCE WAYNE ANNOUNCED HE WILL SEEK THE DEMOCRATIC PARTY'S NOMINATION FOR PRESIDENT IN NEXT YEAR'S ELECTION.
WAYNE, WHO HAS NEVER HELD PUBLIC OFFICE, WAS A MAJOR SUPPORTER OF PRESIDENT DOLE IN HER PRESIDENTIAL RUN FOUR YEARS AGO.
PAMELA ACKROYD
I INTEND TO RUN ON A BROAD PLATFORM OF SOCIAL REFORM--
--TO RETURN TO THE PEOPLE OF THIS COUNTRY THE ECONOMIC RIGHTS THEY SO RICHLY DESERVE.
WAYNE FOR PRESIDENT
WE'LL BE BACK, RIGHT AFTER THIS...
ACTION NEWS
PAMELA ACKROYD

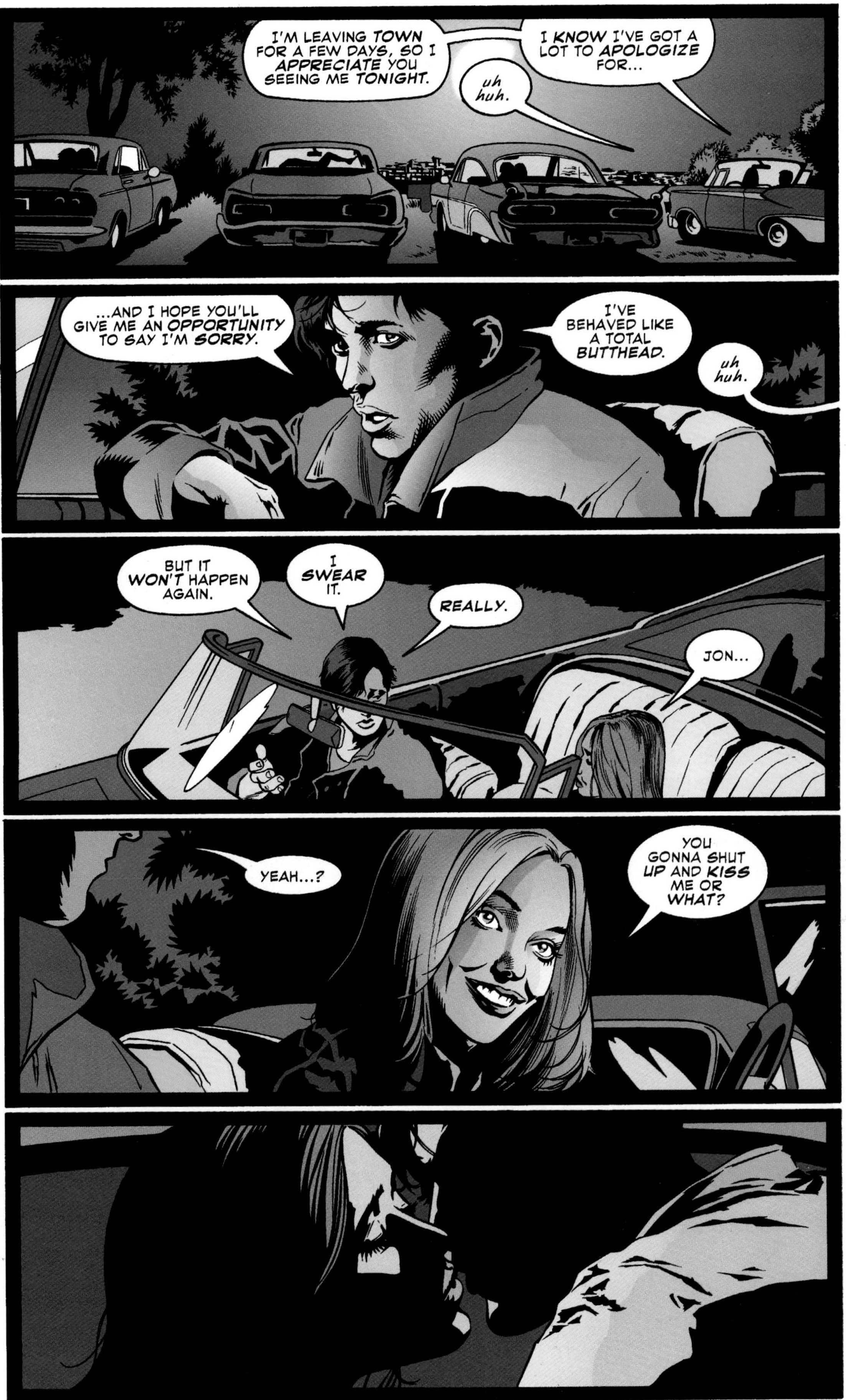

I'M LEAVING TOWN FOR A FEW DAYS, SO I APPRECIATE YOU SEEING ME TONIGHT.
uh huh.
I KNOW I'VE GOT A LOT TO APOLOGIZE FOR...
...AND I HOPE YOU'LL GIVE ME AN OPPORTUNITY TO SAY I'M SORRY.
I'VE BEHAVED LIKE A TOTAL BUTTHEAD.
uh huh.
BUT IT WON'T HAPPEN AGAIN.
I SWEAR IT.
REALLY.
JON...
YEAH...?
YOU GONNA SHUT UP AND KISS ME OR WHAT?

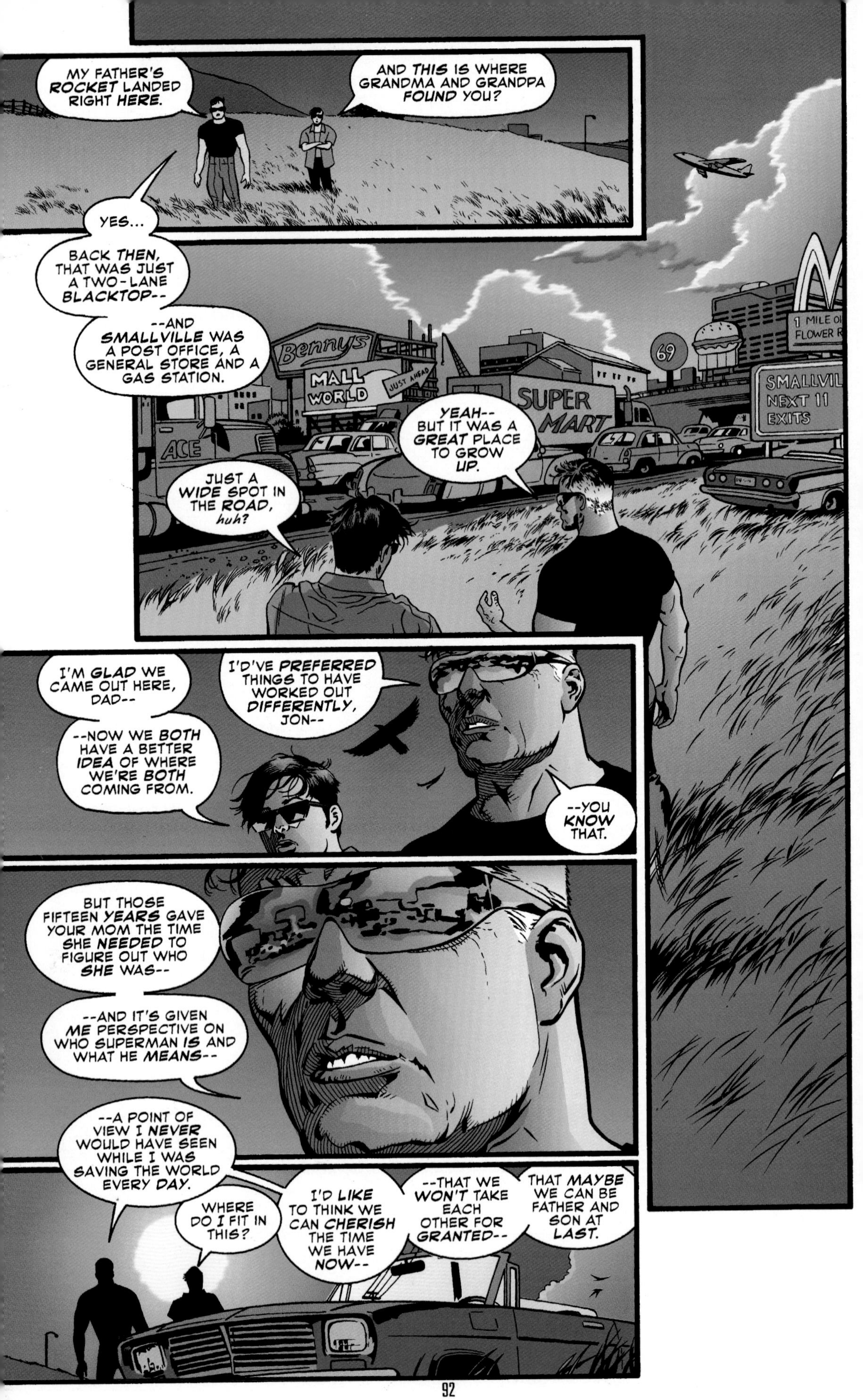
MY FATHER'S ROCKET LANDED RIGHT HERE.
AND THIS IS WHERE GRANDMA AND GRANDPA FOUND YOU?
YES...
BACK THEN, THAT WAS JUST A TWO-LANE BLACKTOP--
--AND SMALLVILLE WAS A POST OFFICE, A GENERAL STORE AND A GAS STATION.
Benny's
MALL WORLD
JUST AHEAD
69
1 MILE O
FLOWER R
SMALLVIL
NEXT 11
EXITS
SUPER MART
ACE
YEAH-- BUT IT WAS A GREAT PLACE TO GROW UP.
JUST A WIDE SPOT IN THE ROAD, huh?
I'M GLAD WE CAME OUT HERE, DAD--
--NOW WE BOTH HAVE A BETTER IDEA OF WHERE WE'RE BOTH COMING FROM.
I'D'VE PREFERRED THINGS TO HAVE WORKED OUT DIFFERENTLY, JON--
--YOU KNOW THAT.
BUT THOSE FIFTEEN YEARS GAVE YOUR MOM THE TIME SHE NEEDED TO FIGURE OUT WHO SHE WAS--
--AND IT'S GIVEN ME PERSPECTIVE ON WHO SUPERMAN IS AND WHAT HE MEANS--
--A POINT OF VIEW I NEVER WOULD HAVE SEEN WHILE I WAS SAVING THE WORLD EVERY DAY.
WHERE DO I FIT IN THIS?
I'D LIKE TO THINK WE CAN CHERISH THE TIME WE HAVE NOW--
--THAT WE WON'T TAKE EACH OTHER FOR GRANTED--
THAT MAYBE WE CAN BE FATHER AND SON AT LAST.

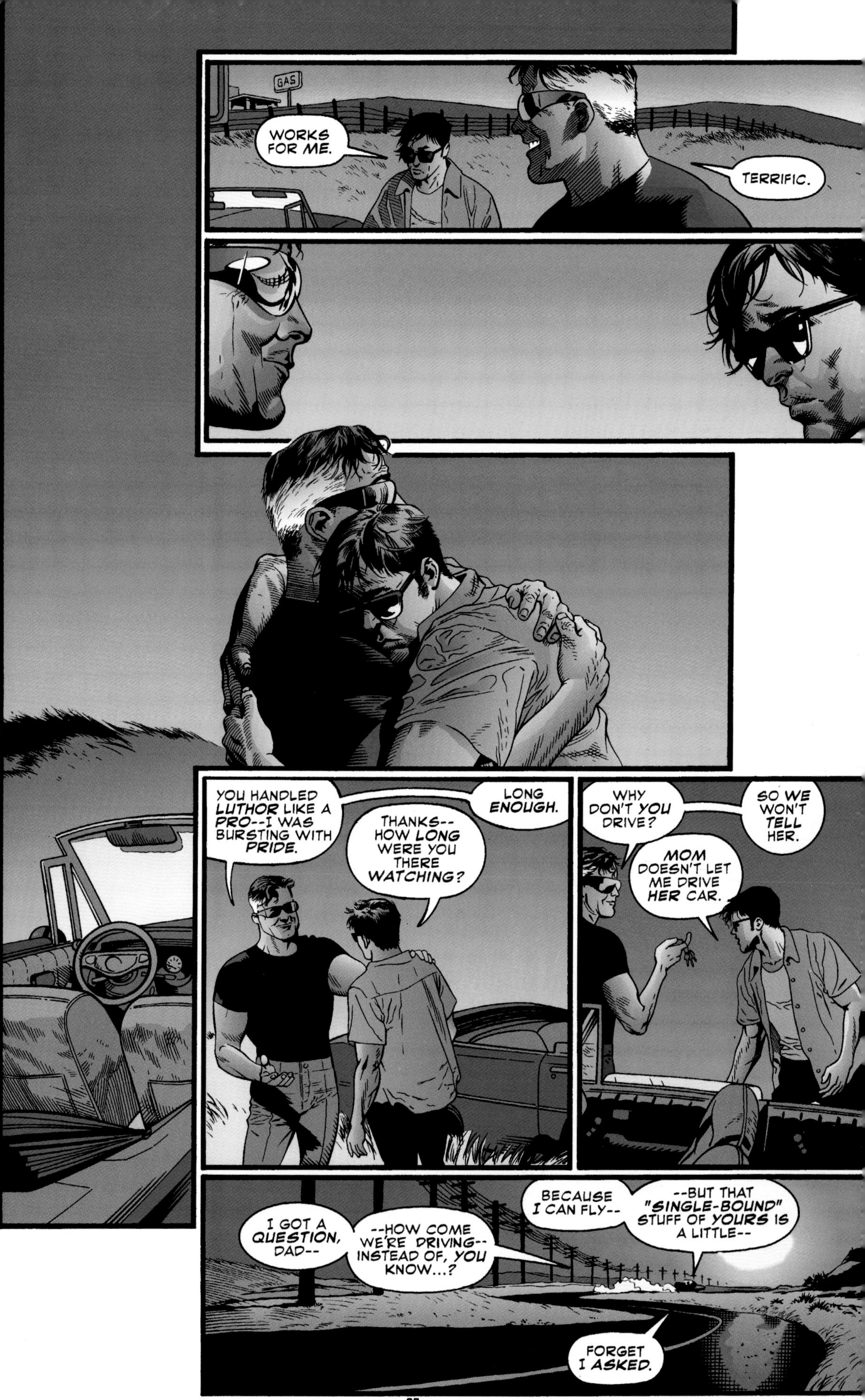
WORKS FOR ME.
TERRIFIC.
YOU HANDLED LUTHOR LIKE A PRO--I WAS BURSTING WITH PRIDE.
THANKS-- HOW LONG WERE YOU THERE WATCHING?
LONG ENOUGH.
WHY DON'T YOU DRIVE?
MOM DOESN'T LET ME DRIVE HER CAR.
SO WE WON'T TELL HER.
I GOT A QUESTION, DAD--
--HOW COME WE'RE DRIVING-- INSTEAD OF, YOU KNOW...?
BECAUSE I CAN FLY--
--BUT THAT "SINGLE-BOUND" STUFF OF YOURS IS A LITTLE--
FORGET I ASKED.

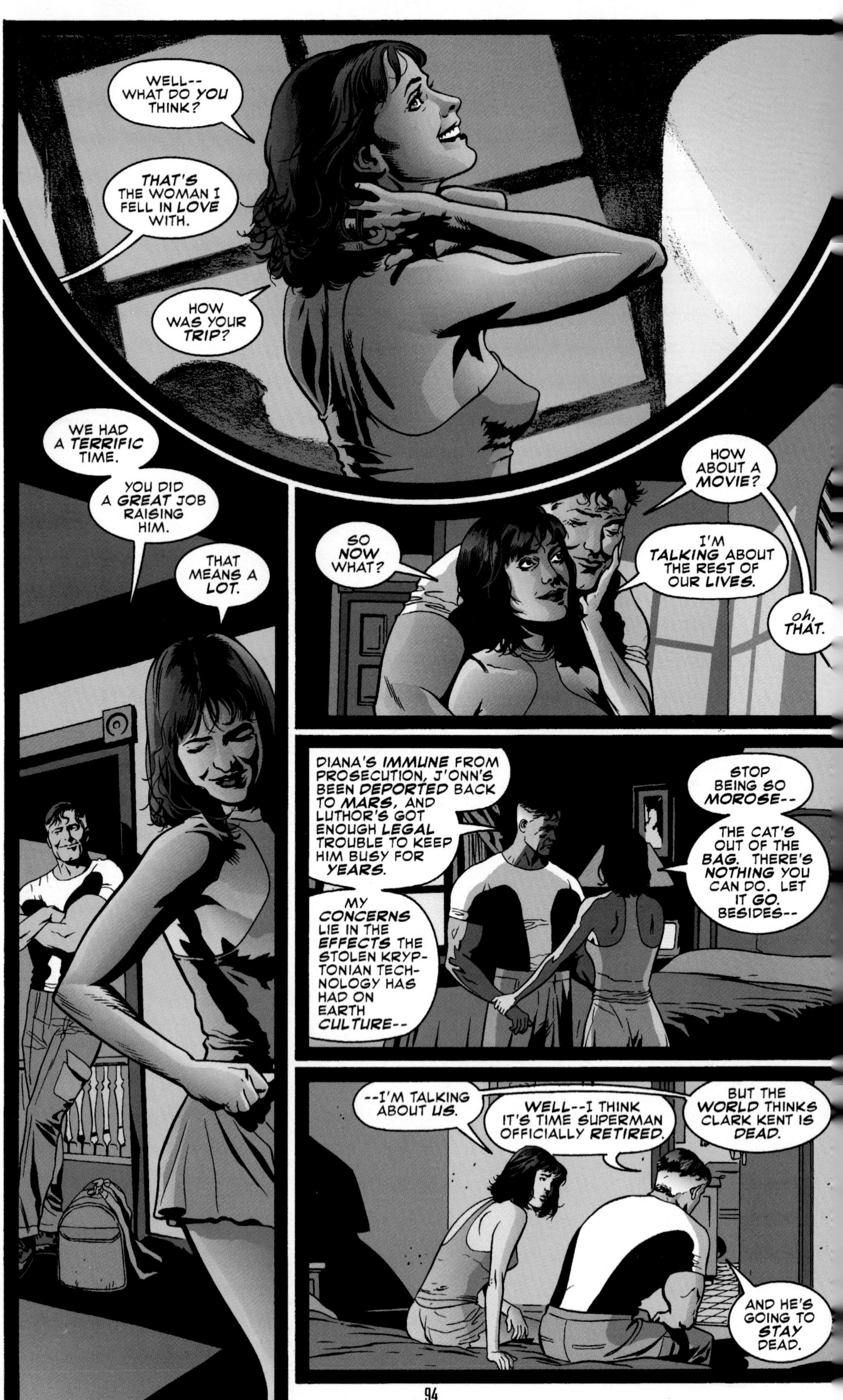
WELL-- WHAT DO YOU THINK?
THAT'S THE WOMAN I FELL IN LOVE WITH.
HOW WAS YOUR TRIP?
WE HAD A TERRIFIC TIME.
YOU DID A GREAT JOB RAISING HIM.
THAT MEANS A LOT.
HOW ABOUT A MOVIE?
SO NOW WHAT?
I'M TALKING ABOUT THE REST OF OUR LIVES.
oh, THAT.
DIANA'S IMMUNE FROM PROSECUTION, J'ONN'S BEEN DEPORTED BACK TO MARS, AND LUTHOR'S GOT ENOUGH LEGAL TROUBLE TO KEEP HIM BUSY FOR YEARS.
MY CONCERNS LIE IN THE EFFECTS THE STOLEN KRYPTONIAN TECHNOLOGY HAS HAD ON EARTH CULTURE--
STOP BEING SO MOROSE--
THE CAT'S OUT OF THE BAG. THERE'S NOTHING YOU CAN DO. LET IT GO. BESIDES--
--I'M TALKING ABOUT US.
WELL--I THINK IT'S TIME SUPERMAN OFFICIALLY RETIRED.
BUT THE WORLD THINKS CLARK KENT IS DEAD.
AND HE'S GOING TO STAY DEAD.

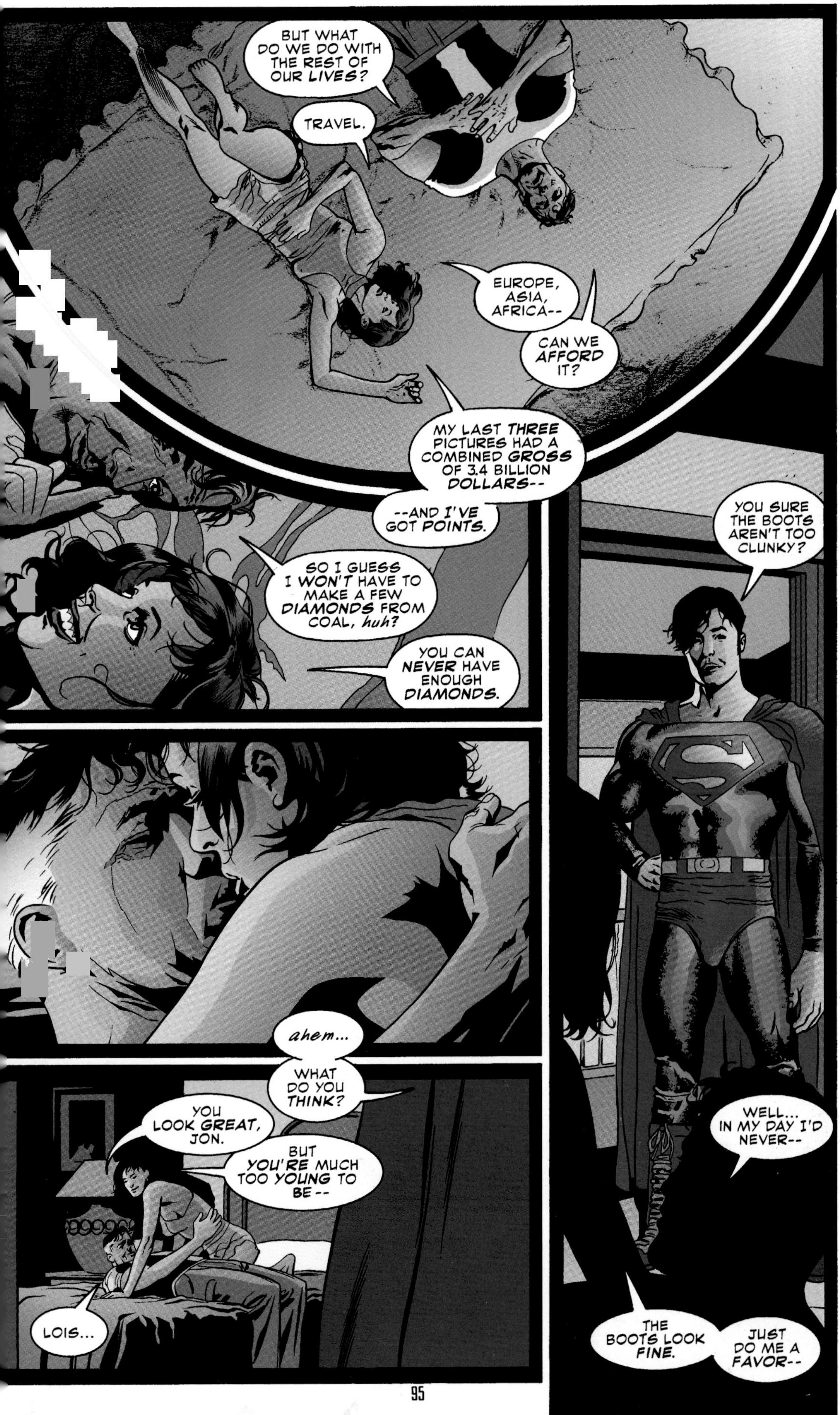
BUT WHAT DO WE DO WITH THE REST OF OUR LIVES?
TRAVEL.
EUROPE, ASIA, AFRICA--
CAN WE AFFORD IT?
MY LAST THREE PICTURES HAD A COMBINED GROSS OF 3.4 BILLION DOLLARS--
--AND I'VE GOT POINTS.
SO I GUESS I WON'T HAVE TO MAKE A FEW DIAMONDS FROM COAL, huh?
YOU CAN NEVER HAVE ENOUGH DIAMONDS.
ahem...
WHAT DO YOU THINK?
YOU LOOK GREAT, JON.
BUT YOU'RE MUCH TOO YOUNG TO BE --
LOIS...
YOU SURE THE BOOTS AREN'T TOO CLUNKY?
WELL... IN MY DAY I'D NEVER--
THE BOOTS LOOK FINE.
JUST DO ME A FAVOR--

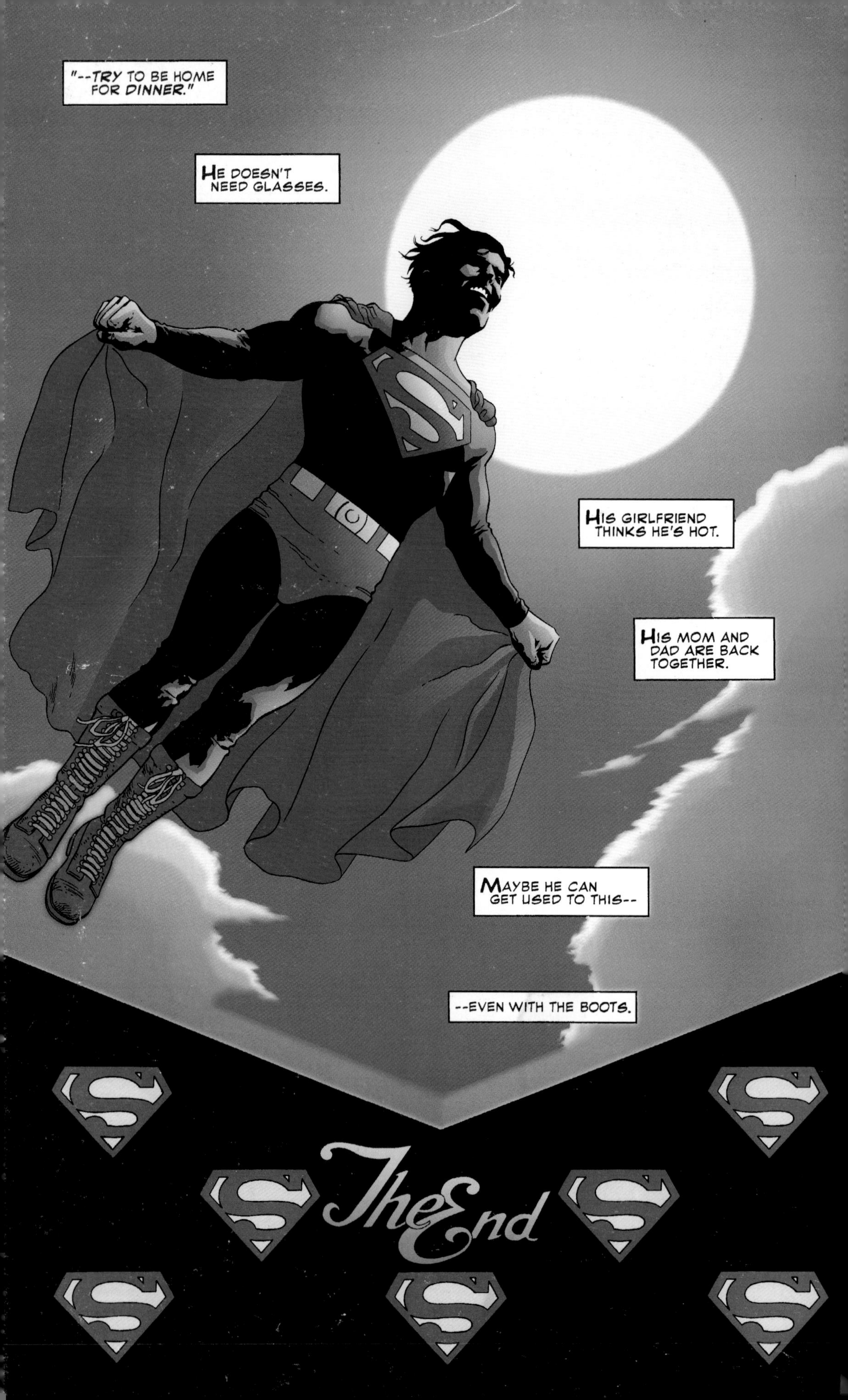
"--TRY TO BE HOME FOR DINNER."
HE DOESN'T NEED GLASSES.
HIS GIRLFRIEND THINKS HE'S HOT.
HIS MOM AND DAD ARE BACK TOGETHER.
MAYBE HE CAN GET USED TO THIS--
--EVEN WITH THE BOOTS.
The End